Social Transformations and Revolutions

Annual of European and Global Studies

An annual collection of the best research on European and global themes, the *Annual of European and Global Studies* publishes issues with a specific focus, each addressing critical developments and controversies in the field.

Annual of European and Global Studies

Social Transformations and Revolutions

Reflections and Analyses

Edited by Johann P. Arnason
and Marek Hrubec

EDINBURGH
University Press

centrum im. willy brandta
willy brandt zentrum

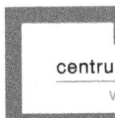

Edinburgh University Press is one of the leading university presses in the UK. We publish academic books and journals in our selected subject areas across the humanities and social sciences, combining cutting-edge scholarship with high editorial and production values to produce academic works of lasting importance. For more information visit our website: www.edinburghuniversitypress.com

Edinburgh University Press Ltd
The Tun – Holyrood Road
12(2f) Jackson's Entry
Edinburgh EH8 8PJ

Typeset in Minion Pro and Gill Sans by
Servis Filmsetting Ltd, Stockport, Cheshire

A CIP record for this book is available from the British Library

ISBN 978 1 4744 1534 7 (hardback)
ISBN 978 1 4744 1535 4 (webready PDF)
ISBN 978 1 4744 1589 7 (epub)

Contents

1

Introduction

Johann P. Arnason and Marek Hrubec

PROBLEMS OF SOCIAL revolutions and/or transformations belong to the classical agenda of social inquiry, as well as to the most prominent real and potential challenges encountered by contemporary societies. Among revolutionary events of the last decades, particular attention has been drawn to the changes that unfolded at the turn of the 1990s and brought the supposedly bipolar (in fact incipiently multipolar) world to an end. The downfall of East Central European Communist regimes in 1989 and of the Soviet Union in 1991 marked the beginning of a new era, originally characterised on the one hand by the relaxation of international tensions and on the other by the ascendancy of Western unilateralism.

The twenty-fifth anniversary of the Soviet collapse prompts the authors of this book to reflect on revolutions and transformations, both from a long-term historical perspective and with regard to the post-Communist scene. The social changes unfolding in Eastern and Central Europe are not only epoch-making historical turns; their economic, social and political aspects, often confusing and unexpected, have also raised new questions and triggered debates about fundamental theoretical issues. Moreover, they have had a significant impact on developments elsewhere in the world, in both Western and developing countries.

In another context, military actions of the United States after the terrorist attacks on 11 September 2001 have also had a major and controversial impact on the global arena. More recently, the economic crisis that began in 2007–8 can be seen as a historical watershed; it caused a series of breakdowns and provoked demands for social and political transformation, so far unfulfilled. The wave of protests and mostly abortive revolutions, known to optimists as the Arab Spring, is certainly not unconnected to crisis dynamics in the centres of the world economy, but it also reflects regional trends of a specific kind. Finally, internal and external transformations linked to the rise of new powers (such as the BRICS group, to which we could add Turkey, Indonesia and Mexico, and possibly others) are altering the patterns of international and global relations.

All these processes have unfolded within the framework of unchallenged global capitalism, whose reproduction on an expanding scale involved multiple economic, political, ecological and civilisational transformations. The aim of the present volume is not to attempt a survey of these changes; rather, we take them as a background to more selective discussion of theoretical and historical questions. In particular, we seek to problematise the relationship between revolutions and transformations. The attention of citizens, politicians and the media tends to focus on dramatic events of more or less genuinely revolutionary dimensions; but more gradual and therefore less noticeable social changes, extending over decades or even longer, may result in radical transformations that turn out to have lasting revolutionary impact. On the other hand, spectacular upheavals can quickly lose their aura and give way to disillusioned resignation: *plus ça change, plus c'est la même chose*. Examples abound in recent history. Perceptions of revolutionary and transformative processes are thus often out of tune. But when it comes to concrete analyses of historical trends and patterns, it will be necessary to deal with interconnections and mixtures of the two levels. Such observations give rise to disputes about short-term and long-term conceptions of revolution, but also to controversial attempts to integrate the study of revolutions into the interdisciplinary social research on long-term processes. These issues arise in the context of past and contemporary history, and in connection with the great European revolutions as well as the unfinished changes now unfolding in emerging great powers, notably India and China.

The arguments developed in the following papers reflect theoretical orientations as well as geographical locations of the authors. The book has a Central European core; that is where the largest group of authors comes from, especially from the Czech Republic. But other parts of the world are represented, and the contributions add up to a cosmopolitan exchange of views. A brief survey of successive chapters will highlight their shared horizons.

In the first text, a trialogue on revolution and transformation, Vladimíra Dvořáková, Marek Hrubec and Jan Keller open the discussion and suggest themes that are then taken up in the following chapters. This is a conversation between a philosopher, a political scientist and a sociologist. The trialogue focuses mainly on the significance and the consequences of social changes after 1989. It also proposes more general conceptual analyses of revolutions and transformations in social, economic and political spheres, and draws attention to revolutionary transformations that may be less striking but in the long run all the more important. Finally, some scenarios for further social development are noted, ranging from positive to dangerously agonistic perspectives.

The following chapter, written by Johann P. Arnason, focuses on revolutions in the traditional sense of major and relatively abrupt upheavals, and outlines the main conceptual alternatives that are still central to debates on the subject, on the levels of definitions as well as explanatory theories. Particular attention is paid to controversies about the respective roles of power and ideology. Against that background, the paper then turns to a brief exposition and discussion of the civilisational approach to revolutionary phenomena, outlined in late writings of S. N. Eisenstadt but so far less developed than mainstream views.

Jerry Harris discusses the current prospects for a democratic transformation of capitalism. He recalls the historical sources of such efforts and traces the changing forms of social movements involved in demands for economic and social rights. He stresses that neoliberal forces have applied new technologies in the global arena and effectively undermined the social norms previously imposed by various reform movements. The paper concludes with a discussion of ways to reverse the current regressive trends and prepare the ground for a New Deal of global dimensions.

Oleg Suša's contribution deals with the multiple crises of contemporary capitalism, seen as aspects of a complex civilisational predicament. The author links up with the idea of 'civilisation on the crossroads', introduced by theorists of Czech reform Communism in the 1960s, but now applicable to a very different historical environment, characterised by new problems of capitalist development, a much more visible environmental crisis and the empirical absence of a non-capitalist alternative. The problematic of risk, somewhat one-sidedly emphasised in recent Western diagnoses of the times, should be considered in this context.

Richard St'ahel's paper on environmental crisis and political revolution links up with the preceding chapter and focuses on the connection between multiple crises of capitalism. St'ahel returns to Jürgen

Habermas's much-discussed theory of legitimation crisis in late capitalism and applies it to a more comprehensive and contemporary crisis of industrial civilisation. Its most important aspects have to do with the environment, especially with excessive growth of production and consumption and its social as well as ecological consequences: the rapid extinction of animal and plant species, over-exploitation of natural resource, pollution and the threat of overpopulation. To conclude, he raises the question of whether the multiple crises can be overcome without social and political revolution.

The sixth chapter, by Gábor Gángó, is a case study of a very complex and often misunderstood revolutionary episode. Gángó interprets the Hungarian revolutions, the 'bourgeois' one at the end of 1918 and the 'proletarian' one of 1919, as a single transformative process. He shows that although the attempt to establish a Soviet republic is commonly identified with a Bolshevik revolution, the real story is much more complicated; social democratic forces played a decisive role, and their sources of strength, as well as their internal conflicts, must be analysed more closely than mainstream scholarship has done.

Emil Sobottka discusses the Brazilian experience of democratic transformation during the last three decades. The growing involvement of citizens in economic and political life, on local, regional and national levels, was facilitated by such institutional measures as participatory budgets. But, as Sobottka explains, the transformative strategy as a whole was not institutionalised in a satisfactory fashion, and the concrete measures taken could be turned to advantage by those who opposed it. He thus develops a critical reflection on the changes so far realised and on further prospects.

Jiří Krejčík's paper deals with the question of revolutionary transformations in India after independence, and with particular emphasis on changes between 1990 and 2015. In this context, he also draws on the Gramscian concept of passive revolution. He shows that from the early 1990s onwards, India underwent a silent revolution through the transformation of formerly state-controlled companies into private-owned corporations. This trend also involved changes to the structure of class domination, now characterised by a coalition of neoliberalism and cultural-religious nationalism. The paper also deals with concomitant social processes, such as the transformation of the middle classes and attempts to emancipate backward castes.

The final chapter, by Wei Xiaoping, discusses the fundamental economic transformation of China during the last decades and links it to the question of an incipient political one. Before the economic transformation, centralised public ownership and central planning corresponded to a centralised political system; the economic changes have raised expectations of a political reform, and this is to some extent being implemented. The whole process is affected by transformations from below and by the demands of multiple interest groups.

To sum up, individual contributions highlight the general theme of the book, social revolutions and transformations, from various angles. They do so from the viewpoint of different disciplines, but also with reference to interdisciplinary and transdiciplinary perspectives. Connections between philosophy, sociology, history and political science are of particular importance; they also reflect the fact that the majority of the authors could exchange views and ideas prior to the production of the book.

In conclusion, we wish to thank all authors for their cooperation and for background discussions; and also those colleagues who provided valuable critical comments. Last but not least, thanks are due to our home institutions, the Centre of Global Studies in the Institute of Philosophy at the Czech Academy of Sciences in Prague, and the Faculty of Human Studies at Charles University in Prague.

2

A Trialogue on Revolution and Transformation

Vladimíra Dvořáková, Marek Hrubec and Jan Keller

KELLER: *W*ERE REVOLUTIONS *only a passing fad? Prior to the beginning of modernity, it was impossible to speak of revolutions in the true sense of the word. What if modernity has changed so much that the concept of revolution is again becoming meaningless?*

Dvořáková: I have often asked myself the same question. Revolution introduces radical change and dismantles certain barriers blocking the way forward, and yet the system is always newly institutionalised in one form or another (and sometimes completely contrary to the goal and values of the change that has been heralded). The question is whether there is still room for 'reform' within the framework of a particular system. I would say that there is. The liberal democracy and social market economy we have created are, if anything, a caricature. Root-and-branch change is essential, if only so that further (revolutionary?) changes in society are not based on caricature, but are derived from the pursuit of fundamental values and goals.

Hrubec: Classic modernity can definitely claim a monopoly on the concept of revolution in the strict sense. Ever since Copernicus, we have had a modern notion of substantial change, which has come to be characterised by the word 'revolution'. Socially and politically, this change needs to involve a mass movement or a popular or civic insurrection in the way we associate with the French, American or Russian revolutions. One of the preconditions, then, is mass society, but in the West – not least in our own peripherally Western country – this has become fragmented and splintered in recent decades. We can add to that the institutionalisation of crises, resulting in frequently less dramatic, but bureaucratically more regulated and longer-term propensities for crisis than in the past. In this sense, it is true that, in some societies, this precondition for modern social and political revolutions to be feasible has faded somewhat.

Nevertheless, the pre-modern stages of human history had their own functional equivalent of revolution in a broader sense, in practice and in theory, in Western societies at least from the time of ancient Greece. The point is that revolution is associated with radical change which, as a rule, is not only quick, but also often violent and unconstitutional. We can argue over the vocabulary, but the content remains the same: a fundamental, rapid sociopolitical change as witnessed not only in modern times, but throughout the long history of human civilisation. And by that I mean not only in Western societies, but in other cultures, too. This radical change, revolution, even without its current modern Western sense, remains a matter of great turbulence that plays – and is likely to continue playing – a major role in people's lives.

Hrubec: *How would you distinguish revolution from transformation? What defining characteristics should these events have? Weren't there also important (counter-)revolutionary changes during transformation in the 1990s, when neoliberalism began to set up a new structure?*

Dvořáková: Terminology is always a problem because the different scientific and, especially, ideological approaches have differing perceptions. I would say that a revolution involves fundamental and systemic regime change. In that sense, the revolutions in the Central European countries in 1989 were clearly not only political, but also social, overhauling the social structure, wealth and, in part, the economic and political elite.

I view transformation, on the other hand, as the specific procedures behind these revolutionary changes that are intended to lay the foundations of the new system. Here, the ideology of neoliberalism certainly played a very negative role because the rule of law and the functioning of institutions are issues that have been disregarded. It could have had a positive effect, to some extent, in lambasting some excesses of welfare states, but, applied to post-Communist countries and even the countries of Latin America (neoliberalism was primarily a fixation of Pinochet and the Argentine military, where the regime was held in place at the cost of thousands or – in Argentina's case – tens of thousands of human lives), it clearly delivered no forward-looking benefits and, thanks to primitive ideological handling, established a system of unbridled profiteering at the expense of societal advancement. It is no coincidence that East European proponents of this primitive neoliberalism include those who, in the late 1980s, promoted an equally primitively grasped Marxism.

Keller: I'm afraid that, in practice, there is only one real difference between revolution and transformation. Revolution is radical. Machiavelli's lions are utterly reckless as they settle scores while Machiavelli's foxes hang back in the background waiting to pounce on the spoils. New atrocities abound, but when, after a while, we sober up, we start to correct the blunders made during the revolution. That is no consolation to the victims, but it means that a bigger hunk falls off the revolutionary table to be gobbled up by the patiently waiting foxes.

In the 1990s in particular, there was a big misunderstanding. In one of southern Czech district towns we conducted a survey in order to gauge, among other things, how locals thought everything would play out. Basically, they believed there would be a combination of themes from the wistfully nostalgic popular memory of the good old days and democratic socialist ingredients of the Prague Spring 1968. Everyone would have their own small store or workshop and we would hand over our surpluses to build up the country's hoards of treasure. A middle-class idyll. This must have been hilarious to the neoliberals.

The changes that took place were happening against a background where, west of our borders, the middle class had already started changing themselves. They had written off those lower down in the pecking order, replacing them with the much cheaper labour available in third-world countries. During Czechoslovakia's privatisation of assets, which effectively belonged to no one, it was essentially a case of how much the indigenous population could grab without paying a penny, and how much would be snapped up well below the actual value by foreign corporations. It was difficult to back anyone in this race, knowing that the end result would make no difference to anyone else. They could either work for foreign companies for wages cheaper than those in the West, which meant they would have a job, or they could be the butt of insults from the domestic nouveaux riches complaining that they were benefit scroungers living beyond their means. Roughly speaking, what had originally appeared to be free choice boiled down to this.

Dvořáková: *There is talk of change. People are looking for a new vision. But how to size up any new vision? What value or significance is attached to the concept of 'progress'? All spheres of society are in flux, but sometimes it is difficult to decide whether changes are a force for 'good' or* 'bad', and whether we are witnessing progression or regression. Besides, evolution is never linear.

Keller: The problem lies in the very notion of 'progress'. This concept was created when the Enlightened secularised the Christian concept of linear history. Antiquity, subscribing to a cyclical concept of time, lacked this notion. Rather than progress, it dwelt on the receding Golden Age and the gradual spoiling of what had been at the beginning. Christianity came up with what was perhaps excessive optimism, unrolling the circle of time into an ascending line. In this respect, bright tomorrows were invented by Christianity. The Enlightened did nothing to alter this logic. They simply added that we would be guided out of dark beginnings by the light of knowledge, which they also patented for themselves and incorporated into their name as a logo (not to be confused with 'logos').

One of the problems of assessing changes as positive or negative is the principle of the unintended consequences of actions. Unfortunately, this is evident most often in the sense that an innovation which is inherently positive triggers problematic consequences if adopted by a large number of people. The fact that increasing numbers of people are university educated is positive. An unintended consequence of mass enlightenment is the devaluation of all levels of diplomas and education per se. Another example: the development of the welfare state made a significant contribution to the advancement of individualism. The generous welfare state goes some way to extricating individuals from the risks that they would otherwise have to bear due to poor decision-making. This reinforces in them a sense of the social unconditionality of their existence. Individualists who, in this way, are not conditioned by anything believe they are a victim of a huge injustice if they are called upon to contribute to the financing of the welfare state. And a welfare state to which no one wants to contribute will collapse. This brings us back, by regression, to the situation in place before the emergence of the welfare state.

Therefore, not only is evolution not linear, it may even be something that ultimately denies itself.

Hrubec: I believe that the term 'progress' is readily defensible, although there is no way the complex historical development of society can be adequately described using simple geometric shapes such as a circle or a straight line. That would be misleading, as we have had the opportunity to see in various religious or political dogmas in the course of history. On the other hand, nor is there any need to succumb to absolute relativism, which abandons all attempts to formulate what at least some groups of people consider to be progress, i.e. positive aspects of social development. At least from the perspective of social constructivism and historical realism, we can formulate what certain groups of people regard, at a particular time, to be good or bad, and, on this basis, in historical development, they make a distinction between positive and pathological tendencies or between progress and regression in that period. Long-term struggles for social recognition engender developmental societal tendencies and promote certain values and institutions embodying them. If we were to forego this looser concept of good and bad, too, we would be unable to criticise and refuse even the most pathological of societies, such as genocidal societies, cannibalism and Fascism. Naturally, what is fair and what is not becomes redefined over time, but this should not deter us from trying to distinguish between tendencies towards just and unjust development in different periods, between progress and regress.

But, as has already been noted here, nothing is only black and white. From the perspective of a critical social theory, Axel Honneth and his research team in Frankfurt explored the paradoxes of capitalist modernisation. They argued that certain positive developmental trends in society could be simultaneously accompanied by negative tendencies, producing ambivalent developments. They point out that, despite these ambiguities, people can weigh up the pros and cons of such contentious developments and decide whether to evaluate them as positive or negative within a certain period. Let's not be afraid of saying, then, that both progress and regress may exist. That the idea of progress has been trivialised and misused in the past does not change anything. This approach, however, does not stop us from describing some historical periods as ambivalent and contradictory.

Hrubec: *This year marks a quarter of a century since the revolutionary events of 1989 in Central Europe. Viewing those events from such a distance how do you evaluate them and the period immediately afterwards in which a new societal structure was established? What are the causes of their negative aspects? How was the greatest naivety – whose inauspicious fruits we are reaping today – manifested?*

Keller: No matter what the backdrop to 1989 was, it opened up a huge opportunity. The previous regime was utterly untenable, a mixture of, on the one hand, meetings for meetings' sake and, on the other hand, underhand wheeling and dealing. No one took the language of politics seriously. Certainly not those who were using it. It was a great opportunity which has been unbelievably wasted and frittered away. In the 1960s, convergence theories arguing that the best of the Western and Eastern Blocs could be interwoven were in vogue. This would nurture a thriving, yet socially just society. We, on the other hand, managed to clump together the worst of both regimes. We viewed capitalism merely as an opportunity for unlimited racketeering, and violent force (which held the Eastern Bloc together) was not rescinded, but privatised. Anyone today who becomes truly troublesome need not fear the secret police. Rather, they would be dead vainly waiting for an initial interrogation.

I am not sure this is solely a matter of naivety. The naive were those joining the post office queues for privatisation voucher books in the hope that they would subsequently only have to spend their lives cutting out vouchers. I opted against buying one of these books, not because I thought I would fail to transform my thousand-crown outlay into ten thousand crowns, but because I believe standing in a queue at the post office for the sake of money when I am healthy and capable of work is parasitic. Unfortunately, the new regime here was based on this principle and it is the height of irony that the right, which pushed this through and profited from it enormously, now dismisses those who cannot work as parasites. This is not naivety. It is an agenda.

Dvořáková: I view the events of 1989 in a positive light in the sense that they were an opportunity for change and brought down the curtain on the 'inflexibility' characteristic of the Brezhnev period, when efforts to promote anything (e.g. in science) came up against immense bureaucratic and ideological barriers. There was also much more room for personal freedom, with the chance to travel, take decisions on our lives, elect political representatives, publish at our own discretion and speak openly about social and political issues. Naturally, even these freedoms are partially restrained by the societal environment (e.g. if we have a job and are able to draw on financial resources), and we witness manipulation, untruths and dogmatic assertions by certain representatives of 'free journalism', as well as targeted campaigns against proponents of other views. Nevertheless, it is largely up to us whether we allow ourselves to be intimidated or disgusted, and whether we accept the prevailing phrases and clichés without flinching.

I would say that the biggest problem in the post-1989 period was the refusal to set up the basic principles of the rule of law and establish regulatory institutions and mechanisms to keep politics under control. Some politicians undeniably knew why they opposed the rule of law. At the time, they even enjoyed the backing of many intellectuals, who were expecting a moral revival to roll in when new people took to the stage. This is unworkable. Most people do what the system lets them get away with. A handful of individuals making a stand is commendable, but this seldom changes anything.

Keller: *What chance is there, not only for revolutions, but also for serious reform in a country which cannot defend itself against major multinational corporations or large financial capital?*

Hrubec: The fact of the matter is that small countries have very little chance of implementing successful social change in the face of transnational capital. The way, for example, that the Czech Republic has evolved thus far is sound proof of this. If we are to have the capacity to counter the power of global capitalism, it is necessary, in relation to major social upheaval, to begin at the grassroots level in civil society, while thinking and acting also macro-regionally and globally within social and political movements.

However, there may be exceptions where, above all, engagement is essential. Opportunities for social change spread in countries affected by various kinds of crisis and ensuing social conflicts. Furthermore, social changes in some smaller countries originate in or are reinforced by developments in stronger neighbouring and similarly socially oriented countries, especially those with rich natural resources. Thus the sparks ignited, for example, in Bolivia and Venezuela, where the concept of a low-intensity revolution seems to be applicable, owe something to changes in neighbouring Brazil, a much more powerful country, even if the policies of its leaders are more moderate. Significant potential can also be identified in certain African countries.

Therefore, especially in a period of stagnation, it is important to realise the significance of gradually implemented revolutionary transformation in the sense of fundamental social and political change with a set of arrangements: for example, the introduction of participatory budgeting; unconditional basic income; the de-privatisation of many companies and the governance thereof by the employees; pluralism of ownership at the level of villages, towns, regions, nation states and macro-regions; additional tax charges for companies established in tax havens; the prohibition of political corruption known in plutocratically deformed countries as the sponsorship of political parties, etc. This could be a good springboard for major changes to overcome global capitalism.

Dvořáková: We need to split the answer into two parts. The first comprises changes responding to the international environment and to the way globalised capitalism looks today. Opportunities for individual countries (especially smaller ones) are few and far between here; the major players and international social movements, on the other hand, have the clout to push certain issues through. 'Political consumerism' could also play a role. There are examples where companies that behave unethically (animal experiments, child labour or environmental pollution) have been hit globally via social networks. However, a nation state faces a considerable problem here – independent economic policy leaves it very limited space and public policies must be implemented without much opportunity to obtain resources for them.

Nevertheless, I think that certain possibilities are available but, intentionally or out of stupidity, have not been used. The first thing is to configure conditions for companies to do business – frankly, it is enough to watch how supermarkets behave in developed countries, including in relation to employees, the environment and the quality of goods on offer (e.g. vegetables, fruit and meat). They simply behave in the way society allows them to.

Secondly, there is the quality and price of labour. This means investing in education and a concept for the development of the education system, which is completely absent in many countries. I know I am not really answering the question, but many of the problems that we have here are not a direct result of the actions of a globalised environment; rather, they can be attributed to the way our environment has been set up, generating a specific type of economic and political elite, where the key to rising in status is to jettison ethical scruples rather than to gain skills and education.

Dvořáková: *In politics, the word 'reform' has become almost sacred and inviolable. Everything is subordinate to the fact that reforms are essential. Then it turns out that the advocated reforms have ultimately dismantled something which more or less worked. When I speak to our teachers, they often dream of being able to teach in the same way for a few years, according to the same methodology and curriculum, and only then assess the situation. Is constant reform merely a ploy by certain groups to make money and not actually necessary?*

13

Hrubec: Reforms have become part and parcel of governmental work in many countries. The election campaigns waged by political parties are based on promises that are generally formulated in the context of such-and-such a reform in their programmes. Reform even tends to be the main element in the administrative implementation of a policy agenda. The rhetoric of reform is played out, the importance of transformation is over-emphasised and even minor tweaks are often passed off as very significant changes. This allows political parties to avoid fundamental transformation and sidestep revolution.

The leitmotif of the neoliberal governments' reforms was the dismantling of the state, as neoliberal ideology wants only a minimal state. This is best for big firms and the wealthiest groups, who are not then required to pay the highest taxes to maintain the state. Accordingly, neoliberal reforms were aimed at taking apart not only the welfare structure, but also the state in general. The economic and political 'elites' benefited in two ways here. First they weakened the enemy, i.e. the state, and secondly they misappropriated considerable finances. However, since the 2007–8 global economic crisis, banks and other large corporations have been hoovering up the remnants of nation states, which, thanks to the taxes of ordinary citizens and sovereign debt, have been compelled to bail out companies which are 'too big to fail'. Future historians of economic crime are sure to have plenty to feast on.

Keller: Reforms invented by our governments so far have followed, to the letter, the principle described by Michel Crozier in relation to efforts at reforming bureaucratic institutions. Reforms of bureaucracy regularly disable what, even in bureaucratic conditions, has more or less functioned satisfactorily, while those areas meriting reform increase their stranglehold. Crozier, using specific institutions as an example, was actually simply describing what Max Weber had claimed about bureaucracy in general: efforts to reform the bureaucracy can only have two outcomes. Either they will result in chaos, or even more rigid bureaucracy will emerge. The only area in which our government reformers have distinguished themselves is that they have achieved something that not even Weber could have imagined. They have allowed rigid political bureaucracy to survive and grow in the centre of expanding societal chaos. This is something so unusual historically that our governments should have patented it.

Nevertheless, it would be a mistake to consider the resulting mix of bureaucracy and chaos only as a consequence of the impotence of right-wing governments. They have proved themselves highly capable in one respect: they exploited reforms to privatise entire swathes of the public sector. They used the chaos and density of bureaucracy as a smokescreen to make their actions as opaque as possible, enabling the public sector to be divided up among private hands at prices far below its actual value. In this light, their reforms were actually just a continuation of privatisation by other means. In the 1990s, businesses were placed in private hands very easily in the 'large-scale privatisation' scheme. First, formerly thriving businesses were deliberately pushed into the red and then sold at prices far below their true value. Then, once privatised, there was no longer any need for this artificial suppression and they made their new owners lots of money. The reforms of right-wing governments were supposed to do the same with the public sector. First, they stifled it and pushed it into financial difficulties. Then the plan was to privatise it for a song. After this, when public-sector services were definitively in private hands, we would be surprised to learn that they were delivering profits to their 'saviours' on a scale that those doing business in industry or agriculture could only dream of.

Hrubec: *A lot of people in the European countries and the USA are disillusioned with politicians, political parties and politics in general. On the other hand, there are still relatively few people active in civil society and social movements. Mobilising other members of the public has proved difficult, so the problems persist. Why do you think so few people are engaging in social change?*

Dvořáková: There is no single answer. There are numerous causes which, in each country, reflect previous trends and the experiences of their citizens. For citizens to become involved, the important factors are always whether it is generally thought that change is possible and what the specific ideas for such change are. Of course, there will always be individuals who make sacrifices even in situations where the chances of winning are very small, but with mass movements we are on another plane altogether. Naturally, we can think about strong individuals capable of mobilising the public, and these days there is no problem creating a 'media' persona tailored to a particular social group, but perhaps this society is rather 'over-mobilised'. Let's just think back to how many 'false mobilisations' there have been, when elements of the population were mobilised to enforce certain changes (especially those representing values or morals), and after their failure and the internal disintegration of their movement they no longer trust themselves to embark on anything similar.

Keller: The answer would have to be very extensive, as there are many underlying reasons. Look at it in terms of social stratification: the few per cent of people who are really prospering have no reason to become engaged other than to protect and reinforce their positions. Those at the bottom, on the other hand, have so many other concerns that changing society is the least of their worries. In 1990, there were precisely five homeless people in the Czech city of Ostrava. I know the social officer who was in contact with them. Today, there are just over 2,000 homeless in the same city. Looking at them (and they really are everywhere), you would have to say that you're not so badly off after all. The middle classes, whether employees, owners of small businesses or self-employed traders, are on the go all the time just to stop themselves from sinking. They are acutely aware of the fact that they will never clamber to the top. Yet they would not waste time and energy if there was no risk of landing among those below them. In our city, there are now several university-educated engineers among the homeless.

Or you can take it by age cohorts: the youngest generation has great expectations. Here in the Czech Republic and some other neighbouring states, they find themselves in a situation similar to that of young people in the West in the 1980s, who still believed that they would make their way up the ladder like their parents. They do not know that there is no more room up there. The oldest generation is resigned to its fate and has completely different problems to deal with, mainly regarding their health and often related to subsistence. And then there's the middle generation, the generation of young people from 1989, which is internally the most disparate. Some of them learned their way around. Let's not forget that when we talk about corruption, we are referring almost exclusively to the middle-aged. There is little fertile ground for corruption in schools or retirement homes. Most of the middle generation is being squeezed in a vice: they need to keep pace to provide for their children and, at the same time, not end up like their parents in old age. They are kept in line not by fear of the secret police, but by the fear that they will become superfluous to their employer's needs.

Dvořáková: *If trust is disappearing from ordinary relations and authority is fading entirely, what might the ramifications be? This goes beyond our own society, blatant though this factor is here. Crises of confidence and crises of authority are a problem in many countries. Is this one of* *the reasons for a fear of openly subscribing to values – because we have experience of large-scale hypocrisy? Such experience has origins both before and after 1989.*

Hrubec: Interpersonal trust is an important part of any cultivated society. Economic and political systems that are based on circumventing cultivated rules of justice or on aggression require different, harsher relationships between people. Where people ignore, cheat, rob or attack others, there is little room for trust. Should I trust a minister, for example, who traitorously attempts to exploit or dismantle the state? This takes us down the path towards a crisis of confidence, with the danger of political turbulence. Therefore, even aggressive and violent regimes need at least basic manifestations of interpersonal trust in order to survive. Otherwise they would harm their own interests and, sooner or later, collapse. In this sense, we can say that neoliberalism and capitalism have a tendency to undermine their own foundations.

This is where the crisis of authority comes into play. In recent decades of neoliberal capitalism, the exaggerated and distorted emphasis on the idea of freedom has formed the notion that some people and corporations can do virtually anything they want. Yet should people be entitled to boundless freedom? For example, the freedom to be corrupt, strip assets or murder? Should not the freedom of one person end where the freedom of another begins? Boundless freedom effectively equates to arbitrariness or aggression, not liberty. Freedom should have limits defined by the authority of justice, including just laws of political and economic democracy. The authority of rules, however, should be guaranteed by legitimacy conferred by the public and its ethos of political and economic justice, otherwise such authority could easily spiral into authoritarianism.

Keller: The intensity of trust in specific individuals and in people in general, and even in institutions, is something we can measure. We are finding, with reasonable precision, that in all these forms trust is, if anything, contracting. Regrettably, we do not know how to bolster that fading trust. One of the main problems here is that, in everything we do (whether individually or institutionally), we must be dedicated to profit in keeping with the imperative of the time. However, nurturing friendship, love or trust just because we will benefit from it automatically destroys the essence of such love, friendship and trust. We are stuck in a trap that we laid ourselves in our selfishness. It is an unsolvable problem: capitalism cannot function without trust. Capitalism can only work on the principle of profitability. Trust cannot be built on the principle of profitability. Without trust, there can be no capitalism. Anyone who cannot remember what a real and genuine blind alley looks like needs to carefully run through this chain of truths once more. Inventing a vision within a capitalist structure is a rather meaningless activity. However, for those who would like to come up with a vision outside of such a structure, our democracy has created a number of provisions under criminal law.

The weakening of trust is regrettable not just in terms of interpersonal relationships and the quality of human life. Capitalism needs trust primarily from an economic perspective. Trust reduces transaction costs. If you cannot trust your business partners, guarantees via legal channels become all the more important. You need to take out more insurance and create more reserves in case you are cheated. This all drains money from the productive economy and transfers it into 'insurance' in the broader sense of the word. Those who measure gross domestic product growth gloss over such trifles. Society is getting richer regardless of whether we invest in the production of a new effective drug or in a network of consultants who are paid to call our attention to increasingly sophisticated tricks used by our business partners to exploit us. Nevertheless, we all feel that the first type of growth is more desirable than the second. Unfortunately, we live in a society where health is diminishing but the numbers of consultants are rocketing. Lamentably, none of them has been able to advise us on how to restore dwindling trust.

Dvořáková: *Every schoolchild knows that there is no point in playing a game if it is not played by the rules. Why, then, do we engage in games where others are constantly disrespecting the rules or interpreting them in different ways to suit their current circumstances?*

Keller: When rules are broken, ignored or transgressed by unprivileged individuals and groups, we call this social pathology. When the power-holding elite and the strongest financial groups of all time do the same, we call it deregulation. In cases of social pathology, a group usually unites in defence of the infringed rules, but in cases of deregulation those who protest are portrayed as deviants. In the media age, the elite and those who serve them have ample resources to present this reversal of values and the dismantling of rules as the shortest and surest path to freedom and prosperity.

Deregulation is not the work of anarchists. Rules that are purportedly overly prescriptive should not be abolished so that everyone can do what they want without interference. Only those rules that protect employees from employers, small businesses from large multinational colossi and nature from devastating practices are singled out for abolition. Removing them would not leave a vacuum in the domain of standards and rules. New rules would immediately surface. And this time they would be tailored completely to the financially strong and powerful. Deregulation is nothing other than the elimination of safeguards designed to protect the interests of the weak. Levers to help the powerful become even more powerful are installed in their place. Deregulation would not result in a freer world, but in a world in which the weaker have no recourse at all against the despotism of the powerful.

Hrubec: A major problem with adherence to rules in the economic and political sphere is that the economic and political 'elite' believe that their role is to set rules, but that they themselves do not have to observe them, or that they are above them. Rules are for their inferiors, for citizens. Supermarket cashiers whose cash drawer is out at the end of the evening are required to pay for the missing hundreds or thousands out of their own pocket. When ministers are found to have diverted hundreds of millions, or billions, the most we can often expect to hear is that it might be a good idea to organise things better next time. If anyone is prosecuted, it is the small fry – the subordinates.

The same applies on the transnational stage. Although we assume that all firms have to pay taxes that have been democratically set by parliament, large multinational corporations who choose to do business here often operate outside of governing law. The government arranges exemptions and tax breaks for them that are beyond the reach of ordinary small businesses. And to make it clear who's who and where a line is drawn between the lords and the rabble, the government even has an industrial zone built for the corporation with taxpayers' money. Therefore, maladjusted citizens indeed exist – many of them are managers and owners of large companies and the politicians serving them.

Keller: *It has always tended to be the young and the educated who entertain notions of social change. Why, today, do these two categories belong among those for whom the word 'vision' has often a hint of the senseless and inappropriate?*

Hrubec: The power-holding 'elites' have often resorted to deterrents in pursuit of their visions. However, after the horrors of World War II, people once again dared to dream of creating a better society, in both the West and the East. This was an era of hope and ambitious visions. Yet young people in the 1960s rightly decided that this was not enough and staged student revolts. At the same time, there was a surge in the feminist movement, the movement of African Americans in the USA, etc. But then, after 1969, so-called 'normalisation' descended on Czechoslovakia and neoliberalisation spread in the West, expanding globally after 1989. We live in an era of disillusionment and discontent. Sooner or later, the struggle against injustice will once again engender revolt and an intensified search for alternatives and visions.

Those young people who appear to be hopeless products of today's era of disillusionment in the West need not necessarily be a lost generation. They may come good. Nor can we generalise; even among university students I can see active young people, although I realise that this is just a small minority. But it is impossible to live for long without hope and at least minimal vision. After all, even today citizens take at least a modestly conceived vision for granted. Politicians, for example, who promised nothing in their election campaigns and failed to formulate at least some form of vision would not be elected. That said, it is true that these days many people expect very little, and sometimes even nothing, of elections and politicians. But when they do realise that they have been seriously marginalised, or when they see examples of social change abroad, they will demand more. Fortunately, the West is no longer the centre of the world from this point of view. For example, in Latin America many young people have been highly active in recent decades. They have inspirational visions of social and political justice which have spread around the world: for instance, they have been at the forefront of the organisation of local and global social forums, they have made major contributions to the formulation of participatory budgeting, etc. Many young people are also engaged in social change in other places around the world. They criticise the contemporary unjust reality and the coming dystopia, and they know that it is not necessary to be passive pessimists. They want at least to try to change the unjust status quo, some of them by long-term social changes, others by short-term ones. History is not over.

Dvořáková: Visions in themselves have been very vulgarised because all sorts of atrocities were committed in the twentieth century in the name of realising visions and changes in society. Even the transformation of the 1990s took place in tandem with a sort of ideological short-cut that ultimately concealed large-scale larceny and the dismantling of essential state capacities, where not only the vision but also the values were almost aggressively presented.

A vision is itself a problem, in that it may create the illusion that a society can be built where difficulties will be resolved once and for all. Yet this can never happen. Every development, every change addresses one issue while simultaneously opening up other problems. Incidentally, the fact that a vision can never be entirely realised and an 'ideal' community can never be created is heavily exploited in populist strategies and policies. They vaguely formulate a vision and the efforts to realise it legitimise the reason why a charismatic leader, the stand-ard-bearer of this vision, must constantly extend his or her power – in order to bring his or her vision to fruition.

I think that the 'rejection' of a vision, the rejection of the notion of profound changes, is related not so much to the fact that society has become more cynical, but perhaps to a weakening of normal interpersonal trust and to the loss of authority – both the authority of institutions and the authority of individuals. Experience has led us down a path where we often view a 'vision' only as a smokescreen for completely different goals.

Keller: *It is often said that society cannot be changed unless the people change for the better. Do you feel that this is just an excuse? After all, psychologically speaking it is likely that appeals for improvement will be heard by those who are the most morally upright. Those who desperately need a moral awakening are, by definition, somehow deaf to such calls. If those full of promise were to improve, wouldn't life with those who reject improvement be completely unbearable? How could society then evolve in this situation?*

Dvořáková: This problem accurately captures the widespread absurd-ity. What is better and what is worse behaviour largely depends on social conditions and culture. There is no rapid upheaval; culture has long-term effects and only long-term efforts can lead to certain transformations. In our environment, many of the ways of thinking and value-based approaches from the time of 'normalisation' of 1969 onwards have not only been retained but have also deepened to some extent. Aggressive ideologisation that, perhaps, some of the standard-bearers did not even believe in, using it instead as a cover to further their personal interests, reproduced an environment where a variety of services and favours formed a basic economic setting in which ethics were completely excluded from the value system; this was accurately expressed, for example, by the adoration of racketeers as the symbol of modern entrepreneurs.

It is difficult to change. Sometimes the trigger can be the way institutions are configured, sometimes the behaviour of the individual. Socialisation processes, especially education, are also significant. Here, it is not just the form of education (knowledge, skills, cognitive development) that is important, but also the methods of communication and conflict resolution in a particular community. If you look at many schools' rules, unlike the previous regime you will often encounter a long list of rights, but many fewer obligations – yet these should be balanced. Above all, you will rarely find 'what if' procedures – what action will be taken and who will be the judge. In schools, 'pupil parliaments' are often set up, but these often reproduce a caricature of the previous regime's parliament in terms of what is submitted to them and what they vote on. At universities, we often see caricatures of 'academic senates' – either the senate is hostile to the leadership (the dean or rector) and acts to destabilise it or, conversely, is entirely devoted to the leadership and approves of everything it wants. Not to mention the fact that sometimes loyal decisions or elections of the leadership by the senate are actually bought in return for positions, status and success in examinations. Following the political model, this is taken for granted and regarded as a political deal even though it is clear-cut corruption. It is very difficult to set up an academic senate as a partner that controls and monitors, but also cooperates and provides feedback, and this is often undesirable for many anyway.

Children and young people can best learn about living in a democracy by being in a democratic environment which, while obviously conflicted, is a setting where they find a civilised means of addressing conflicts. Today this is not something they encounter at school or even, ultimately, in life – research shows that relationships in the workplace in many places are now even worse than before.

Hrubec: Previously there was a reliance on changes in institutional structures. Now, the individual freedom of action of individuals is over-rated. Both, of course, are extremes. People are not deterministically confined to institutions and their structures, nor can they completely break free from social norms and act in any arbitrary manner. Rather, it is necessary to take comprehensive account of the institutional structures and human action in them and to grasp how they interact. This is the only way of coming to grips with true opportunities and achieving any meaningful social change.

While further developments in the BRICS countries will follow their own relatively alternate path, capitalist normalisation temporarily has the upper hand in Western countries, but it will not last forever. In principle, several scenarios of further societal developments in Western countries are possible, the first two of which are a nightmare.

The first scenario is the effort to revive the economy and political legitimacy through hyper-neoliberalism, which would attempt to build on the neoliberalism in place prior to the global economic crisis. Various banks and other companies have tried their hand at this, forcing national governments to implement state capitalism by means of bailouts or financial incentives, or, conversely, by making numerous financial cuts with negative impacts on the lower and middle classes. Although hyper-neoliberalism would make various ownership relations and financial products more transparent, this transparency could trigger even greater financial and other economic speculation and another crisis, but potentially with a far more drastic impact on the lives of the lower and middle classes in Western countries, combined with intensified extreme poverty in developing countries.

The other adverse scenario is economic and political revitalisation through nationalism, xenophobia, fascisation and war. Investment in wars could pathologically stimulate the economy and, after the war, much of what has been destroyed could then be rebuilt, again stimulating economic development. This agonising neoconservative scenario would probably be the worst way forward.

The third scenario is what we face now. It is a defence of the status quo or simply mild neo-Keynesian attempts to improve the situation. In the shorter or longer term, another crisis would surface that would essentially duplicate the previous crisis.

The fourth scenario, the positive one, would be the effort to overcome the plutocracy or oligarchy (formal democracy) in Western countries by the materialisation of democracy, i.e. by introducing strong elements of economic democracy which, in turn, could strengthen political democracy. In favour of political and social justice, I have already talked about participatory budgeting, the deprivatisation of companies, genuine pluralism of ownership, etc. A prerequisite for a more equitable structure of society is the elimination of ownership extremism, where certain companies and individuals have such extreme sources of ownership and income that they can block or even incapacitate the lives of other people, including the exercise of their freedom. The introduction of democracy in the economic, political and cultural spheres would facilitate advancements in the lives of all people.

Hrubec: *And what is your opinion? What further developments can you see happening? Do you think that, in view of the developments so far, contemporary society is headed towards stagnation, i.e. towards capitalist normalisation, or do you expect any dramatic changes, whether for the better or for the worse? Surely we should not simply gawp in surprise at future events without having engaged in any forecasting, and without considering what action could and should be taken in such circumstances?*

Keller: I think that there are three risks, which – especially if combined – could be devastating. The first is that the system has been set up in a way that has steadily ruined the middle class, entailing a transition from a society of inequality to a society of asymmetry. There is a danger that the middle classes will slide downwards at an ever faster pace. The result would be worse than ordinary polarisation. In a polarised society, those at the top need those down below to work for them, to buy their goods and to provide them with services. Today, those at the top behave as if they do not need those at the bottom or in the middle for anything at all. In a globalised economy, people in any one locality are not important as it is always possible to go elsewhere.

The second threat is xenophobia and racism. People who already know that they are not important look for scapegoats to take the blame. They look for them not above, but below. Therefore, I would rather not theorise about revolution because our society has fallen so deep that, for many people, the only meaningful revolution would take the form of a pogrom.

The third threat is ecological. The deepening of the asymmetry and the guidance of people's resentment towards those who are even worse off perfectly draw attention away from a ticking environmental time bomb. At a time when the scope for survival in the environment is shrinking, things are seething as though they were about to explode in that corner of the former nature and landscape that we so nicely civilised. Where are those times when we had the consolation that, at least in the medium term, there were no threats?

If citizens want to be active, then they should be active mainly in seeking ways and means to change what is bothering them. I can only give one piece of advice. It is pointless for anyone to try to change the system themselves. It is better and more opportune to fight the small evils we encounter directly around us. If a lot of people were to resolutely fight these small evils they see around them, this would be the best change in the system we could imagine.

Dvořáková: Originally a historian by education, I would say that the 'world' community and individual countries are at a crossroads. There are many critical phenomena here and it is difficult to say at this time which ones are permanent and indelible and which ones may, if addressed, calm the situation for a while. It is difficult to predict how things will develop. There is always a risk of disaster, of the breakdown of civilisation or the extinction of humankind, but there is also the possibility that something will come to the fore that creates the conditions (seeds) for further development. We cannot say in advance what will happen.

However, not to be so fatalist, it is important for society to defend certain core values that it does not want to abandon; in this way, it is in a position to influence future developments. The problem is that everyone has a different view of what positive social change is. Of course, the legitimacy of interests cannot be boundless; thieves – even those in suits – have their own specific interests and we should not tolerate these. Naturally, however, I believe it is possible for society to agree on certain issues. First and foremost, most agree on what they do not want. I am not the only one who is worried that there are hungry children whose parents cannot afford school lunches. I am not the only one who is uncomfortable living in a country where, rather than engage in legitimate debt recovery, it is possible for people to be artificially cast into ingeniously set debt traps. And I am not the only one bothered when the logic of 'reform' is determined by opportunities to channel money into private hands, when decisions on the political direction of the country are taken by arrogant 'nabobs' or 'empresses', and the economy and politics are influenced by the various racketeers.

To extricate ourselves, we should build the state apparatus (and prevent its further privatisation), rehabilitate the notion of public interest and reclaim public space. Everyone can contribute. Let's keep control of politicians, demand information and insist on compliance with the rules. Let's not underestimate the setup and functioning of institutions. We are the ones who must deliver the values lacking in society. No saviour will do it for us. We must all strive for change and fight for change.

3

Revolutions, Transformations, Civilisations: Prolegomena to a Paradigm Reorientation

Johann P. Arnason

ATTEMPTS TO DECLARE an end to the era of revolutions have proved as futile as the efforts to develop a consensual model for their study. Unexpected turns of history have brought revolutionary phenomena back to attention and, at the same time, have raised fundamental questions about definitions and demarcations in the field. That applies, in very different ways, to the Iranian revolution of 1979 and the collapse of Eastern European Communist regimes a decade later. In both cases, aspects indicative of a properly revolutionary dynamic (such as the exceptionally high level of popular mobilisation in Iran, or the liquidation of an entire ideological, political and economic order in Eastern Europe) seemed to combine with more disconcerting features (hierocratic politics in Iran, proposed adaptation to an older and globally dominant order in Eastern Europe). More recent developments have also underlined how far the mythologisation of revolution can outrun real history. The changes brought about by the 'Arab Spring', at first grossly exaggerated by Western liberals and radicals alike, now appear very insignificant. Only two cases can at all be claimed as evidence. In Tunisia, a fragile parliamentary regime still faces unsettled questions about the place of Islam in political life; as for the upheaval in Egypt, where the military state seems to have survived and given its main rivals just enough time to stalemate themselves, the only question is whether we want to describe the whole process as abortive or illusory. Another example is the imagery of 'colour revolutions' in post-Soviet states. The events in question did not amount to more than skirmishes within the ranks of unstable power elites, and the main reason for mythologising them is that it helps to justify a revival of cold war politics. But such vicissitudes may also serve to remind us of further sides to the problematic of revolutions. The revolutionary imaginary is a significant part of the story, and not only because of its impact on revolutionary processes; its disembodied offshoots include sectarian subcultures and quixotic adventures as well as geopolitical masquerades of the kind just mentioned.[1]

The following discussion does not aim at a broad overview of current debates. Its main purpose is to highlight some basic points of dispute in the historical and sociological research on revolutions; they have to do with the definition as well as the explanation (or, for some authors including the present writer, the understanding) of revolutions, and can be formulated in terms of conceptual alternatives. Against this background, the final section of the paper will then consider the case for a particular approach to the study of revolutions: the civilisational one, so far rather marginal to the field but in my opinion a very promising line of argument.

Categorising revolutions: dichotomies and their problems

If we first consider descriptive categories, ways of defining revolutionary phenomena and demarcating them from other types of historical events or social processes, it seems appropriate to start with the very elementary distinction between short-term and long-term transformations, also discussed in some other contributions to this volume. A familiar understanding of revolution applies the term to abrupt turns of events with wide social ramifications, such as those of 1789 in France or 1917 in Russia, and sometimes to very short but crucial episodes, such as the February and October revolutions in Russia. On the other hand, the concept of revolution is commonly used to describe transformations unfolding over much longer periods of time; the industrial revolution is a classic case, and so is the modern scientific revolution, understood as an ongoing process beginning in the sixteenth and seventeenth centuries. Although it is very unlikely that these conventions can be changed, we can neutralise the issue by redefining the transformations in question as long-term processes with more or less pronounced breakthrough or renewal phases. The same applies, for example, to the 'legal revolution of the Middle Ages' (Berman 1983); it is best understood as a take-off to a long-term process of juridification. More ambiguous is the term 'urban revolution'. If it is used to describe urbanising processes, it falls into the same category as the cases just cited. But it can also, especially in the medieval context, refer to the emergence of autonomous urban communities, and thus to more short-term changes with political impact.

On closer examination, the difference between short-term and long-term perspectives reappears within the more circumscribed category of political revolution. Key examples will illustrate this point. The French revolution has often been dated from 1789 to 1799, and taken to end with Napoleon Bonaparte's coup d'état; if we want to stress the imperial turn of the revolutionary process, the end of the Napoleonic wars in 1815 may seem an appropriate final date; but a strong case has been made – notably by François Furet (1988) – for a longer period ending with the consolidation of the Third Republic around 1880. Only then was the contest between monarchy and republic settled, with the accompaniment of major sociocultural shifts. In the Russian case, there are obvious reasons to go beyond the events of 1917 and consider the end of the civil war in 1921 as a defining culmination of the Bolshevik takeover. But it may also be argued that Stalin's 'second revolution', beginning at the end of the 1920s, was the final twist to the Bolshevik project: it imposed the regime of state-controlled accumulation on rural society. Then the end of the 'second revolution' remains to be dated, and the termination of the Great Purge in 1938 is perhaps the most plausible choice. It marks the self-destruction of the Bolsheviks and the final consolidation of a totalitarian regime. It is more difficult to define a long revolution beyond that point – unless we want to interpret the whole Soviet trajectory as a road from one imperial collapse to another, which may not be an idea to be dismissed out of hand.

Finally, the Chinese revolution appears easier to grasp in a long-term than a short-term perspective. The events of 1911–12, sometimes described as a revolution, do not fit the term: they exemplify the breakdown of an old order accompanied by the failure to establish a new one. The Communist victory in 1949 ended a process of fragmentation, power struggles and bids for reunification; reconstructions of that background tend to prolong it into the past. John King Fairbank (1986) developed the idea of a long Chinese revolution, from 1850 to 1949. In fact, the title of Fairbank's book suggests a beginning in 1800; but the real starting point is the Taiping rebellion, a veritable historical cataclysm that weakened the apparently victorious old order beyond repair; later internal crises and geopolitical setbacks led to its collapse, and it took several decades for a unified successor state to emerge. This periodisation is easy to justify in terms of geopolitical aims and achievements. There is no doubt that efforts to reunify the Chinese imperial state and re-establish it as a great power were central to the revolutionary process. But if we also consider the quest for a new social order and a model of development, a shorter process following Fairbank's long one may be identified. For a quarter of a century after the Communist victory, social and developmental goals were pursued through a combination of exaggerated Soviet prescriptions with home-made excesses and derailments (such as the Great Leap and the Cultural Revolution). This phase came to an end in the late 1970s, and Deng Xiaoping's return to power marked the beginning of a pragmatic but sustained reorientation.

To sum up, the demarcation of politically centred and socially significant revolutions from long-term transformative processes seems justified, but it still leaves us with a distinction between shorter- and longer-term sequences within the former category. Moreover, a very brief comparative reflection is enough to show that this contrast must be redefined for each specific case. Taking that point on board, we can move on to the next dichotomy.

It has often been suggested or assumed that to qualify as revolutions in the full and proper sense, radical political changes must involve high levels of popular mobilisation. The term 'social revolution' is sometimes used to stress this aspect. On the other hand, the notion of a revolution from above is widely current, and attempts have been made to defend it as a special category of revolutionary phenomena (e.g. Trimberger 1978, explicitly conceived as a complement to Theda Skocpol's work (1979) on states and social revolutions). Revolutions of this kind are supposedly carried out by elites in control of state power, with minimal or non-existent input from social movements. Standard examples from modern history are the Meiji revolution of 1868 in Japan and the Kemalist revolution in Turkey after World War I. The early phase of the military regime in Egypt, from 1952 to 1970, earlier seen as a major case in point, now appears less significant.

Two trends seem especially characteristic of the debate on these issues, and both lead to a certain relativisation of the difference between social revolutions and revolutions from above. Doubts have been cast on both Turkish and Japanese experiences of revolution from above. Historians now emphasise continuities between modernising currents under the Ottomans, from the early nineteenth century onwards, and the post-imperial Kemalist phase; a nationalist turn was already evident in the Young Turk revolution that preceded imperial collapse. And later developments have shown that the Kemalist state did not settle the question of Islamic involvement in politics as conclusively as was widely assumed when revolutionary secularism seemed in control. In short, the revolution from above now looks more like an episode in a long-term process of imperial modernisation and its nation-state aftermath. As for the Japanese example, the events of 1868 and their sequel have proved susceptible to very different interpretations. Apart from Marxist attempts to portray them as an incomplete and deformed bourgeois revolution (at one stage widely accepted by Japanese scholars), a provocative reassessment was proposed by an author who saw the role of lower samurai in the Meiji revolution as a particularly pronounced case of global modern trends (Huber 1981). On this reading, the managerial-bureaucratic logic of modern revolutions, obscured by Western constructs of bourgeois and proletarian stages, was implemented by a samurai stratum mutating into a service class. But such arguments invite an objection: if the making of modern Japan was – at a decisive juncture – a matter of following a mainstream path in an exemplary fashion, why were the political and cultural patterns of Japanese modernity so markedly different from those prevailing in the West? A closer look at that aspect may lead to the conclusion that Japanese transformations should be judged in the context of indigenous traditions and their cultural premises. That is the view taken by S. N. Eisenstadt, on the basis of a civilisational approach; the point to be noted here is that he prefers the Japanese term *ishin*, underlining the traditionalist claims of the 1868 activists, rather than any Western notion of revolution. To put it another way, this view suggests that the Meiji experience blurs the distinction between revolution and restoration, rather than exemplifying any kind of revolution from above.

On the other hand, advancing historical research on social revolutions has highlighted the fact that they include elements and episodes of revolutions from above. The French revolution is an obvious starting point for clarification of that problem. It gave rise to the Jacobin paradigm, convincingly described by Eisenstadt as an ideologically convertible model that recurs in movements otherwise as different as Communism, Fascism and Islamic fundamentalism (Eisenstadt 1999). Admittedly, the notion of an enlightened or spiritually qualified political centre, capable of regenerating society, does not constitute a blueprint for revolutions from above. But the historical trajectory of the Jacobin model (including its influence on Napoleon's version of imperial rule, already noted by Karl Marx) reveals its ability to adapt to circumstances and at the same time to acquire specific contents. In the Russian revolutionary tradition, Bolshevism represented an explicit renewal of Jacobin visions, reinforced by claims to a scientific grasp of history. The potential for a 'substitutionist' recentring of revolution was later – after the upheavals of 1917 – maximised by a whole concatenation of events, culminating in Stalin's second revolution; the latter is often, and for good reasons, described as a revolution from above, but detailed analyses of the record suggest a somewhat more nuanced view, stressing urban support for Stalin's offensive against the peasantry. China may be described as an even more pronounced case of a revolution from above, absorbing inconclusive beginnings of a social revolution. Neither February nor October 1917 had a parallel in China; a whole cultural, social and political order collapsed, and there was, after World War I, a temporary upsurge of social movements. The organisation that ultimately restored the centre came out of this crucible; but, in the first instance, the post-imperial transition was followed by a struggle between rival successor states, primarily the Guomindang and Communist ones (although alternatives supported by Japan also came into play), and the power balance between these two main contenders was decisively affected by regional geopolitics. The Japanese bid to conquer China did massive damage to the Guomindang regime, and the triumph of the Communist counter-state can only be understood in this context. Obviously, the ability of the Communists to attract peasant support (varying in kind and degree across the different regions of China) counted for something, but so did the perceptions of their local regime as a more promising model for state rebuilding, and therefore a more credible nationalist force. The interpretation of the Communist takeover as a peasant revolution belongs in the realm of political mythology. And contrary to another myth still widely accepted by the Western Left, the Chinese Communists did not succeed primarily as 'fighters for national independence against the Japanese' (Therborn 2008: xvi); they succeeded as more effective and credible state builders against an adversary who had borne the main brunt of the war with Japan and been weakened beyond repair.

The upshot of all these considerations is certainly not that the notion of revolution from above should be dismissed; rather, we need to rethink the experiences associated or connectable with it and their relationship to social revolutions. A further subject for reflection and controversy, not unrelated, is the question of violence and its role in revolutions. Here, too, it seems useful to define contrasting perspectives. One approach takes a violent transfer of power as a defining feature of revolutions; for others, the absence or involvement of violence is a question of historical circumstances, and not to be prejudged on the conceptual level. If we consider the exemplary and most extensively studied cases of modern revolutions, there can be no doubt about the matter. Violence has been a very central part of the picture, although not always to the same degree or in the same form. But it may be helpful to broaden the focus and take more original or atypical constellations into account. On the one hand, there are situations characterised by a far-reaching collapse of established power structures and an unleashing of violence, without this breakdown leading to the emergence of a new order. Such episodes occur in various historical settings. One of the earliest cases may be the disintegration of the Old Kingdom in ancient Egypt in the late third millennium BCE. This intermediate period, as it is now known, was clearly an unravelling process of major dimensions, although historians still disagree on the extent of regression and the level of violence; but nobody now argues, as some early Marxists did, that it was the earliest known social revolution. The restored monarchy of the Middle Kingdom was a somewhat modified version of the pharaonic regime, but certainly marked by basic continuity. A much later example is more relevant to the study of modern revolutions. The early-seventeenth-century Russian 'time of troubles' (*smuta*) led to an all-round implosion of state power, accompanied by widespread violence; but in the end, core structures of the Muscovite state were restored, though without the excessive twists taken under Ivan IV. Memories of this breakdown have played a certain role in perceptions and interpretations of twentieth-century Russian revolutions. Some realignments after 1905 had to do with the fear of a *smuta*-style breakdown, seen as a possible outcome of the interrupted revolution. The application of this model to the events of 1917 and their sequel allows for more variations. If the focus is on the civil war from 1918 to 1921, the analogy serves to stress the distance between the process that unfolded in St Petersburg in 1917 and the regime emerging victorious in a ruined country. A different picture is evoked as a looming threat in the later months of 1917, in the end only avoided through the Bolshevik seizure of power. The timing of the latter has even been ascribed to premonitions of an uncontrollable and destructive revolt (Rosenberg 1962 is an example of this argument). The debate on possible alternative outcomes is still open, but it seems in any case clear that Lenin's strategy was not aimed at the prevention of collapse. This prospect was not yet in sight when he proposed a short path to power.

On the other hand, there are cases of major and rapid macro-social changes with little or no violence involved. Here the Eastern European transformations at the end of the twentieth-century are of exemplary importance. Admittedly, they did not result in the smooth transfer of Western models that was widely expected at the outset, but the upshot was nevertheless a rapid and sweeping replacement of core institutions and a complete disintegration of the imperial regime that had controlled the region. Apart from the marginal case of Romania, this was a non-violent revolution (the later conflicts and changes in Yugoslavia unfolded in a different, non-imperial context); the role of popular mobilisation varied from one country to another. The most markedly non-violent turn, and the least dependent on any broader mobilisation, occurred in Hungary, where the ruling party renounced its monopoly of power. Since this was the beginning of a chain reaction in the central and south-eastern part of the Soviet Bloc, it can hardly be dismissed as a minor or atypical event. And it may be added that the longer-term Hungarian experience of Communism deserves more attention: this was the only country that twice put an end to party-state rule, through popular rebellion in 1956 and elite abdication in 1989. The asymmetric compromise between the party-state (restored by invasion) and society did not achieve its stated aim: no viable or transferable model of reform Communism emerged. But it seems, in retrospect, to have paved the way for a particularly smooth exit. How this whole trajectory relates to the later nationalist revival is another issue, not to be explored here.

To sum up, this aspect of a more general problem – defining revolutions – remains controversial. There is a strong and still widely accepted tradition of including violence as a key factor, and this would make the concept inapplicable to the Eastern European events of 1989. Given the radical character and the exceptional rapidity of the changes in question, that seems counter-intuitive. But purely definitional disputes are not fruitful. The substantive lesson from the debate summarised above is best put in conditional terms: if we retain the definition of revolution as major and rapid social change by violent means, we must locate the relevant cases within a broader spectrum. At one end we find explosions of violence with destructive but not transformative impact on social patterns, at the other constellations of actors and structures that eventuate in vast but non-violent changes, such as the regional concatenation of 1989.

The fourth and last pair of alternatives is most closely linked to underlying visions of history. Revolutions have often been associated with progress, most emphatically in the Marxian tradition, but more conditionally by those who stressed the enlightening and liberating

34

effects of some revolutions while condemning others for deviating from that course. Some earlier comparisons of the late-eighteenth-century democratic revolutions with the twentieth-century Communist ones took this line: developments in Russia, and to some extent in China, were portrayed as taking off from democratising and potentially Westernising beginnings, but then, due to ideological, structural or situational factors, lapsing into less promising ways (Malia 1980). More recently, one of the recurrent comments on the Iranian revolution is that it has dealt a blow to Western assumptions about the affinity of revolution and progress. But the contrast to be noted here is not between an indiscriminate and a selective identification of revolution and progress. Rather, it concerns the very commensurability of the two concepts. To the claim that revolutions are more or less progressive, we can oppose the idea of revolutionary episodes as – first and foremost – problematising turns of social-historical processes, terminations of certain patterns and at the same time openings to multiple possibilities. They entail breakdowns of previously dominant institutions, though not always to the same degree; by the same token, they provide space for new expressions of instituting capacities, and an arena for actors with strategies of alliance as well as conflict. They lead, more or less circuitously, to the restructuring of states and societies. To put it another way, they involve dynamics of collapse and regeneration, further complicated by heightened contingency and open alternatives. It cannot be said that this view of revolutions has, as yet, been formulated with the same clarity as the much older association with progress. But it seems implicit in major reappraisals of major cases, especially the French and Russian ones: their complexity and irreducibility to any linear logic is now better understood. If we want to retain at least the possibility of asking questions about the connection to progress, they can only relate to particular aspects of the revolutionary process. And that presupposes a scaled-down idea of progress, perhaps best summed up in Norbert Elias's observation that 'es gibt Fortschritte, aber keinen Fortschritt'. Freely translated, this means that we can speak of advances in specific areas, but not of any all-round and ongoing trend that could be equated with progress *tout court*. With such considerations in mind, it would still seem meaningful to distinguish between progressive and regressive developments within a revolutionary transformation – but, needless to say, with all due awareness of their often complex intertwinings.

Explanations and interpretations: alternatives in debate

The conceptual issues discussed above have to do with ways of defining revolutions. On another level, we find similar contrasts between attempts to account for them, sometimes in terms of causes, but in other cases through interpretive models. Here, too, I shall distinguish four types of controversy, and although there are no close correspondences to the definitional questions, some affinities will be noted.

The most marked disagreement among theorists of revolution is about the respective roles of power and ideology, and there is no doubt that power-centred approaches have been more strongly represented in recent debates. Their ascendancy and their specific thrust are best understood in the context of moving beyond Marxian ideas, and the shift from Barrington Moore (1967) to Theda Skocpol (1979) seems crucial. Marxian views of revolutions as the highest level of class action were influential far beyond the limits of orthodox Marxism, and Moore's comparative history was still within that broader orbit: he argued that an explanation of transitions to the modern world, and especially to political modernity, could only be explained in terms of a more complex analysis than Marx or his disciples had developed. In particular, landlords and peasants, on their own or in changing class alliances, played more important roles than had generally been recognised. Skocpol moved beyond class-centred perspectives towards a more comprehensive focus on social power, and the main counterweight to class had to be the state. Hence the emphasis on several aspects of state dynamics that characterises Skocpol's comparison of three great modern revolutions. In France, Russia and China, revolutionary crises engulfed states whose capacities were overtaxed by their involvement in international affairs; the crises led to a mobilisation of social forces whose conflicts and initiatives resulted in major transformations of the social order; the revolutionary processes were then brought to an end by a reconstruction of the affected states in new and stronger forms.

Skocpol's book on revolutions seems to have been more central to subsequent debates than any other single work on the subject. Some responses have aimed at a more precise definition of powers and problems attributed to the state. In that context, a few comments on Jeff Goodwin's arguments (Goodwin 1997: 12–13) may be useful. He distinguishes four versions of a 'statist model' in the theory of revolutions. The state autonomy perspective emphasises the specific 'identities, interests, ideologies and . . . lines of action' developed by state officials; a second approach stresses the capacities and resources mobilised by states; a third one focuses on the political opportunities that states can create for social groups; finally, a 'state-constructionist' perspective puts the main emphasis on state involvement in the formation of civil society. But on closer examination these are not so much different models as different implications of one basic perspective, and we could add to the list; for example, Michael Mann's comments on the internal conflicts and dysfunctionalities of state structures, often very important for the course of historical events, certainly has some bearing on the analysis of revolutions. But the common denominator is the state autonomy perspective, which would be incomplete without a reference to capacities and resources, one-sided if it dealt only with the characteristics and possibilities of elites and did not take into account the logic of institutions, and oversimplified if it did not allow for disruptive factors at work within the state. The role of the state in the constitution of civil society is a particularly important aspect of the former's autonomy.

More critical reactions to Skocpol's work, too varied to be discussed here in detail, have noted one-sided claims and thematic omissions. Her comparative approach met with twofold criticism: the search for lawlike correlations on the basis of three examples seemed misguided, but each of the latter was also found to need more contextualisation. For those who insisted on the complexity and uniqueness of each revolutionary constellation, it was natural to foreground two factors marginalised by Skocpol's effort to shift the framework from theorising from actors to structures: leadership and ideology. The latter is, for present purposes, more important. If ideology is understood in a broad sense, it shapes the visions of leaders as well as their appeal to their followers. But it can also be analysed at a more general level, as a constitutive correlate of power, inasmuch as the latter is always culturally defined. Until now, however, the ideological dimensions of revolutions have mainly been explored in relation to particular cases. François Furet's reassessment of the ideological background and legacy of the French revolution is in this vein: the revolutionary myth – including, most importantly, the Jacobin phantasm – is a unique historical formation, and the twentieth-century Communist myth is a derivative version (Furet 1981). Similarly, those who analyse the Bolshevik takeover and its Stalinist sequel as a turn to 'ideocracy' stress the imposition of an ideological project on a ruined and fragmented society (the most systematic version of this argument is Malia (1995); to the best of my knowledge, it has not proved at all possible to make the same case about Chinese Communism). The militantly Islamic ideology of the Iranian revolution has been emphasised by some authors writing on the subject (Arjomand 1989), whereas others have tried to show that the dynamics of state building and state crisis were more fundamental (Skocpol 1982), even if they took a turn that enabled a traditionalist religious elite to take control of a revolutionary alliance. There seems to be no comparative discussion of the ideological factor in revolutions that could be confronted with Skocpol's analyses of power structures in crisis and transformation; and no properly systematic attempt to combine and theorise the results of advancing historical research on these two aspects of revolutionary phenomena.

There will be more to say on the relationship between ideology and power. At this point, we may note some basic conceptual preliminaries. A quick look at classical sources suggests that the question could be linked to Max Weber's much-quoted distinction between interests (material and ideal) and ideas. As Weber puts it, interests are direct determinants of human action, but ideas (including, to use a non-Weberian term, ideologies in the broader sense of comprehensive interpretive frameworks) shape the options and paths seen as available by interest-driven actors. It is easy to add the point that the pursuit of interests involves power, and that despite changing ways of conceptualising power, the ability to achieve goals guided by interests is always included. The next step is to stress the cultural variability of power, recognised by some authors (such as Pye 1988) on the empirical level but not yet theorised in an adequate fashion. Perceptions, understandings and uses of power are culturally patterned, and a theoretical approach can begin with a brief survey of elementary alternatives, all of which combine dichotomous patterns with ambiguous, discontinuous and non-deterministic processes. An obvious starting point is the distinction between embodied and disembodied visions of power. Claude Lefort (1994) applied this conceptual pair to the democratic revolution against the early modern monarchy as well as to the totalitarian turns of twentieth-century revolutions. But it is also relevant to the long-drawn-out process that culminated in a de-personalised notion of the state. If the emergence of the state is inseparable from kingship, de-personalisation is a secondary process and, as Lefort's analysis of the totalitarian experience shows, visions of re-embodiment within a changed sociocultural world can lead to extreme consequences. A second key distinction, between the sacred and the secular, has similar implications. The sacral context of early state formation seems well established. At the same time, a minimum of self-contained structural cohesion is always required and, in that sense, there is a constitutive secular side to state power. The complexity of the processes supposed to strengthen it becomes clear when we consider the meanings attached to the concept of secularisation: it refers to a rollback of religion as well as to the permanence of religious significations in worldly guise and to their transformation through projection onto social or (more importantly) political actors and institutions. The last aspect is notoriously disputed among historians and sociologists of modern revolutions. Finally, political power – in our context the most important type of power – implies a distinction between a political centre, for present purposes identifiable with the state, and a political community recognising the authority of the centre (with varying degrees of ambiguity) and to some extent involved in its activity. Interconnections and tensions between the two poles are omnipresent in history (Eisenstadt tends to subsume them under the interaction of centre and periphery). Archaic states developed aspirations to unconstrained power, but in practice their reach was limited by various counterweights. The Greek polis represented a new turn, minimising the social distance between state and society, and further steps towards democracy may be seen as efforts to merge the two. Modern revolutions invented representative democracy, as a new way of asserting the sovereignty of the political community, but they also strengthened political centres in multiple regards. The trajectory of the Russian revolution illustrates the most extreme possibilities within this spectrum. Its early phase gave rise to radical visions of absorbing state power into the political community (by transferring all power to the councils, thus lending a semblance of content to the notion of 'withering away'), but later developments led to the formation of an ultra-autocratic state. Lenin's *State and Revolution*, perhaps best described as a borderline case of self-deluded demagogy, served to appropriate and subvert the utopia of a self-governing society, in such a way that it did not clash with the principle of party leadership, and could on that basis be gradually neutralised.

To round off this comment on ideology and power, one more point should be added. If power is always culturally defined, it is also true that cultural patterns are power-backed. If we briefly recall Weber's distinction between ideas and interests, the ideas in question appear as interpretations of underlying and encompassing cultural orientations and, as such, they affect social life through power; that general claim makes no specific assumptions about the bases or holders of power. As noted above, the upshot of debates on power in social theory seems to be that the concept is not separable from the context of a plurality of actors intervening in the world. Their interaction, further complicated by the involvement of various situational factors, gives rise to constellations that acquire their own dynamic, neither reducible to the structure of action nor to any kind of collective macro-actor. Analyses of social power call for a relational approach, and the main discussions now in progress are about different versions of this view. For our purposes, Norbert Elias's concept of figuration – the first attempt to explicitly foreground the relational character of power – will suffice to outline some general conclusions. Figurations are power balances in flux; in that sense, the concept applies to all levels of social relations, from the interaction of individuals to the rivalries of institutionalised power centres. It also allows for interconnected formations of varying size and cohesions from small-scale groupings to global networks. And although that was not part of the original conception, figurations can easily be understood as frameworks including natural and sociocultural factors (a point developed from another angle by actor-network theory). The coalitions and confrontations of actors in figurations draw on different 'sources of social power', to use Michel Mann's term, and affect the dynamics of their overlapping networks. By the same token, these multiple intertwinings involve changing spatial and temporal contexts, never reducible to a standard self-contained model of society as a system. To sum up, there are weighty reasons to reject the idea of cultural models, programming social order and development; rather, we are dealing with an open-ended interpenetration of cultural patterns and power constellations, whose fusion gives rise to emergent structures and events, as irreducible to a programming logic of one side as to causal forces of the other. From this point of view, social analysis can make use of theoretical insights into the creativity of culture and the productivity of power.

The reason for including these general considerations in our argument is that they have direct bearing on the dispute outlined above: should comparative histories of revolutions place their main emphasis on ideologies or power structures? As we have seen, conceptual grounds speak for an interactive view. The notion of a revolution aiming at or resulting in ideocracy is as implausible as the claim that all revolutions move within a closed circle of perpetual and uniform oligarchy (if the former approach has found its favourite terrain in the Soviet experience and its revolutionary origins, the *locus classicus* of the latter is Ronald Syme's (2002) work on the revolution that destroyed the Roman republic). As for the more nuanced perspective that seems to prevail in recent and contemporary scholarship, it does not dismiss the ideological dimension out of hand, but there is a decided preference for power-centred explanations. For the abovementioned reasons, it seems preferable to avoid such preconceptions; and that means, more precisely, accepting three main principles of interpretation. Intertwinings of culture and power should be seen as a fundamental feature of the social-historical world, and ideologies – in the sense of interpretations inscribed in power structures and translated into strategies of social actors – as an aspect of that dual pattern. Within this general framework, we should allow for different large-scale and long-term configurations (the relationship between culture and power is not the same in the orbits of universal religions as in more particularistic traditions, nor in empires and clusters of city-states), as well as successive variations resulting from relatively rapid changes. Finally, *prima facie* evidence from the history of revolutions suggests a distinction between situations where acute power struggles predominate over everything else and others where concentrated expressions of ideological visions have the upper hand. To mention only two well-known examples, the Russian civil war exemplifies the first type, whereas the turn taken by the Stalinist dictatorship at the end of the 1920s seems best understandable as a case of the second. Comparative research on revolutions has not yet reached a stage that would allow grounded generalisations on this subject.

Other explanatory choices can be discussed more briefly; they are, in fact, more or less implicit in the problematic of ideology and power. On the side of power, we should note a difference of emphasis, potentially far-reaching when it comes to the question of wars and revolutions. The double-edged role of wars in the process of state formation is a familiar theme: they can accelerate such processes, but they can also lead to the breakdown of state structures and result in situations that necessitate a new beginning. Both aspects enter into the comparative analysis developed in Skocpol's work. However, historical scholarship on major revolutions seems to have brought another perspective to the fore. It links revolutions more closely to wars, integrating both into narratives of escalating violence and placing more emphasis on particular historical constellations than on the direction of long-term processes. A brief glance at key cases will clarify the meaning of the new approach. It is a commonplace that since the eighteenth century, major revolutions have not only been linked to civil wars, but also to wars between great powers; Mark Aldanov (1921) may have been the first to draw attention to differences resulting from the fact that the Russian revolution was triggered by a pan-European war, whereas the French one had preceded such a conflict. More recent work tends to underline certain similarities between late-eighteenth-century and early-twentieth-century configurations. The global dimensions of the Seven Years' War (1756–63) are now so well researched that it is widely seen as the first world war; on the global level, British victory over the French was decisive, but it had two complicating consequences. The reinforced British empire tried to assert more effective control over its trans-Atlantic possessions, and this brought the question of power balances between colonies and homeland to the fore (Theodore Draper (1997) made a forceful case for this geopolitical view of the American revolution, but his argument has not been duly integrated into main-stream accounts). A rapid escalation of this imperial crisis then led to French attempts at revanche through support for the American rebels; the operation proved costly and became a major contributing factor in the pre-revolutionary crisis of the French state. This course of events is generally acknowledged as a central and integral part of the genealogy of the French revolution. It is more debatable whether the sequel has been properly taken on board.

Efforts to rebuild and strengthen the French state were on the agenda of the revolution throughout its trajectory, despite political twists and in conjunction with changing ideological models. The process culmi-nated in the Napoleonic imperial venture; this was a new round of rivalry with British power (in the event leading to a second flowering of the British empire), but also an attempt to roll back the Habsburg and Russian continental empires. The failure of this last French bid for hegemony led to a reconstruction of the European state system, with results solid enough to avert the outbreak of another major multi-power war for the rest of the nineteenth century (the Crimean war was the semi-exception that proves the rule), and of major importance for the containment of the evolutions that broke out in 1848. But it should also be noted that the disappointments of that year lent force to a radi-calised revolutionary myth that compensated for defeat by the promise of a more epoch-making breakthrough.

Another wave of war and revolution shaped the course of European

– and less directly global – history in the first half of the twentieth century. The interconnections have been most convincingly traced in the case of the Russian revolution, where the complete breakdown and the uniquely rapid power shift of 1917 were in all essentials due to the impact of World War I (see, most recently, Lieven 2015). As historians have shown, the disintegration of the imperial order was not simply a matter of a backward society destroyed by modern war. Late Tsarist Russia was not a uniformly backward state, and the war years saw some positive economic developments. The collapse was a concatenation of specific problems, from the traditionally difficult task of provisioning the cities to the inability of the political centre to organise an unprecedented military effort with the necessary cooperation of social forces. The result was an explosion of movements contesting the regime in place: actions of elites in quest of political reform intersected with (and gave way to) those of the peasantry, non-Russian nationalities, urban workers and – last but not least – soldiers in revolt against military discipline. The notion of 'peasants in uniform', a partial truth but far from the whole story, tended to obscure the last point, but it is now more readily given its due. To sum up, the final victory of the Bolsheviks was facilitated by the temporary confluence as well as the ultimate divergence of these movements. The liberal-socialist coalition that had at first seemed to come out on top was most decisively damaged by its attempt to continue the war in the name of a more democratic Russia.

In short, this was a revolution wholly conditioned by the environment of war. It can of course be argued that the Russian imperial order was ripe for a revolutionary upheaval, and that a reformist way around that was in any event very unlikely; but it seems equally clear that a revolution unaccompanied by defeat in war would have taken a different road. This perspective on the Russian upheaval raises questions about broader contexts and longer processes: there was another world war, and its impact on Europe is widely seen as revolutionary, even if not quite in the same sense as the events of 1917. Here I will only briefly mention the most systematic interpretation so far developed along these lines. Andrea Graziosi (2001) dates a period of 'war and revolution in Europe' from 1905 to 1956. The first date is approximate, but the author is alluding to a whole cluster of landmark events, most obviously the Russian revolution of 1905, but also the beginnings of the Young Turk revolution in the Ottoman empire, the escalation of Habsburg-Russian rivalry in the Balkans and the looming collision between Serbia and the Austro-Hungarian empire. The year 1956 is, by contrast, a precise chronological divide. Developments of that year can now, in a double sense, be seen as the beginning of the end for political and ideological legacies of the Russian revolution. The half-baked but irreversible demythologisation of Stalin at the twentieth congress of the Soviet Communist Party let loose a de-legitimising process that could be temporarily obstructed but not brought under control; the Hungarian revolution showed that a Communist regime could be destroyed from within. We may add – although Graziosi does not make the point – that the geopolitical sea change foreshadowed by these events was further underlined by the Suez crisis, which put an end to imperial ambitions of European powers in the Middle East.

Graziosi's view of the period in question is that it experienced uniquely massive, rapid and violent transformation of social, ethnic and regional structures in the eastern part of the European continent, and that the overall context is best described as a civilisational break-down. He explains the political forces most involved in this process in terms of extreme statist and nationalist projects; but he dismisses the concept of totalitarianism as unhistorical, minimises the significance and originality of imperial dynamics as distinct from national ones and finds the interwar liberal notion of 'an era of tyrannies' (Halévy 1990) useful. To my mind, Graziosi's arguments on the last three points are less than convincing, but more detailed discussion is beyond the scope of this paper, and the general reference to a twentieth-century historical field of wars and revolutions can certainly be accepted as a theme for further debates.

The question of relations between war and revolution, with particular emphasis on periods of heightened interaction, leads onto a broader problematic. Those who take this line are critical of the traditional focus on internal social roots of revolutions, and wars between states are the most visible aspect of the transnational context to be brought into the picture. An enlarged geopolitical perspective will highlight this point. The serial military conflicts mentioned above as motive factors of eighteenth- and twentieth-century revolutions were part and parcel of modern European expansion, a long-term process that shifted boundaries and affected neighbouring regions, but in varying ways on different sides of the main powers involved. In west and east, across the Atlantic and on the Eurasian frontier, the intensified pursuit of power by European states had direct and indirect effects accompanied by diffusion and adaptation of cultural models. Conquests in America gave rise to settler societies, whose relative weight vis-à-vis the metropolitan centres was bound to increase (in the Latin American case, the early-nineteenth-century wars of independence were not triggered directly by that process, but by the temporary collapse of the Spanish imperial centre under the impact of the Napoleonic wars). On the eastern side, the most decisive development was the ongoing modernisation of the Russian empire. This emerging state, a crossroads formation in both geopolitical and civilisational terms, drew on European innovations and experiences, albeit in selective and discontinuous ways, and launched its own version of imperial expansion into the inner Eurasian regions. In the long run, the changing mixture of Westernisation and indigenous imperial modernisation led to the differentiation of three sociocultural currents. For one camp, empire building was the primary imperative; it was the meaning of Russian history and the principal goal to be pursued in the modern context of interstate competition. Another trend put the main emphasis on political and social reforms that would bring Russia closer to perceived European patterns of modernity. Finally, a tradition committed to revolutionary Westernisation, drawing on ideological countercultures of Western origin to construct strategies for a frontal attack on the existing order. This constellation emerged against a social background fraught with conflicts that could derail all three alternatives and combine them in unforeseen ways. This was the internal situation on the eve of the twentieth-century geopolitical upheaval; as the Russian example underlines, the international settings of revolutionary transformations are not least important because of their role in the transmission of ideologies.

The expanded perspective on transnational and in key cases global constellations can serve to clarify a last question about explanatory models. Visions and theories of revolution are bound to involve more or less explicit assumptions about revolutionary actors. A particularly influential line of thought defined this issue in terms of a unified or even – in the most ambitious versions – universal revolutionary subject. *The Communist Manifesto*, proposing a reading of European history from the High Middle Ages onwards as a succession of two such macro-historical subjects, the bourgeoisie and the proletariat, was no doubt the most widely known formulation of this view, and its influence reached far beyond the movements directly inspired by its political message. The idea of a bourgeois revolution, often with major modifications, was acceptable to some of those who rejected the proletarian one as a mirage; and substitutes for the latter seem to be envisaged even by some of those who reject Marxian class analysis; it is hard to explain the conjuncture of 'civil society' and the readiness to see it behind the most disparate happenings, unless the concept is understood as an alternative vehicle for hopes previously invested in a universal revolutionary subject. Michael Mann's reminder of Nazi roots in the civil society of Weimar Germany is a useful antidote against such notions (Mann 2004; see also Riley 2010).

All the empirical and conceptual shifts discussed above – in particular the emphasis on multiple factors, complex historical constellations, and the ramifications of ideology and power in interaction – suggest a different approach to the question of revolutionary actors. The forces and processes that enter into the making of a revolutionary situation lead to the formation of shifting coalitions. The Gramscian concept of a historical bloc might seem applicable in this context, but it implies a more solidly integrated alliance than historical experience has – in the case of revolutions – so far substantiated. Revolutionary transformations are set in motion by multiple collective actors, elites as well as more broadly based groupings, and their interrelations are a mixture of convergence, rivalry and conflict. To recall the Russian example once more, the crucial phase was marked by multiple and intersecting initiatives of political movements and social forces; the decisive turn was the Bolshevik achievement of control over urban and military rebellions, with partial support from but much less power over a peasant revolt that was following its own course. Official ideology then transfigured the problematic conjunction of urban and rural revolution into a durable worker-peasant alliance; but the reality seems to have been closer to what a prominent historian of the Soviet Union (Graziosi 1997) calls a great peasant war, lasting from 1919 to 1933.

The civilisational approach

It remains to add a few words on the civilisational approach and its relevance to the comparative study of revolutions. But a link to the above discussion is most easily established through a historical argument. If we accept that revolutions are a particularly pronounced case of phenomena defined by 'family resemblances' (Kumar 2008), we can add that they also exemplify the pattern of a few paradigmatic instances shaping the contours of a broader field. The above reflections have repeatedly returned to the outstanding examples of revolutionary transformations, more revealing of basic patterns than are episodes of more limited significance or local reach. Scholarly research on revolutions seems to confirm a near-consensus on properly labelled great revolutions. There is some doubt whether the late-sixteenth-century revolt of the Netherlands should figure as an early modern precursor, and less than complete agreement on the seventeenth-century English revolution; but in the latter instance, the case for inclusion has been strengthened by recent work showing that the 'Glorious Revolution' of 1688 was more radical than mainstream accounts tended to admit (Pincus 2009). The American, French, Russian and Chinese revolutions are uncontroversial. A few obvious candidates for a second but still select circle are easily identified. The Mexican, Cuban, Algerian, Turkish and Vietnamese revolutions vary widely in regard to context, unfolding and impact, but all must be seen as important historical experiences. At least two singular but very instructive cases, far apart in time and space, might be added: the events of 1868 in Japan and 1979 in Iran, both very resistant to Western-based interpretations, but the latter more commonly classified as a revolution.

A focus on paradigmatic and path-breaking cases is characteristic of the civilisational approach to revolutions, as developed by S. N. Eisenstadt. His earlier work on the subject (Eisenstadt 1978) had dealt with revolutions as a mode of social transformation; but as the civilisational perspective took shape, the emphasis shifted to privileged examples that can then help to delineate a broader field. Given the extreme proliferation of actors, events and processes that besets attempts to construct a general definition of revolutions, it seems reasonable to try an alternative approach through eminent and generally acknowledged historical types of revolutionary change; and the civilisational frame of reference lends added force to this proposal. Eisenstadt's main interest was in the great revolutions, and although there are some variations in his list of them (for example, he sometimes wants to include the Vietnamese and Iranian revolutions), the primary cases are those mentioned above as belonging to that category. It may, however, be added that Eisenstadt was clearly more concerned with the democratic revolutions of the Atlantic world than with the twentieth-century Communist ones, and some conceptual implications of closer attention to the latter will be noted. But to begin with a general characteristic of the great revolutions, they constitute 'a distinct type of macro-societal change', one that combines 'a change of regime with the crystallisation of new cosmologies and ontological conceptions with far-reaching institutional implications, i.e. of new civilisations' (Eisenstadt 2006: 4).[2] They are, in other words, key episodes in the formation and institutionalisation of the 'cultural and political program of modernity' (ibid.: 4). The latter formulation seems misleading, but easy to correct in light of Eisenstadt's more detailed arguments. To speak of a cultural and political programme is to rely on the conceptual tools of older theoretical traditions, unfit for the new ground broken by civilisational analysis. On both cultural and political levels, the understanding of civilisations that emerges in Eisenstadt's work would be better expressed through the concepts of cultural and political problematics. A problematic is a constellation of themes, problems and perspectives, open to different and often antagonistic interpretations; it can crystallise into relatively stable alternative patterns and its components include peripheral and contestatory aspects that can in specific circumstances assume more central roles. In short, a problematic has dimensions of indeterminacy and creativity, not adequately reflected in the functionalist notion of a programme.

In amended terms, then, we might say that great revolutions are not so much expressions or repeated confirmations of a civilisational blueprint, as different developments of a shared but disputed problematic, defined by cultural orientations that characterise modernity as a new civilisation but are at the same time conducive to ideological conflicts, most sharply articulated in the realm of politics. The civilisational core of modernity is a constellation of meanings that amounts to an epoch-making upgrading of human autonomy. This new emphasis on autonomy is, however, inseparable from the 'antinomies of modernity' that figure prominently in Eisenstadt's analyses; the term is borrowed from philosophical sources and used to describe divergent interpretations of common cultural premises. Liberal, democratic socialist and totalitarian versions of political modernity exemplify this constitutive discord, and their changing configurations are reflected in trajectories of modern revolutions. On the other hand, the revolutions – in particular the great ones – that unfold in different contexts at different historical junctures can nevertheless be seen as successive manifestations of a macro-historical trend; the experiences of earlier revolutions, variously interpreted and more or less mythologised, enter into the theoretical and practical profiles of later ones. A diverse and contested but distinctive revolutionary tradition is an integral part of modern history. The question of non-revolutionary roads should be considered in that light. Transitions through reform, sweeping or piecemeal, are a recurrent feature of the modern world, but they occur in an increasingly global setting marked by the revolutionary breakthroughs. Eisenstadt's analysis of the great revolutions as crystallising moments of a new civilisation seems convincing.

This brief summary of the civilisational view suggests a few comments on the issues outlined in the first two sections of the paper. Most obviously, we should relativise the distinction between internal and external factors leading to revolutionary upheavals. The civilisational context of revolutions is, by definition, multinational and marked by interstate rivalry; to put it another way, geopolitical and geocultural processes are always involved, and it is a matter for comparative historical analysis to assess their weight in relation to crises and conflicts within the societies at the centre of events. As noted above in various connections, the main arena of the great revolutions was the expanding European world, together with the crisis zones created by its collisions with other civilisational domains; the impact on East Asia, with very different consequences in China and Japan, was particularly significant. If we consider the roughly two centuries in question (one possible periodisation would begin with the outbreak of the American revolution in 1776 and end with the evaporation of Maoism in 1976), it seems clear that international constellations and dynamics became increasingly salient in the background to revolutions. They certainly had more to do with the course of revolutions in Russia and China than in North America and France. It is less clear that the same applies to the outcomes of revolutions. The American revolution set the scene for a geopolitical power shift so far unequalled in history (this trend is particularly marked if the civil war of 1861–5 represents, as some historians have argued, the final revolutionary episode). During the second half of the twentieth century, it seemed at times possible that the Russian revolution might result in a comparable or more definitive shift, but the end of the cold war put paid to such expectations. The long-term geopolitical and geo-economic impact of the Chinese revolution is still uncertain.

The great revolutions are specific and prominent landmarks on the roads to modernity (for the original use of the plural, see Nelson 2011); as such, they respond to and intertwine with the long-term processes that shape the modern world. To avoid terminological confusion, it would seem preferable to label the latter as transformations, but the notions of industrial, democratic and scientific revolutions are probably too entrenched for a clear distinction to be possible. In any case, the revolutions properly so described, and most of all those singled out in Eisenstadt's work, stand out as social-historical phenomena in a class of their own, and the reappraisal of crucial experiences helps to correct some traditional but one-sided or prejudicial assumptions. Revolutions that combine new articulations of the world and the human condition with institutional mutations are inseparably political and social: political centres are their primary targets, but their intentions go beyond the political sphere, and their repercussions affect the whole social order. The interplay of elite actions and broader social movements, varying from case to case, is always important enough to blur the distinction between social revolutions and revolutions from above; but inasmuch as politics is ultimately 'in command', to quote a Chinese revolutionary-turned-emperor, all revolutions are revolutions from above. And if all great revolutions involve violent conflicts and changes, their record also shows that violence is not simply a recurrent historical fact. It enters into cultural contexts, and each revolution develops its specific ideological ways of transfiguring violence.

The variety thus apparent should be seen from a broader angle. The idea of multiple modernities presupposes and qualifies the conception of modernity as a civilisation; as noted above, a horizon of variation is built into the core problematic that defines modern cultures, but concrete articulations depend on historical factors. Diverse pathways and patterns of modernity affect all its levels and components, including revolutionary dynamics. Revolutions with civilisational impact were in the first instance products of the European complex, as Eisenstadt calls it (ibid.:4; in this context, it includes Russia and the Americas), but the Chinese revolution also belongs in that category, and sometimes adds the Vietnamese one, with a passing reference to the Confucian background of the two later cases.[3] This point raises a question about long-term pre-modern roots of revolution. Eisenstadt's comparative perspective on that field is based on the concept of axial civilisations, which I cannot discuss here; suffice it to say that the 'axial' aspect of civilisational patterns has to do with innovative visions of order, conducive to distance from given reality and to a search for alternatives ranging from reform to salvation. Traditions of this type go back to cultural transformations of the last millennium BCE, and one of the criteria for distinguishing them from each other is the weight and meaning given to action and cultivation in the political sphere. Eisenstadt claims that Greek and Chinese versions of the axial breakthrough share an emphasis on the political, albeit with very different intentions and connotations. In the Chinese case, he proposes to trace the concern with political themes through the Confucian tradition; on the Western side, matters are more complicated. The Greek sources of political thought entered into European traditions through a complex interaction with Christian themes, and the picture is further complicated by another line of cultural descent. Eisenstadt emphasises the role of Christian heresies in the formation of revolutionary ambitions and imaginations; heterodoxies are, as he sees it, an important feature of all axial civilisations, but the exceptionally vigorous Christian tradition of heresy is one of the factors that help to account for Europe's unique record of revolutionary change. This is, for Eisenstadt, a matter of structural characteristics rather than specific doctrines: heresies translate more or less directly into visions of a radically new order. It should, however, be noted that one aspect of this genealogy becomes less important as Eisenstadt's argument develops. The book discussed here (Eisenstadt 2006) places less emphasis on gnostic sources than some earlier essays did, and this caution is well-founded. Research on Gnosticism has highlighted the complexity and diversity of the religious currents in question, and their later influence is a very controversial subject, not least after Hans Blumenberg's attempt to show that modernity, including its revolutionary versions, represents the overcoming of gnostic trends in late medieval religion and culture (Blumenberg 1985).

All these suggestions about long-term ancestry of the modern revolutionary tradition should be seen as hypotheses that call for much more historical and comparative research. But they testify to the new horizons opened up by civilisational analysis, even in its present tentative phase. To round off the discussion, I shall briefly indicate some questions left open in Eisenstadt's work. If the civilisational sources of revolutionary traditions go back to axial sources, the comparative analysis of revolutionary processes presupposes the framework of multiple modernities. Eisenstadt referred to the Americas as the first multiple modernities, on the grounds that the two sixteenth-century reformations, Protestant and Catholic, developed a new civilisational potential across the Atlantic and translated into different roads to modernity. The North American experience is duly included in his typology of great revolutions, but it is less clear where Latin American revolutions would fit into his frame of reference. It would seem clear that they are not in the same class as the great ones of the northern hemisphere, but they may still be important for comparative study, inasmuch as they sometimes took trends known elsewhere to unusual lengths. For one thing, the Mexican revolution represents an extreme case of national and political unity breaking down in face of multiple, disparate and predominantly rural popular movements, but then reconstructed by turning the revolution into the founding myth of a developmental state. If we allow for some scepticism as to the revolutionary character of the wars of independence, four cases are commonly cited as major revolutions: Mexico (1910–20 and beyond), Bolivia (1952), Cuba (1959 and beyond) and Nicaragua (1978–9). On the other hand, these revolutions and other less conclusive examples should, as Vayssière (2002) has shown, be studied in relation to a distinctively Latin American tradition of authoritarian rule (often outright dictatorship), known as *caudilloismo*. The most accomplished fusion of the two currents occurred in Cuba, which must – because of the much later liberation from Spanish colonial rule and the very limited independence that followed – be regarded as an atypical offshoot of the Latin American complex. In the three other cases mentioned above, the caudilloist alternative was – for a variety of reasons – blocked or rejected. In Cuba, it took the spectacularly unique turn of embracing the Soviet model. Other Communist regimes had, for longer or shorter periods, turned the party-state into an autocracy; in Cuba, a charismatic autocrat coming from outside the party subordinated it to his personalised version of its programme. The result was not a great revolution in Eisenstadt's sense, but it was briefly mythologised into a new chapter in the history of Communism (a 'revolution in the revolution').[4]

Another key question concerns Fascist movements and regimes, and their claims to revolutionary significance. Here Eisenstadt makes two points worth further elaboration. First, the Fascist projects turn particularistic components of Western traditions, massively radicalised, against the universalistic ones (Eisenstadt 2006: 210). This analysis links up with Kolnai's early and classic interpretation of National Socialism as a 'war against the West' (Kolnai 1938; there is, however, nothing to show that Eisenstadt has drawn directly on this work); but the war against the West is also a war within the West. Second, Eisenstadt sees the Jacobin component of political modernity as – with appropriate modifications – adaptable to Fascist projects. Finally, there is the issue of Islamic revolutions. In this regard, the comments in Eisenstadt's last statements on the subject do not go beyond observations. On the one hand, he repeatedly mentions the eighth-century 'Abbasid revolution' that changed the character of the early Islamic caliphate as a plausible example of a genuine pre-modern revolution (Eisenstadt 2006: 13, 80); on the other hand, a brief excursus on Islam as a civilisation invokes

Ibn Khaldun's account of a sectarian-innovative tradition. Whether this adds up to a specific revolutionary tradition remains unclear, and is certainly not the least interesting theme waiting for a more systematic civilisational analysis.

Notes

1. For an excellent study of an extreme case, see Koenen 2008; the fundamentally oniric character of Ernesto Guevara's revolutionary imagination is convincingly shown.
2. The book quoted above is in many ways an incomplete work, and successive chapters are unequally developed. But it represents the opening of a new phase in Eisenstadt's exceptionally ambitious research project, and a very rich array of themes for further discussion.
3. There are good reasons to doubt the inclusion of the Vietnamese revolution of 1945–6 among the great ones; its impact was not of the kind associated with the term. But there is no doubt that this was a distinctive and important episode, so far under-represented in comparative research. It was the first wholly independent and ultimately successful Communist seizure of power after 1917; it created a new state in a very peculiar power vacuum, resulting from the conflict and very brief coexistence of rival colonialisms, French and Japanese; moreover, it was the first successful fusion of Communism and nationalism, and arguably the most enduring of its kind (by contrast, the Algerian revolution was characterised by repeated failures to achieve that kind of fusion).
4. The Haitian revolution at the end of the eighteenth century is a very peculiar case, and hardly to be counted among the Latin American ones. If we consider its impact on social structures, Jürgen Osterhammel (2011) may be right in describing it as the most radical revolution of all times. But in ideological terms, it was within the orbit of the French revolution.

References

Aldanov, M. (1921) *Deux révolutions: La révolution française et la révolution russe.* Paris: Imprimerie Union.

Arjomand, S. A. (1989) *The Turban for the Crown. The Islamic Revolution in Iran.* Oxford: Oxford University Press.

Berman, H. (1983) *Law and Revolution. The Formation of the Western Legal Tradition.* Cambridge, MA: Harvard University Press.

Blumenberg, H. (1985) *The Legitimacy of the Modern Age.* Boston, MA: MIT Press.

Draper, T. (1997) *A Struggle for Power: The American Revolution.* New York: Vintage Books.

Eisenstadt, S. N. (1978) *Revolution and the Transformation of Societies. A Comparative Study of Civilizations.* New York: Free Press.

Eisenstadt, S. N. (1999) *Fundamentalism, Sectarianism and Revolution. The Jacobin Dimension of Modernity.* Cambridge: Cambridge University Press.

Eisenstadt, S. N. (2006) *The Great Revolutions and the Civilizations of Modernity.* Leiden and Boston, MA: Brill.

Fairbank, J. K. (1986) *The Great Chinese Revolution 1800–1985.* New York: Harper.

Furet, F. (1981) *Interpreting the French Revolution.* Cambridge: Cambridge University Press.

Furet, F. (1988) *La révolution: 1770–1880.* Paris: Hachette.

Goodwin, J. (1997) 'State-centered approaches to social revolutions: Strengths and limitations of a theoretical tradition', in J. Foran (ed.) *Theorizing Revolutions.* London: Routledge, pp. 11–37.

Graziosi, A. (1997) *The Great Soviet Peasant War. Bolsheviks and Peasants, 1917–1933.* Cambridge, MA: Harvard University Press.

Graziosi, A. (2001) *Guerra e rivoluzione in Europa, 1905–1956.* Bologna: Mulino.

Halévy, E. (1990) *L'ère des tyrannies. Études sur le socialisme et la guerre.* Paris: Gallimard.

Huber, T. (1981) *The Revolutionary Origins of Modern Japan.* Stanford, CA: Stanford University Press.

Koenen, G. (2008) *Traumpfade der Weltrevolution. Das Guevara-Projekt.* Köln: Kiepenheuer & Witsch.

Kolnai, A. (1938) *The War Against the West.* London: Victor Gollancz.

Kumar, K. (2008) 'The future of revolution: imitation or innovation', in J. Foran, D. Lane and A. Zivkovic (eds) *Revolution in the Making of the Modern World.* London: Routledge, pp. 222–36.

Lefort, C. (1994) *L'invention démocratique. Les limites de la domination totalitaire.* Paris: Fayard.

Lieven, D. (2015) *Towards the Flame. Empire, War and the End of Tsarist Russia.* London: Allen Lane.

Malia, M. (1980) *Comprendre la révolution russe.* Paris: Seuil.

Malia, M. (1995) *The Soviet Tragedy. A History of Socialism in Russia, 1917–1991.* New York: Free Press.

Mann, M. (2004) *Fascists.* Cambridge: Cambridge University Press.

Moore, B. (1967) *Social Origins of Dictatorship and Democracy. Lord and Peasant in the Making of the Modern World.* Boston, MA: Beacon Press.

Nelson, B. (2011) *On the Roads to Modernity. Conscience, Science and Civilizations.* Lanham, MD: Lexington Books

Osterhammel, J. (2011) *Die Verwandlung der Welt. Eine Geschichte des 19. Jahrhunderts.* München: C. H. Beck.

Pincus, S. (2009) *1688: The First Modern Revolution.* New Haven, CT and London: Yale University Press.

Pye, L. (1988) *Asian Power and Politics. The Cultural Dimensions of Authority.* Cambridge, MA: Harvard University Press.

Riley, D. (2010) *The Civic Foundations of Fascism in Europe: Italy Spain and Romania, 1870–1945.* Baltimore, MD: Johns Hopkins University Press.

Rosenberg, A. (1962) *Geschichte des Bolschewismus.* Frankfurt: Europäische Verlagsanstalt.

Skocpol, T. (1979) *States and Social Revolutions. A Comparative Analysis of France, Russia and China.* Cambridge: Cambridge University Press.

Skocpol, T. (1982) 'Rentier state and Shia Islam in the Iranian revolution', *Theory and Society* 2(3), 256–83.

Syme, R. (2002) *The Roman Revolution.* Oxford: Oxford University Press.

Therborn, G. (2008) 'Foreword', in J. Foran, D. Lane and A. Zivkovic (eds) *Revolution in the Making of the Modern World.* London: Routledge, pp. XIV–XVII.

Trimberger, E. (1978) *Revolutions from Above: Military Bureaucrats and Development in Japan, Turkey Egypt and Peru.* Livingston, NJ: Transaction Books.
Vayssière, P. (2002) *Les révolutions d'Amérique latine.* Paris: Seuil.

4

The Transformation of Capitalism and the Limits of Democracy

Jerry Harris

CAPITALISM HAS UNDERGONE a number of important transformations and challenges. Wars, depression and imperialism created
the socialist revolutions of the twentieth century. But within the
West, capitalism responded to these problems with Keynesian solutions, creating an expanded social contract and growing middle class.
Perhaps with the fall of the Soviet Union capitalism became drunk
with victory. But alongside its triumphalism, capitalism was reaching
its own limits of expansion within the Keynesian model. Without an
external threat, capitalism was free to focus on the wage structures and
social benefits that restricted corporate profitability. The middle class
had reached their limits and the working class had overreached theirs.
Neoliberalism, led by financialisation, transformed capitalism into an
updated model of its pre-Keynesian existence. Austerity, the export of
jobs, privatisation and attacks on unions overwhelmed the working
class.

The Washington Consensus was not just about the United States.
In reality it was a capitalist consensus developed as an economic and
political strategy by the emerging transnational capitalist class (TCC)
(Sklair 2001; Robinson 2004; Harris 2008). Capitalism was rapidly
transforming from a nation-centric system into a global structure of
accumulation and power. Austerity in the developed North and structural adjustment programmes in the developing South resulted from
a break with industrial-era national capitalism by a hegemonic TCC.

The democratic dialectic

The bourgeois democratic revolutions in the US and France were based
on a revolutionary alliance between the capitalist class, craftsmen,
workers, farmers and peasants. This created a historic dialectic that

encompassed a contradictory and tension-filled relationship, but that nevertheless allowed for the incorporation of popular demands into capitalist society. As a result the working-class opposition has always existed inside the capitalist dialectic to produce democratic outcomes. These movements took shape not only inside the factories, but also as social movements that have encompassed the demands of women, minorities and other identities.

Antonio Gramsci's theory on hegemony best explained the twin aspects of consent and coercion that have characterised bourgeois rule. While force and violence was always present, consensus was the main tool of more developed capitalist societies (Gramsci 1971). This contradiction, built into the very origins of political institutional structures, produced the flexibility that allowed capitalism to adopt and continue to evolve. In examining great social upheavals we can see they were always met with levels of violence that included police repression, government spying, imprisonment and sometimes state executions. The struggles for unions, women's rights and civil rights are saturated with such experiences. (Zinn 1998). But the government and capitalist class eventually conceded to many of the demands that had motivated these oppositional movements. These concessions created a formal legal structural that expanded democratic rights, and an economic and social contract that produced the middle class.

Socialist activists in these movements always saw reforms as a stepping stone to revolution. They sought to transcend the capitalist dialectic that contained the labour movement and other social forces within the existing system. The revolution was to take a qualitative leap into a new dialectic based on working-class state power. Socialists argued that economic equality and social justice would only be fully realised with such a historic break. Yet socialist and working-class demands were sooner or later enfolded into an ever-evolving capitalism, never in the way envisioned by and called for by revolutionary activists, but in a way that allowed for continual gains in both the economic and the social contract. This was particularly true after the Great Depression and war against Fascism, both of which pushed the capitalists into further concessions.

The left has viewed the working-class opposition, its strikes and social rebellions, as belonging to the socialist side of history rather than as an essential feature held within nation-centric capitalism. Yet the very definition of the modern nation state revolves around citizenship, and the political and economic rights that became part of modern society. This was an essential expression of one's national identity. That identity, of the working class as stakeholders, was present from the first days of the barricades in Paris or guerrilla fighters in the woods of North America. From the moment the Parisian masses read the Declaration of the Rights of Man they took liberty, equality and fraternity as their own, not as rights exclusively reserved for property owners. When Thomas Jefferson declared that 'all men are created equal' and endowed with 'unalienable rights', farmers and workers took possession of those ideas to define their own future. Consequently, the working masses have always been the contradictory democratic opposite that creates the dialectic to bourgeois rule. The long and neverending struggle over citizenship and social justice arose from these revolutionary beginnings.

Modern revolutionary leaders have also been influenced by these democratic principles of earlier insurrections. Malcolm X argued that the black liberation struggle in the US should demand human rights rather than civil rights. Like Jefferson, Malcolm maintained people were born with 'unalienable rights', while governments only granted more limited civil rights. Ironically, Malcolm was firmly within the democratic tradition first established by the slave owner Jefferson. Also influenced by early democratic philosophy was Mao Zedong, whose favourite philosophers in high school were Locke, Rousseau, Jefferson and Benjamin Franklin (Rittenberg and Bennett 1993).

Just as socialists have sought to resolve this contradictory historic relationship, the capitalist class has also wished to escape it. This is where globalisation comes to bear, because it allows capitalism to advance that goal. World financialisation and global production has meant the capitalist class can at long last jettison the burdensome relationship with their own national working class. Nation-centric capitalism was historically, and by economic and political necessity, based on a tension-filled alliance with its own working class. This relationship has been ruptured by the reorganisation of capitalism on a transnational level. The consensus side of Gramsci's hegemonic relationship, as the key feature of nation-centric capitalism, is being replaced by a new technocratic authoritarianism (Harris and Davidson 2013; DuRand and Martinot 2012). Democratic will is pushed aside by transnational bodies such as the International Monetary Fund (IMF) and World Trade Organisation (WTO) that enforce austerity over popular opposition. Millions have demonstrated in Greece, Spain, Portugal and Ireland. The Occupy movement spread across the US and then throughout Europe. Yet austerity and neoliberalism marches on. Coercion, the threat of unemployment, poverty, police repression and spying have become the weapons of choice. The Associated Press reported that over their working life 80 per cent of adults in the US will live in near poverty or be jobless or on welfare (Yen 2013). The litany of attacks on public institutions, jobs and the environment doesn't have to be repeated here. Just read your daily newspaper, no matter the country in which you live.

The global shift in power is not the strategy of any single nation or hegemonic state. Nor is it the result of a weakly organised and incomplete transnational capitalist class. It is the strategic objective of a capitalist class transformed by globalisation. The manner in which production is organised and value expropriated allows the capitalist class to break out of its historic nation-centric dialectic. It was trapped within a formal relationship of equal citizenship, and burdened with concessions conceded to its nationally organised labouring classes. But capitalism has succeeded in creating a new dialectic. Not by one state, nor for one state, but for the class as a whole on a global scale.

Nevertheless, some sections of the TCC are beginning to propose the outlines of a Green New Deal. In important ways this differs from the neoliberal authoritarian regime that has engulfed global governance. It would return capitalism to the consensual side of the dialectic, using green technologies to create a new cycle of accumulation and bolster the system's legitimacy. In the following sections we will explore neoliberal financialisation, how modern technology helps to structure patterns of accumulation and the politics of a Green New Deal.

Democracy, technology and labour

A fundamental characteristic of transnational financialisation is cross-border flows of money. This crucial activity of global capitalism has expanded immensely through the use of information technology, creating enormous wealth with the use of minimum amounts of labour. Bain Capital, the hedge fund of Mitt Romney, issued a report on the remarkable over-accumulation of capital that uncovers the extent of this contradiction. As Bain stated:

> the relationship between the financial economy and the underlying real economy has reached a decisive turning point . . . By 2010 global capital had swollen to some $600 trillion, tripling over the past two decades. Today, total financial assets are nearly ten times the value

of the global output of all goods and services [creating] a world that is structurally awash in capital. (Bain & Company 2012)

Bain's 'decisive turning point' marks the rupture between socially necessary labour and the accumulation of capital. It has inflated speculative activities that feed financialisation. It also allows investment bankers to claim billions of dollars in annual salaries and the sky-rocketing wealth of the top one-tenth of 1 per cent. On one hand technology has reduced the need for labour, while globalisation has opened access to a mass of super exploited workers. The result in the US and EU is that millions are expelled from the labour force, and face a broken social contract that the TCC no longer sees any need to maintain.

The contradiction between the socialised nature of work and the private ownership of the means of production is accentuated by the technological tools of financial production. The problem is not that workers are alienated from their production of value, but that mass labour is no longer needed to create wealth. The work involved in trillions of dollars in speculative finance is carried out by a very small section of the global workforce. Moreover, about half of all daily trades are done by computer algorithms written by a handful of experts and run without daily human input. The former chief technical officer at Goldman Sachs reported that trading strategies were done by '50,000 servers just doing simulations', and he noted that many more had been added since 2006 (Hardy 2013). So important is the speed of the technology that a number of trading firms have moved from New York to Newark to be within a few blocks of SWIFT, the company that runs the supercomputer through which world trades are processed. Fibre-optic cables transmit data at about a metre every three-billionths of a second. That means that in one second data can travel the circumference of the Earth 7.6 times. Consequently, physical closeness to the big financial servers creates a microsecond advantage in receiving information and the ability to profit from it. These huge data centres have no workers but are filled with racks of servers in vast rooms lit only by the gold and blue lights of computers.

The money markets are one way to examine this phenomenon. This means traders, or actually algorithms, buying and selling currencies across borders and around the world. In effect, money becomes a commodity rather than a form of exchange. Algorithms look for arbitrage, or the very small differences in the price of a currency that exist at the same moment in time but in different places. When the algorithms read the mathematical formulae and figures they are programmed to look for, transnational trades are conducted in less than a second. Billions flash back and forth over borders to totals that hit $5.3 trillion a day. It is difficult to understand what 'one trillion' means; to get an idea, one trillion seconds equals 36,000 years, while one million seconds is only twelve and a half days.

The wealth of Henry Ford depended on the day-to-day expropriation of value created by tens of thousands of car workers. This expropriation could only occur when workers took their place on the assembly line. But Goldman Sachs gains vast riches from the operation of its computers working without the input of daily human labour. This rupture between socially necessary labour time and wealth is one element that gives the TCC growing freedom from any nationally based working class. It inflates the space between the real economy and finance capital, and between the capitalists and the working class. In reducing the socialised nature of work information technology has changed the relations of production.

Marx defined socially necessary labour time as 'the labour-time required to produce any use-value under the conditions of production normal for a given society and with the average degree of skill and intensity of labour prevalent in that society' (Marx 1990). But speculative economic activity such as money markets produce no use-value, no commodity that can be used or consumed. It merely circulates currency which algorithms appropriate through arbitrage, producing wealth but nothing of use. The software itself condenses centuries of useful knowledge. In that sense algorithms contain the historic culmination of social labour. But capitalists only pay for the labour of programmers who write the software. The algorithms then work essentially independently of concrete labour time. As a result cognitive capitalism largely escapes its relationship to living labour, creating what Bain Capital called a 'decisive break' between the financial economy and the real economy, the real economy consisting of socially necessary labour time producing socially useful commodities that are used or consumed, such as cars, food or the health care system.

A further indication of the change in the relationship between capital and labour induced by financialisation and technology can be found in the rate of profit per employee. Table 4.1 compares some of the world's major financial, industrial and technology corporations. As we see, mass concentrated labour plays a reduced role in today's global capitalism. Over the past thirty years, older industrial corporations

Table 4.1 Global corporations and their income per employee, 2012

Corporation	Revenues in millions	Income in millions	Employees in thousands	Profit per employee
Goldman Sachs	34,160	7,480	31,495	$237,498
JP Morgan	99,900	21,300	180,000	$118,333
Google	50,200	10,740	32,467	$330,797
Microsoft	74,260	28,500	94,290	$302,225
Ford	136,254	5,700	166,000	$34,337
GM	150,276	7,600	250,000	$30,400
Toyota	258,845	6,170	300,734	$20,516

Sources: M. Zeitlin, 'Goldman and JP are still tops – but Dimon takes pay cut', Daily Beast (16 January 2013), available at www.thedailybeast.com/articles/2013/01/16/goldman-sachs-and-jp-morgan-see-profits-surge-in-2012.html; http://money.cnn.com/magazine/fortune500/2012; www.media.gm.com/media/gm/news.details; www.job.gm.com; http://www.microsoft.com/en-us/press/2012

have begun to make use of information technology. Since 1980 the car industry has increased production while cutting its labour force by two-thirds, yet it still lags far behind finance and technology corporations. Accordingly, union membership has dramatically dropped, the social contract has weakened and capital has migrated out of manufacturing. This underlines the inability, and even the lack of need, to create employment for millions of laid-off workers. In Table 4.1 we can see the large differences in profits per employee between financial, technology and traditional manufacturing corporations.

Finance does not exist simply in an isolated electronic realm of virtual money. The speed at which funds can be invested and withdrawn is key to its power over manufacturing. This power can push stock prices up or down and ensure that primary concerns are neoliberal efficiencies. Consequently the holders of stocks, bonds, equities, securities and derivatives can determine the decision-making process of corporate boards. Finance capital, whose use of labour is minimum, now drives the real economy where the vast majority of the labour force is engaged. It is no wonder that this mode of accumulation has produced a TCC wedded to the ideology of austerity. Keynesianism has little to offer in a world where the distance between capital and labour stands like a new Berlin wall.

Financialisation has been fabulously successful for the top 1 per cent of the global economy and even more so for the top one-tenth of 1 per cent. With their enormous political and economic power they have maintained the grip of neoliberalism on government policy in most major economies. Even as stagnation marches on year after year the global elite continue to advocate the same ideology and practice. And why not, when it has resulted in soaring fortunes.

For the working and middle classes even as jobs slowly recover incomes do not. This is the new neoliberal reality that also seeks to permanently cement cuts to social services. In the US 25 per cent of national income goes to the top 1 per cent, while the mean family income is lower today than twenty-five years ago (Stiglitz 2014). A report from the National Bureau of Economic Research goes beyond even the top 1 per cent stating that, 'The rise in wealth inequality is almost entirely due to the rise of the top 0.1 per cent wealth share, from 7 per cent in 1979 to 22 per cent in 2012' (Cohen 2014). The same conditions exist in Europe. Writing for *The Financial Times*, Gideon Rachman noted that 'Britons born in 1985 are the first cohort for 100 years not to be experiencing better living standards'. Rachman also noted that in Germany neoliberal reforms have benefited those 'at the top end of the wage scale [while] holding down wages, cutting social benefits and employing many more temporary workers' (Rachman 2013).

The explosion of temporary work and part-time jobs is one of the fundamental changes in the labour market brought about by neoliberalism and globalisation. Kelly Services, a leader in the temp industry, ran an ad for the 'Never-Never Girl' that set down the principles for the industry. The ad read:

Never takes a vacation or holiday. Never asks for a raise. Never costs you a dime for slack time. (When the workload drops, you drop her.) Never has a cold, slipped disc or loose tooth. (Not on your time anyway!) Never costs you for unemployment taxes and Social Security payments. (None of the paperwork, either!) Never costs you for fringe benefits. (They add up to 30% of every payroll dollar.) Never fails to please. (If your Kelly Girl employee doesn't work out, you don't pay.) (Hatton 2013)

Although run in the 1970s, the ad foretold the future direction of capital's relationship to labour *sans* the social contract. It also emphasised the feminisation of part-time and temp labour, another trend that grew stronger throughout the world.

But a future of such great inequalities with its dystopic dangers has created a growing neo-Keynesian opposition. Nobel Prize-winning economist Joseph Stiglitz has declared that 'wealth at the top of the ladder arises from exploitation [and] because of our tolerance for inequality, even the quintessential American Dream has been shown to be a myth' (Stiglitz 2014). Bank of England governor Mark Carney aimed his criticism at the very foundations of neoliberalism, stating:

> All ideologies are prone to extremes. Capitalism loses its sense of moderation when the belief in the power of the market enters the realm of faith. In the decades prior to the crisis such radicalism came to dominate economic ideas and became a pattern of social behaviour . . . Just as any revolution eats its children, unchecked market fundamentalism can devour the social capital essential for the long-term dynamism of capitalism itself. (Monaghan 2014)

Green capitalism

As problems and worries pile up, some among the elite have begun to promote an alternative strategy, one that centres on the environmental crisis and worries about inequality. These are not always one and same, and in fact neoliberal practices already exist in the alternative energy industry. Those who are most concerned about inequality have made *Capital in the Twenty-First Century* by Thomas Piketty a worldwide best-seller. Their thinking often turns to promoting alternative energy as a path to new jobs and a renewed manufacturing base, a reframe often heard in the US.

Former prime movers of the neoliberal economic and political onslaught have begun to add their voices. An op-ed piece in *The New York Times* by a trio of billionaires urged a tax on carbon emissions, indicating that some on Wall Street are ready to shift to green capitalism (Jasper 2014). The trio consisted of Hank Paulson, ex-CEO of Goldman Sachs and Secretary of the Treasury under George W. Bush; former mayor of New York and political independent Michael Bloomberg; and San Francisco liberal Democrat Tom Steyer. Both Bloomberg and Steyer are already big-time funders of environmental groups and political candidates.

Robert Rubin, an architect of financial deregulation, Citicorp CEO and President Clinton's Treasury Secretary, joined the choir, writing in *The Washington Post*, 'We do not face a choice between protecting our environment or protecting our economy. We face a choice between protecting our economy by protecting our environment – or allowing environmental havoc to create economic havoc' (Rubin 2014). Even some major figures within the oil industry have come to accept global warming as a planetary threat. Lord Browne, former CEO of BP, stated that the scientific basis for global warming is a settled issue, but critically noted that 'this conclusion is not accepted by many in our industry, because they do not want to acknowledge an existential threat to their business' (Clark 2014).

There are also liberals who advocate green capitalism as a way to revive US global hegemony. In his state of the union speech, President Obama asserted, 'the nation that leads the clean-energy economy will be the nation that leads the global economy, and America must be that nation' (Schwartz 2010). Environmentalist Hunter Lovins has called on the US to lead the world in green technologies because 'they'll rule the world, economically, politically, and probably militarily' (Samuels 2009). And Thomas Friedman wrapped green capitalism in red, white and blue, calling it the new currency of power. 'It's all about national power . . . what could be more patriotic, capitalistic and geostrategic than that?' (Friedman 2008).

The green wing of the TCC is developing a strategic vision that may solve three major problems facing the system: stagnation, legitimacy and defence. In terms of economic stagnation new investments in green technologies can set off a renewed cycle of accumulation, creating an expansion of new industries, jobs and profits. The next problem, rapidly disappearing political legitimacy and trust in government, is, in Gramscian terms, a crisis in the ideological hegemony of the ruling class. But green capitalism can re-establish the system's identification with democracy and extend its political legitimacy to the grand issue of saving the planet and building a better future. This would also include coopting sections of the environmental leadership into their hegemonic project. Last is the question of defence and stability. For the past decade the Pentagon and CIA have been warning of possible social and political chaos as the result of global warming. They have predicted economic collapse in ecologically vulnerable countries and instability created by the movement of environmental refugees across wide areas of the planet. Addressing the most pressing environmental issues can help reduce this threat and create a more stable and manageable state of affairs.

But for all the rhetoric, international conferences and treaties generated over the past twenty years, little has been accomplished. In the last ten years fossil fuel emissions have risen at almost double the rate as during the preceding decade. In addition, $600 billion a year is still spent to subsidise fossil fuels, more than six times the level of subsidies going to renewable energy. Leading United Nations scientist Dr Ottmar Edenhofer has claimed the world is 'in the middle of a fossil fuel renaissance' (Gillis 2014). In fact, the UN has warned that renewable energy is being overwhelmed by fossil fuel emissions and the rapid growth of fracking. The true revolution is not taking place in sustainable energy, but in the use of natural gas which increased ten times faster than wind power in 2012. If there is any hope of keeping to internationally agreed limits of a 2° Celsius rise in global temperature, 75 per cent of all fossil fuel reserves need to stay in the ground. But much of these huge reserves are already on the books of oil and energy transnationals, and account for billions in the valuations of these corporations.

Replying to the UN, Exxon issued a report which stated, 'The scenario where governments restrict hydrocarbon production in a way to reduce GHG [greenhouse gas] emissions 80 per cent during the outlook period is highly unlikely . . . We are confident that none of our hydrocarbon reserves are now or will become "stranded"' (Crooks 2014). In other words, oil majors intend to put every tonne of fossil fuel underneath the Earth's surface into our atmosphere. The G20 governments seem to agree and have committed $88 billion of taxpayers' money to the exploration for oil, gas and coal. The highest subsidies are from the UK, US, Australia, Saudi Arabia, Brazil, Japan and South Korea, and are eight times greater than support for renewables in these countries (Lomas 2014).

Another obstacle facing the Green New Deal is the effects of economic recessions. Critics on the left have mainly looked at problems inherent in capitalist-driven growth, including the relentless need for more fuel and for resources of every kind, neverending consumption and constant material expansion (Foster 1999). But perhaps just as serious is the crisis side of the economic cycle. Recessions produce three major problems for green capitalism: cuts in subsides; protectionism; and overproduction resulting in a crisis of profitability. Solar and wind are still dependent on state subsidies for the development of their technologies and gaining market share. Funders also keep a close watch on government support to judge the viability of their speculative investments into the industry. When economic recessions hit subsides tend to disappear or suffer cuts, often resulting in lay-offs and a general slow-down of overall development.

Protectionism also reared its head during the recession, as Chinese solar panels became a hot issue in both Europe and the US. In the space of five years China became the world's biggest producer of solar panels, lowering costs and making them competitive with fossil fuels. Solar World, a German company operating in the US, initiated a suit against the importation of Chinese panels and was joined by other manufacturers. But US companies that install panels opposed the suit because lower prices expanded their market. With much rhetoric about saving American jobs and US companies, the Obama administration put a 27–78 per cent tariff on Chinese panels.

The added charges made Chinese imports significantly more expensive for installers. Mukesh Dulani, president of SolarWorld Americas, claimed victory, declaring, 'The tariffs and scope set the stage for companies to create new jobs and build or expand factories on U.S. soil' (Cardwell 2014a). The creation of US jobs, however, has been less than impressive. Since the first tariffs two years ago, SolarWorld has created only 200 jobs in its factory in Oregon – hardly a big dent in the 11 million people still looking for work. Behind the patriotic smokescreen, protectionist battles in both the US and Europe are about transnational corporations fighting for market share and profits, not employment.

We can gain a further picture of the transnational character of the alternative energy industry by examining the two largest US solar firms. The largest, First Solar, is owned by True North Partners, an investment arm of the Walton family of Wal-Mart, infamous for their exploitative labour practices. Headquartered in Arizona, the company has facilities in Ohio, Malaysia and Germany. Operations in Malaysia have 3,700 employees working in six factories producing 83 per cent of First Solar's global output (Bradsher 2014). When it comes to technology and quality, however, there is no difference between Malaysia and Ohio. Standardisation of production is a benchmark for transnational firms. First Solar's story is not all about Malaysia, however; its connection to Germany is key to its success. CEO Mike Ahearn stated, 'First Solar is to a large extent a German success story . . . we purchase over half of the equipment used in our production lines from German manufacturers and we count suppliers in Eastern Germany as among our most important business partners' (Friedman 2008, pp. 389–90).

The next largest US company is SunPower. It carries out R&D in California, but half of its solar panel production takes place in Malaysia, and its major stockholder is the French oil transnational Total. In addition, the company has three production facilities in the Philippines, one in Mexico and one in France. No manufacturing is carried out in the US (SunPower 2014). Chief Executive Tom Werner praised Malaysia for a 'cross between just a straight low-cost play and a high engineering play' (Bradshser 2014). What this play translates into is an average monthly pay of $765 for technicians and $400 for assembly-line workers. Based on a forty-hour working week, four weeks per month, that amounts to $1 an hour for factory workers and about $4.30 an hour for skilled engineers (Bradshser 2014). It's no mystery why Malaysia has become the world's third largest producer of solar equipment, attracting transnational corporations from Europe, South Korea, Japan and the US.

A final point to look at is the rapid rise in solar panel production that caused overproduction and a profit crisis in the industry. In 2013 global production of panels peaked at 70 gigawatts of energy, but worldwide demand hit only 30 gigawatts. Much of this production was in China where companies received cheap loans from state banks and nearly free land from local governments. This pattern of Chinese state support began in 2009, and by 2012 two dozen solar manufacturers in the US and Europe had gone bankrupt, unable to compete on price and facing worldwide overproduction. With supplies running ahead of the market by over 130 per cent prices crashed, and some of the biggest Chinese corporations, such as Suntech and LDK Solar, were also facing bankruptcy. Chinese state support also led to US and European tariffs and a WTO law suit.

But such a crisis could only happen under capitalism. In reality, to combat climate change the world needs much more than 70 gigawatts per year. The policies of the Chinese government should be praised and followed in every country, not opposed by protectionist manoeuvres. In the US solar power accounts for only around one-fifth of 1 per cent of energy use. Cheaper prices should encourage widespread adaptation, not bankrupt companies and shut down capacity. Research by the University of Delaware and Delaware Technical Community College found that wind and solar power could supply 99.9 per cent of US electrical needs by 2030 (Massey 2012). Moreover, the International Energy Agency reported that up to $2.5 trillion a year will need to be invested in energy for the next twenty years. The agency also notes, however, that fossil fuel investments will outspend renewable energy by a margin of four to one (Reed 2014). There is clearly a need for great expansion of sustainable energy, the technical knowhow for which already exists.

Unfortunately major roadblocks stand in the way. Political problems that saturate the debate over subsidies and protectionism limit the rapid deployment of solar technology. These are based on conservative opposition to government spending and oil industry lobby power. On a deeper level, contradictions inherent in both the growth and crisis cycles of capitalism, leading to overproduction and bankruptcy, reveal some of the fundamental economic problems blocking a Green New Deal. Market forces have to be controlled and capitalist rationality replaced by the rationality of environmental sustainability. Yet it is doubtful that committed neoliberals such as Rubin and Paulson would be won over to such actions. Their preference is for market-based solutions such as carbon trading stocks, a programme that has failed to produce significant results and collapsed with the recession. Moreover, they see no particular contradiction between austerity for the working class and the promotion of sustainable capitalism to address global warming. Lastly, given the highly transnational character of the alternative energy industry, its global outsourcing of jobs and fondness for cheap labour, the Green New Deal appears less promising than hoped for.

Building the democratic alternative

As outlined above, the drive towards green capitalism retains many of the same problems as neoliberal globalisation. Green capitalism, or a neoliberal Green Deal, will present only partial solutions, too weak and slow to address the extent of the environment crisis. Nor will a neoliberal Green Deal be committed to shrinking the ever-growing gap of inequality. On the other hand, a *progressive* Green New Deal, like the New Deal of the Great Depression, would necessitate a virtual political revolution. A green political movement would have to become the dominant wing of the Democratic Party, reach political hegemony in Europe and have major influence in the Chinese Communist Party as well as in other emerging economies. In the US a major roadblock is the anti-scientific faction in the Republican Party that has yet to catch up with the Age of Enlightenment. This would only be possible with a powerful mass movement and a sea change in social consciousness. Currently about half the US population rejects the science of global warming, and provides the social base for political deadlocks and backward economic and social policies.

All the above would entail the defeat of the fossil fuel industry's power over political policies, as well as its social hegemony. Yet the oil industry lobby has huge influence over Congress as well as many state attorneys general who oversee the application of environment laws (Lipton 2014). From 2000 to 2006 political donations included $72.8 million from ExxonMobil, $42.3 million from Chevron, $34.3 million from Marathon, $31.6 million from BP and $29 million from Shell (Roberts 2006).

Yet given economic stagnation, the hopeless political floundering of neoliberal elites, the dangers of another financial collapse and a possible catastrophic environmental future, fundamental change cannot be ruled out. Because of the seriousness of the crisis, sectors of the capitalist class will attempt a move to green capitalism with or without the left. But a progressive Green New Deal depends on the participation of the left and a number of important contributions it can make. This would entail an alliance with the green capitalist sector, particularly with its most progressive and Keynesian wing. Specifically left political forces can make important contributions in three key areas:

- labour rights and the struggle against neoliberalism
- building a broad-based environmental movement
- supporting a decentralised energy system and creating green cooperatives.

James O'Connor wrote about the first and second contradictions of capitalism (Foster 2002). The first was the exploitation of labour, the second the exploitation of the environment. Green capitalism will attempt to solve the second contradiction, but makes no commitment towards ending the exploitation of the working class. Although important voices such as Stiglitz, Paul Krugman and Robert Reich understand the crucial need to lessen inequality, only a red/green strategic orientation will address the problems in a systematic and fundamental manner.

Progressive Green New Deal advocates will be in an arena with a complex array of players: green entrepreneurs and companies with a mission of social responsibility, neo-Keynesian advocates deeply concerned with inequality, neoliberal transnational capitalists and green nationalists obsessed with US hegemony. Addressing both the environment and social justice issues can only be accomplished by building a more powerful and deeply rooted environmental movement, one that understands its links to labour and other social movements. Only by creating a synergy of movements can the left hope to be successful. This was achieved in the 1960s when the civil rights movement, the anti-war movement, insurgent labour rebellions, Native American struggles, Asian activists, feminists, the farm workers' struggle and the Gay Pride movement collectively posed a challenge to capitalism. The green movement needs to be dynamic and independent, linking with all progressive forces. In fact, it is less an environmental movement than a people's movement for sustainability, democracy and social justice, one that activists at the World Social Forum have called a movement of movements. Consequently, a set of relationships emerges that calls for closer affiliation among strategic allies, tactical alliances with others as well as opposition to some players.

One example links sustainable energy to jobs, workers' empowerment, social justice and police repression. If the government encouraged the import of less expensive solar panels, then the installation industry could rapidly expand. In terms of employment this sector creates more jobs than manufacturing panels does. Worker-owned cooperatives, like the Evergreen solar installation company in Cleveland, Ohio, could be created in poor communities throughout the US to install panels on millions of homes and businesses. Local hiring and training could be a requirement in order to receive subsidies, and good wages and health care would be guaranteed by being a member of a worker-owned business. The creation of jobs and the circulation of money would reduce poverty, decreasing the attraction of gangs, and would undermine the excuse for heavy police tactics that condemn so many Black and Latino men to prison. This is certainly not the complete answer to these problems, but it does begin to address class inequality, institutional racism and worker empowerment.

Another important aspect of a progressive Green New Deal would be a national system of energy independence based on solar panel installations. With each home having its own energy system, the utility monopolies and fossil fuel transnationals would become a secondary back-up system, breaking monopoly control over energy supplies including the corporate-dominated solar and wind energy farms. A progressive movement needs to make clear the more democratic choice of community-based development and a citizen-centred economy. Neighbourhood installations would also produce far more jobs because centrally owned solar and wind farms employ only a handful of workers once in operation. A good example is the success of solar power in Germany, which is based on economic incentives for homes and farms to begin using solar panels. The policy requires the utility corporations to buy excess energy, sold to them by home owners above market price valuations. Although Germany is on a similar latitude to the Hudson Bay in Canada, it is the world's leading user of solar panels, with 7 per cent of its energy needs supplied by solar power. The German system, along with its commitment to wind power, has been so successful that the energy giant E.ON is selling off its nuclear, oil, coal and gas operations to focus on green energy and its distribution network (Deutsche Welle 2014).

The competitive position of alternative energy has greatly improved over the past five years with rapidly falling prices. The cost of wind turbines has gone down by 20 per cent and that of solar panels has plummeted by 80 per cent. Lazard, the investment banking firm, reports 'solar energy is as low as 5.6 cents a kilowatt-hour, and wind is as low as 1.4 cents. In comparison, natural gas comes at 6.1 cents a kilowatt-hour on the low end and coal at 6.6 cents' (Cardwell 2014b). Frequently, however, subsidies are the key to lower prices. Without government support, Lazard estimates that solar costs would rise to about 7.2 cents a kilowatt-hour at the low end, with wind at 3.7 cents (ibid.). Consequently the political struggle over government spending, tax policies, subsidies and regulations are key battlegrounds for the progressive movement, particularly in the US, Europe and India. Of all the big fossil fuel emitters, China and Germany have the most forward-looking policies on government support for solar and wind.

Key to the creation of democratic alternatives are ongoing efforts made by Latin American countries in the struggle to expand the solidarity economy and horizontal democracy. Hugo Chavez of Venezuela, who first defined twenty-first-century socialism, has emphasised the state's role in giving resources and power to local communities and worker cooperatives. According to Chavez and his collaborators, the new society was to be rooted in the everyday realities of the working class and poor. The model of large, centrally organised state bureaucracies leading social transformations, as attempted by twentieth-century socialism, has been giving way to greater coordination between a socialist state, civil society and social movements. Within this framework, worker-owned cooperatives are understood as democratically controlled institutions of working-class power.

Also essential are environmentally balanced concepts of human society that reject the destructive relationship between capitalist materialism and the environment. An important contribution is the philosophy of *buen vivir* (live well), articulated by the indigenous social movements in Ecuador and Bolivia. The president of Bolivia, Evo Morales, explained this vision in his speech at the United Nations COP20 climate talks in Lima, Peru, stating:

> The economic model upholding the financial architecture and war politics has as its nucleus the politics of the free market, that is, the voracious capitalist policy that pays no attention to anything other than profit, luxury and consumerism . . . People are treated as things, and Mother Earth as a commodity. Either we change global capitalist society or it annihilates the world's peoples and nature itself. The environment is a common heritage of all the peoples of the world, of the ancient peoples, of the present peoples and the peoples who are to come. (Morales 2014)

Conclusion

Just as the Keynesian model of capitalism became exhausted, so too has neoliberalism crashed against its boundaries of expansion. Another transformation is called for. Currently neoliberalism has refused to recognise the full extent of the cancer eating at its body. Instead it has turned to greater austerity and a growing technocratic authoritarianism grounded in supranational political institutions, military drones and vast collections of personal data of anyone who picks up a phone or turns on a computer.

Capitalism may find a transformative model in the green economy. But the question then becomes: do we want a green deal, or a Green New Deal? In other words, will green technologies be used simply to renew accumulation and mediate aspects of global warming, or do we fight for a socially progressive New Deal with all its implications of mass mobilisation, environmental sustainability and regulations that discipline the destructive habits of capitalism? If a progressive left can play an important role in such a struggle it will open the door to greater social transformations that may take us beyond the limits of capitalism. The most hopeful alternative is a green democratic socialism that builds society around the principles of environmental sanity, human solidarity and popular empowerment.

References

Bain & Company (2012) 'A world awash in money', available at www.bain.com/publi cations/articles/a-world-awash-in-money.aspx

Bradsher, K. (2014) 'Solar rises in Malaysia during trade wars over panel', *New York Times* (11 December).

Cardwell, D. (2014a) 'U.S. imposes steep tariffs on Chinese solar panels', *New York Times* (16 December).

Cardwell, D. (2014b) 'Solar and wind energy start to win on price vs. conventional fuels', *New York Times* (23 November).

Clark, P. (2014) 'Energy groups face "existential" climate threat, says ex-BP chief', *Financial Times* (19 November).

Cohen, P. (2014) 'Fueled by recession, US wealth gap is widest in decades, study finds', *New York Times* (17 December).

Crooks, E. (2014) 'Exxon warns global warming targets "unlikely" to be met', *Financial Times* (21 March).

Deutsche Welle (2014) 'German energy giant E.ON to focus on renewables', available at www.dw.de/german-energy-giant-eon-to-focus-on-renewables/a-18104023

DuRand, C. and S. Martinot (eds) (2012) *Recreating Democracy in a Globalized State.* Atlanta, GA: Clarity Press.

Friedman, T. (2008) *Hot, Flat, and Crowded.* New York: Farrar, Straus and Giroux.

Foster, J. B. (1999) *The Vulnerable Planet.* New York: Monthly Review Press.

Foster, J. B. (2002) 'Capitalism and ecology: the nature of the contradiction', *Monthly Review* 54(4), 6–16.

Gillis, J. (2014) 'Fixing climate change may add no costs, report says', *New York Times* (16 September)

Gramsci, A. (1971) *Selections from the Prison Notebooks of Antonio Gramsci.* New York: International Publishers.

Hardy, Q. (2013) 'A strange computer promises great speed', *New York Times* (21 March).

Harris, J. (2008) *The Dialectics of Globalization; Economic and Political Conflict in a Transnational World.* Newcastle upon Tyne: Cambridge Scholars Publishing.

Harris, J. and C. Davidson (2013) 'Globalization and the crisis of democracy', *Perspectives on Global Development and Technology* 12(1–2), 181–93.

Hatton, E. (2013) 'The rise of the permatemp', *New York Times* (27 January).

Jasper, W. (2014) 'Risky business: billionaires hype climate for power and profit', *The New American* (12 August), available at www.thenewamerican.com/tech/environment/item/18899-risky-business-billionaires-hype-climate-for-power-and-profit

Lipton, E. (2014) 'Energy firms in secretive alliance with attorneys general', *New York Times* (6 December).

Lomas, C. (2014) 'G20 continue to prop up fossil fuel industry', *Deutsche Welle*, available at www.dw.de/g20-continue-to-prop-up-fossil-fuel-industry/a-18060217

Marx, K. (1990) *Capital: Critique of Political Economy*, vol. 1. London: Penguin Books.

Massey, N. (2012) 'Solutions to renewable energy's intermittency problem: more renewable energy', available at www.scientificamerican.com/article/solution-to-renewable-energy-more-renewable-energy/?print=true

Monaghan, A. (2014) 'Bank of England governor: capitalism doomed if ethics vanish', *The Guardian* (27 May), available at www.theguardian.com/business/2014/may/27/capitalism-critique-bank-of-england-carney

Morales, E. (2014) 'Environmental destruction is a result of the capitalist system',

The Bullet 1062 (17 December), available at www.socialistproject.ca/bullet/1062. php#continue

O'Connor, J. (2014) 'James O'Connor: selling nature', available at www.sagepub.com/ upm-data/13298_Chapter_9_Web_Byte_James_O'Connor.pdf

Rachman, G. (2013) 'The west is losing faith in its own future', *Financial Times* (9 December).

Reed, S. (2014) 'Report calls for huge investment in energy development', *New York Times* (2 June).

Rittenberg, S. and A. Bennett (1993) *The Man Who Stayed Behind*. New York and London: Simon and Schuster.

Roberts, P. (2006) 'The United States needs to pursue alternative energy', in Laura K. Egendorf (ed.) *Energy Alternatives*. Farmington Hills, MI: Greenhaven Press.

Robinson, W. I. (2004) *A Theory of Global Capitalism: Production, Class, and State in a Transnational World*. Baltimore, MD and London: The Johns Hopkins University Press.

Rubin, R. (2014) 'How ignoring climate change could sink the U.S. economy', *Washington Post* (25 July).

Samuels, C. (2009) 'The US carbon footprint and good business: the rest of the world gets it, why don't we?', Care2, available at www.care2.com/causes/the-us-carbon-footprint-and-good-business-the-rest-of-the-world-gets-it-why-dont-we.html

Schwartz, A. (2010) 'The green guide to Obama's State of the Union address' (27 January), available at www.fastcompany.com/1529793/green-guide-obamas-state-union-address

Sklair, L. (2001) *The Transnational Capitalist Class*. Oxford: Blackwell.

Stiglitz, J. (2014) 'How inequality is killing the American Dream ... and what we can do about it', Reader Supported News (14 November), available at http://lists. readersupportednews.org/ss/link.php?M=56526&N=13557&C=afb24077225c66c3e a77eec2ac805655&L=17940

SunPower (2014) Annual Report 2013, p. 48, available at http://files.shareholder. com/downloads/SPWR/3724295017x0x733544/FEFEE46D-481B-43DC-917C-C35423CD07E6/685022_002_SunPower_BMK_1_.PDF

Yen, H. (2013) 'Exclusive: signs of declining economic security', Associated Press, The Big Story (28 July), available at http://bigstory.ap.org/article/exclusive-4-5-us-face-near-poverty-no-work-0

Zinn, H. (1998) *A People's History of the United States*. New York: Harper Perennial.

5

From Civilisational Crisis to Revolutionary Transformation?

Oleg Suša

STRONG PERCEPTIONS OF crises have been in the making since the 1970s. The plurality of crises results from dynamic transformations of politico-economic, societal and environmental conditions. Numerous highly problematical consequences of the transformations are produced and reproduced. The crisis of industrial civilisation, related to both social and environmental limits, can be illustrated by a critical analysis of empirical phenomena reflecting the 'creative destruction' brought about by the 'capitalist perestroika' over the last forty or so years. Policies adapting to these crises decisively shaped the 'neoliberal turn' of Western societies, responding to economic, social and technological changes in ambiguous ways: they combine deregulation with new modes of control and certain civilising efforts. In this context, the global expansion of ostensibly free-market capitalism, accompanied by relocations of industries and new directions of technological innovation, has played a key role; to put it another way, the present configuration of capitalism is both conducive to crises of social and environmental reproduction and able to frame responses to them. This configuration affects global civilisational dynamics, now headed either towards further degradation of humanity and the planet or to the generation of something new. To radicalise the issue, the question is whether a revolutionary transformation of both capitalism and civilisation could be on the horizon.

Transformations and risks in global civilisation

It is necessary not only to address the growing problems linked to social changes, but to do so with due regard to their increasingly global dimensions and repercussions. In the late 1960s, the Czech philosopher and sociologist Radovan Richta and his research team formulated an analysis of social and human aspects of the technological and scientific revolution with particular emphasis on its social and human dimensions. Their famous book *Civilisation at the Crossroads* (the most widely translated Czech publication in the social sciences) was an exemplary case of civilisational analysis, in some ways anticipating the crisis atmosphere in the 1970s (Richta 1967). They were writing about 'civilisation at the crossroads' in light of a new transformation of productive forces, based on scientific discoveries and leading, as they argued, to a scientification of society. Almost half a century later, we can still link up with their attempt to locate social transformations and possible alternatives within a global civilisational context, and to grasp the cognitive and technological basis of the latter. But we must take note of other aspects, later highlighted by Western authors working with other models, of which the idea of risk society is not the least important.

Modern civilisation has pursued certainty through growing control of internal and external worlds. However, this control is associated with the en masse generation of risks. Awareness of a rise in uncertainties could appear to be a paradoxical consequence of expert knowledge and reflexivity, but it is also inseparable from continuing political failure when faced with the complexity of the adverse ramifications of modern transformations. Those repercussions then play a role, directly or otherwise, in the emergence of social conflicts, underpinned by the uneven distribution of risks, uncertainties and threats on the one hand and the uneven distribution of opportunities, as well as access to rewards and profits, on the other. Furthermore, ongoing processes of expanding global interdependence and interaction complicate this situation, aggravating the uncertainties and imbalances.

In addition, given the contemporary globalisation of social activities, interactions and changes, there is growing opacity in decision-making processes and in the whole organisation of social behaviour; the highly variable and flexible structures of relations underlying the negotiations of various actors can often be difficult to control democratically by means of existing territorially based procedures of the political process (Sassen 2008). We could refer to this as 'glocal' and in that capacity uncoordinated interactions and relations. Numerous conflicts surface in situations where there is a contrast between the negotiations and decision-making of strong actors in advantageous, perhaps even monopolistic, positions and actors who are affected by and involuntarily exposed to the ramifications of decisions by the elite in which they are unable to have a say. These conflicts feed demands for participatory and resistance-driven politics against 'top-down globalisation' decision-making, or for the establishment of more symmetrical power structures (Beck 2009a: 16; Held 1995). Critical active citizens create and stimulate various activities in civil society, while the majority of citizens are passive even if not satisfied by the contemporary social conditions.

More generally speaking, the risks of global civilisation are linked to the modernising processes involved in the expansion of capitalism, to the transformation of the spatial and temporal organisation of human and social life, and to the technological aspiration to exercise power and control over space and colonise the future. In modern industrial society, risk has essentially depended on the ability or inability to control an unforeseen, unknown event, or to insure oneself against threats of loss or damage. 'Risk' differs from the more commonplace 'hazard' primarily through the concomitant search for the certainty of risk predictability and the reliance on mechanisms and institutions controlling or mitigating the negative impact of risks. The conventional understanding of risk associated negative problems and impacts with external forces; in recent years a new type of risk has emerged that does not just occur but rather is socially or industrially manufactured.

Civilisational risks are no longer a strictly unintended consequence or dysfunction, but rather an increasingly systemic consequence of the global expansion and growth of modern capitalist industrial technological civilisation. This problematic development leads to a crisis of the entire global capitalist industrial civilisation which, despite numerous technological innovations, has produced a number of serious changes and cumulative consequences, and new risks and threats.

Social transformations related to the mentioned civilisational risks are not only visible on the level of historical events, but also have a long-term effect and can remain latent. In a global technological civilisation, the complexity of changes is compounded by the acceleration of technical innovations and interventions. Technology geared towards the purely instrumental handling of problems has resulted in political, social and psychological dependence on technological resources. Examples of this are the business mantra 'innovate or die' and the way the political process and governance have been reduced to technical and economic instrumental procedures. Technical innovations are squeezing human labour out of production and are leading to the overproduction of goods with no one to buy them. Capital is blindly continuing the externalisation of social problems, especially many forms of social exclusion and environmental burdens.

However, the growing uncertainties do not stem solely from scientific and technological progress. In particular, new hazards and high-risk contexts are being generated by economic and political institutions. Individuals are impersonal, anonymous resources forced to lead heteronomous lives in a risky environment. Society, in the form of space controlled by the power elite, is a laboratory in which no one appears to be responsible for the broader societal and global repercussions of experimentation, or for the consequences of decision-making and the implications of conflict-driven strategies pursuing the particular interests of the actors behind them. Individuals are involuntarily deprived of both traditional and modern certainties and protective unions formed on the basis of solidarity. This is particularly true of transformations within the scope of the neoliberal dismantling of the welfare state: an institutional vacuum is created in which there is no civilisational mechanism to absorb the consequences of externalising the risks.[1]

Discussions on risk engender a relationship, based on calculation, between the future and the present. The present is ostensibly rationalised in this way, but the future is hardly predictable. This concerns, for example, the standard discourse on capitalism, in which winners and losers are determined by 'luck' and the 'play of market forces'. This is how the utopianism of belief in winning the lottery is spurred on – it is all about risk-taking and fortune, not about ability, accountability or guilt. The dream is to change the status of an individual (rational) actor in the system, rather than to change the system. Risk compensation can trigger the following effect: the more types of insurance available, the more we are encouraged to gamble. Risk is confrontation with a problem of the future, it is a reified concept of time as a thing, which has fundamental, very serious social consequences from economic, financial and environmental standpoints. Events recurring over time form the basis for norms and fixed expectations that we project into the future. And disappointed expectations are explained by reference to conformity with the norm or derogation from the norm, which we perceive as a risk. Such a misconstrued, reified concept of risk is intended to conceal the fatalism of accepting social inequality. Risk discourses normalise the limited rationality of profit and persuade the actors involved that people must adapt to capital and the capitalist system of objectifying the world, that the misappropriation and manipulation of people and nature in modern technological civilisation are essential. The misplaced objectification of risk conceals its social and environmental conflictual nature (Beck 2009b).

The fact that, starting in the 1970s, people began to realise the problem of the globality of risks can be attributed to numerous factors and transformations, especially the accumulation of the ambiguous consequences of modern scientific, technical and industrial changes, influencing nature and human society: a climate of the certainty of uncertainties began to seep into traditional technical optimism. Other factors included globalisation and globality as a dynamic process and a state of transformation, resulting in the social consequences of comprehensive world metamorphosis and rising interdependence between society and social actors (Appelbaum and Robinson 2005: 23: capitalism is developing into a 'singular global civilization, in which humanity is bound together as never before', and 'the crisis of capitalism is clearly a crisis of civilizational dimensions'). Globality began to be reflected in a subjective consciousness of the time-space compression and a 'diminishing world'. It was also in the 1970s that the syndrome of 'encountering limits to exponential growth' (Meadows 1972) came to the fore, and the energy and environmental crises called for adaptive transformations. Another increasingly significant factor was the process of the protracted crisis affecting political structures and the ideologies of industrial civilisation. In recent decades, there has been an enormous increase in multilateral social inequalities, which have been the source of many crises. The repercussions of the new global and local distribution and redistribution and of resources and opportunities are politically salient. Numerous indigenous movements seeking to combat poverty and champion fairer distributive opportunities and sustainable development, including the right to a healthy environment and socioeconomic reproduction, have emerged. A certain role has also been played by the influence of social movements, which grasped the crisis of modern social structures and institutions, with its socioeconomic and socioenvironmental consequences, primarily as a cultural crisis, as a challenge and opportunity for grassroots cultural politics.

As far back as the 1970s, Joseph Camilleri, in his *Civilization in Crisis*, succinctly summed up the nature and features of the global crisis faced by capitalist industrial civilisation as a concatenation of multiple specific crises threading their way through the entire structure of human relations and institutions and 'destroy[ing] the relationships of humanity and nature'. The worldwide crisis affects everyone living on this planet and is intensifying global interdependence, with the possibility of a looming confrontation between humankind and a crisis of survival (Camilleri 1976: 9–11). This concept of civilisation crisis anticipated and discussed the risks emerging from the technical imperative, associated with domination and power-wielding control over people and nature, and noted efforts to monopolise the exercise of power over resources, flows and profits in the global market and division of labour, which are controlled by the forces of capital, transnational corporations and superpower states. Powerful globalising actors act in line with their narrow interests and intensify the competitive struggle. This increases the potential of risks, while the profit-oriented economic system accentuates their and their uneven distribution and thus accelerates the further increase in social rifts. The interaction of various change-related trends results in a global crisis where each of the critical trends of imbalance 'accentuates the other' (ibid.: 29).

Social crisis: limits to growth, capitalist transformations and social consequences

Contemporary human societies are influenced by the global civilisational configuration shaped by transformations which originated during adaptations to multiple crises from the 1970s. The origins of the transformations can be found in the late 1960s. In 1968, the crisis of Western mass consumer capitalism and the crisis of bureaucratic socialism came to the fore in parallel. Both systems reacted to inner and outer limits, both were repressive to human potential and labour, and both were socially and environmentally exploitative. Crises and transformations were both reactions to and drivers of the further accumulation and acceleration of the limits to growth in both the social and environmental dimensions.

Crises and transformations led to the 'creative destruction' of postwar systems of organised capitalism and bureaucratic socialism, and to the transnationalisation (globalisation) of the capital accumulation process. The globalisation of capitalism (including the collapse of bureaucratic socialism and the accelerated process of the differentiation of 'third-world' developing countries from newly industrialised ones) triggers antagonism between the transnational shift in accumulation and societies organised within a framework of single nation states.

Capitalist adaptation to growth limits saw corporations realign their strategy from long-term to short-term profit, from low risks to high risks, and the new patterns of capital accumulation ushered in a new round of competition and monopoly. Such crisis-adaptive transformations since the 1970s have also included top-down economic-political revolution, taking the form of the restoration of the class domination of capital owners (with free-market neoliberalism as the new dominant discourse), and the reorganisation of capitalist enterprises, including a growing asymmetry of power between capital and labour.

In addition, the information-technology revolution has facilitated the transnational movement of money, information and knowledge as capital – so that capital flows and networks of exchange in trade and production have magnified the flexibility of transnational interaction among economic and non-economic actors alike. Technology has also helped to disseminate the financialisation process. According to William Robinson, capitalist transformations generated two major mechanisms for unloading surpluses that would provide a perverse lifeline to the system: militarised accumulation and financial speculation. 'Military spending skyrocketed into trillions of dollars through the "war on terrorism" and the invasions and occupations of Iraq and Afghanistan . . . Financial speculation was made possible by deregulation of the financial industry combined with the introduction of CIT, giving rise to a globally integrated financial system' (Robinson 2011: 3). This brought about many innovations which made possible a global casino with expansion of fictitious capital.

Adaptation to emerging limits – mostly resulting, in the case of the environmental crisis, from rising prices of resources and energies – to geopolitical transformations and to global financialisation led to another crisis: disinvestment in productive sectors, or the real economy, with adverse consequences for employment and the public sector, including human development, education, health, the environment and so on. This resulted in a deep crisis of the socio-economic reproduction of societies. Globalised financialisation gave rise to the domination of mergers and acquisitions and a debt-based predatory system with the effect of a decline of industrial capacity in many industrial countries: financial speculation became the principal means of making a profit in Europe, in the US, in the West and even in the East, where socioeconomic decline, privatisations and parasitism were connected with the creation of new capital markets, the destruction of real productive forces and negative social consequences (growing unemployment, poverty, crime and a deconstruction of the welfare state). Capitalist crisis-adaptive transformations thus triggered the systemic manifestation of deep-rooted contradictions in the global economy (see North 2011: especially 16–19).

The core crisis problem relates to the main goal of accumulation: to generate financial wealth through a cycle of return to financial markets, and so on ad infinitum. The contemporary model of financialised monopoly capitalism was described by Fumagalli and Lucarelli (2010) as cognitive capitalism, linked to electronic high technologies and knowledge economy. As the newest mutation of the paradigm, cognitive capitalism oriented towards financial speculations instead of real production is unable to protect the socioeconomic system from structural instability. This paradigm is characterised mostly by the fact that financial markets equipped with instrumental knowledge are the drivers of capital accumulation.

In the cognitive capitalist paradigm, financial markets directly influence and condition the process of accumulation and valorisation: this marks the passage from commodity money to sign money. Financial markets play the role of the main multiplier, with the distorted redistribution of revenues leading to the privatisation of social reproduction. Financial markets are a place where the exploitation of social cooperation and the general intellect are measured by stock market values.' 'Profits become rent and labour value is determined and transformed into financial value. Financial markets thus exercise biopower' (Fumagalli 2011).

The vicious circle of money-makes-money transformations leads to speculation, virtual monetary wealth turns to transnational financial flows and its volatility leads to financial crises. The domination of financial capital seriously deforms the priorities of enterprises, states, science and research. With growing risks in global financialisation, the risks of macroeconomic and political destabilisation also grow.[2] Social problems connected with growing inequalities, labour precarisation (and unemployment or underemployment) and environmental damage engender a feedback effect in productivity and low efficiency of the capitalist system as a whole. In summary, '*social crisis* is connected with transformations of capitalism into a system which produces inequality and poverty and generates a process of the *disengagement of human resources*' (Chossudovski 2010).

Moreover, in a neoliberal 'market society', mechanisms of command become even 'more immanent to the social field, distributed throughout the brains and bodies of the citizens' (Kiersley 2011: 36). Every form of human activity is now accountable to metrics of behaviour determined by capitalist rationality, while human creative potential is subsumed to 'human capital'. Within the framework of changing labour practices made possible by communicative technologies and the immaterialisation of labour today, surplus – i.e. rent – is extracted through the production of knowledge, desires and affects. Financialisation uses the unpaid labour and time as well as the lifestyles of consumers – and consumers add value to goods through the very fact of their consumption. This creates a new form of domination over society and human behaviour which can be, following the terms 'cognitive capitalism' and 'biopower', described more sociologically as 'cognitive biocapitalism'.

In cognitive biocapitalism, the condition of the labour force goes hand in hand with mobility and the predominance of individual contracting (precariousness). Work relations based on precarious conditions – the temporal limit and spatial mobility of labour – are a basic feature of the relationship between capital and labour. 'Precariousness becomes a structural, existential and generalised condition' (Fumagalli 2011: 12).

The International Labour Organisation reports steadily growing world unemployment – globally, the estimate is as many as 230 million people within the next five years (ILO Report 2013). It forces many others to accept precarious jobs. Precarisation leads to risks of social conflicts and riots: rising unemployment rates, income inequalities, a decreasing standard of living, low trust in government and politics. These are the main determinant factors of the social risk index (in forty-six out of seventy-one countries, the index has grown). Long-term unemployment – twelve months or longer – is also considered an important social decay factor, with the loss of human social capability to work and to engage socially and politically, eroding the living human potential of democracy.

Furthermore, growing youth unemployment is one of the striking empirical indicators of a complex social crisis in the contemporary capitalist system – the group aged between fifteen and twenty-five is in danger of long-term work exclusion and precarity (ILO 2014: 21).[3] What is more, the average duration of unemployment has gone up, especially in developed economies. This makes job searches harder, with labour skills depreciated. Unemployment comes at considerable personal and social cost, such as decreased life satisfaction and stigmatisation. The unemployed become less healthy on average than the employed, which increases the need for public health expenditures (ibid.: 26).

Stagnation with low investment in the real economy and employment help to reproduce social inequality, with a dangerous split between the minority, which is getting rich, and the majority, which is becoming poor (Piketty 2014). A complex social crisis makes the capitalist system dysfunctional, and the ensuing social limits to growth reproduce the vicious circle of stagnation. Furthermore, growing social inequality and unemployment obstruct political solutions to the social crisis via governmental interventions funded by progressive taxation, which continues to be opposed by ruling capitalist power elites. The distribution of rewards is fixed by power, not by the market (ibid.).

Alternative civilisational and/or political solutions cannot be based on a statistical survey, comparing the numbers of jobs created versus the number of people who need a job, for example. They have to be formulated as complex conceptions of society, economy and politics. The problem calling out for a revolutionary solution is qualitative: the limited valorisation of human collective productive-creative forces – the price of human labour as instrumental to power and domination – continues down the road of further deformations of human development. Reducing use value to exchange value, capitalism reaches its own qualitative social limits, which are based on power-based social relations between capital and labour. Indeed, primitive accumulation extracting financial rent also from the state together with exploitation further divides and divorces human labour from the collective production of common social wealth (Roggero 2010: 360).

At the same time, this underlines the urgent necessity to prepare for a revolutionary civilising transformation. From a normative point of view, revolution here primarily means a redefinition of human work as a sociocultural quality – not the labour force as market commodity but the life-process of communicative action in social cooperation. Work thus understood facilitates moral dignity and the creative satisfaction of self-realisation needs, and the ethical development of social cohabitation, mutual exchanges, cultivation and interaction. Civilisational development in this sense consists of a broad social process of collective support for human social creative potential, not capital investment in financial speculation.

Environmental crisis in progress and violence

There is now a widespread belief that capitalism will not survive the environmental crisis: that the system has reached its ultimate limits. As far back as 1972, the Club of Rome report *The Limits to Growth* stated that we would not run out of minerals and substances in the near future, but recognised that there would be ever higher costs associated with obtaining them.

A recent report to the Club of Rome – more than four decades after the 1972 analysis denouncing the plundering of the planet – points out very clearly that none of the numerous mineral resources that are extracted daily by the 'universal mining machine' (Bardi and Randers 2014) and which are essential to the functioning of our industrial civilisation will run out in the near future. The times of cheap mineral resources will, however, be over soon. The existence of large, easily exploitable deposits will be a thing of the past. Their exploitation will be more costly and more energy-consuming, and will also produce more waste and have a higher negative environmental impact on the future of civilisation, now appearing as a 'mineral eschatology'.

Without natural resources – oil among them – contemporary industrial global civilisation cannot function, and these resources are very quickly becoming depleted. The growing number of ecological disasters, including cumulative pollution and climate change, will push up the cost of maintaining the infrastructures to unsustainable levels. And the impact of a changing climate on food prices will induce riots, rendering societies ungovernable.

On the other hand, there are observations concerning capitalism's ability to adapt and a certain deformed transformative capacity ('creative destruction'): capitalism might well be capable not only of adapting to ecological crisis, but also of profiting from it.

Capitalism is confronted with multiple crises – economic, social and ecological – but one crisis can sometimes be harnessed to address, at least temporarily, another. Each has its own specific way of functioning, and they can sometimes serve to alleviate or spread the rising costs of climate change and the superexploitation of the environment. There are, for example, catastrophe bonds which are linked not to the future as standard bonds, but to the possible occurrence of a disaster (earthquakes or flood). With a growing number of natural disasters due to climate change, catastrophe insurance management has risen to high levels.

As in the case of resource depletion and planetary plundering, which has escalated due to market evaluation through price and profit-seeking by corporate extraction industries and global traders, financial business is – in response to disasters relating to climate change – passively adapting to ecological limits and catastrophes, reproducing, in parallel, its own profit-seeking strategy while worsening the environmental condition of the planet. The profit accumulation of some through the disasters of many others is reproducing the unsustainability of our industrial civilisation. At the same time, it is worsening the social crisis of inequality.

There is clear evidence that such dynamics deliver more destruction than creativity. A global political framework of regulations, for example the UN climate process resulting in a global pact with some substance, is still in the realm of utopia. The UN Climate Panel recently reported that emissions increased 2.2 per cent a year on average between 2000 and 2010 (in the period from 1970 to 2010, the figure was 1.3 per cent a year). In 2010–11, global emissions from the burning of fossil fuels rose by 3 per cent. The most polluting facilities are coal-burning power plants, and there are more than 1,000 new such plants under construction worldwide, mostly in China and India (Stocker 2013: 50).

The call for collective responsibility across governments, businesses and civil society is vital to control emissions and tackle the system of global reliance on fossil fuels, paving the way for revolutionary innovations.

We are currently wrangling about how much to devastate the Earth on an industrial scale and through systemic violence (Helm 2013). Meanwhile, many companies and investors interested in the capitalisation of fossil fuels and searching for new resources continue to dominate political life, blocking socioeconomic change and continuing to profit from the rapid, violent and intentional destruction of the planet. They have no moral justification for continuing to produce fuels they know are changing the climate, but markets and morals are not necessarily natural bedfellows. Corporate responsibility cannot limit itself to responsibility toward investors' or shareholders' profits while breaking environmental limits. The violence behind the plundering of resources also reveals a dangerous near future in the form of geopolitical conflict, wars for scarce resources in the name of the profits of some and the mere survival of others (IPCC 2014: 6).

As pointed out by Dieter Helm, a group of seventy companies has called on governments across the globe to step up efforts to tackle climate change and prevent the risks of disruptive climate impacts, appealing for collective responsibility across governments, businesses and civil society. Such appeals sound good in the media, but there is a powerful coalition between energy (petroleum, coal) and defence businesses, which make a profit from energy production and consumption while at the same time fuelling accumulation through new wars (Nitzan and Bichler 2004: 320).[4] Indeed, the petro-military complex is a major contributor to climate change via direct emissions and the promotion of fake solutions, such as carbon trading, and has a strong interest in the militarist imperial policing of territories with fossil fuel resources.

Today's socioeconomic and environmental dislocations, connected with social inequality and unemployment, expanding populations of the displaced and imprisoned, the accelerating destruction of land and water bodies, and so on, cannot be fully understood in the usual terms of poverty. According to Saskia Sassen, they might be understood as a type of expulsion from one's living space, from one's professional livelihood, from economic and social life, and even from the very biosphere that makes life possible. The dynamics of expulsion from diverse systems – economic, social, biospheric – reveal capitalism as a system that produces devastating consequences and elementary brutalities. This system has evolved into a predatory formation (Sassen 2014). The sophisticated knowledge that created today's financial instruments is paralleled by the engineering expertise that facilitates the exploitation of the environment. Sassen stresses that under the new systemic logic, where global corporations dominate the economy, anybody or anything that gets in the way of profit risks being pushed aside or expelled (Sassen 2014: 213).

Future issues of civilisational transformation

Let us try to define and measure certain outcomes towards which capitalism is headed in its dynamics of 'creative destruction'. Following my conclusions above, we should realise that, without alternative civilisational rules and responsible global regulations, which could be both political and moral, the (relatively) long-term future of capitalist self-market regulation through destruction might entail the failure of humankind to respond (in a civilised, that is, non-violent manner) to the threat of global environmental devastation, as well as social destruction and catastrophes – including wars for scarce resources. In the end, sooner or later, we might face a situation where adaptation for the purposes of survival will no longer be possible.

The crucial question emerges: can we save social and environmental preconditions for the continuity of life on this planet without a revolutionary civilisational transformation? This poses a challenge to human communication and action, and calls for the invention and discussion of anticipative strategies for revolutionary civilisational transformation. In this transformation, a key strategic goal would be to overthrow the dominant power-elite way of thinking – reproducing an antiquated and dangerous narrow instrumentalism which has become unsustainable in conditions of the contemporary civilisational crisis constellation. It is important to realise that neoliberalism, as the dominant discourse and power strategy, causes a host of crisis developments destructive to social, economic and environmental conditions. Neoliberalism and its contemporary surviving stereotypes effectively further the objective undermining of both capitalism and civilisation. Self-destructive consequences are crippling in terms of social and environmental life reproduction.

Are there effective institutional and political means for effective revolutionary transformations? To put it another way, are the institutions of contemporary democracy capable of generating the new rules, goals and values that would be required for a contestation of capitalism and a reorientation of civilisation? Further discussion must begin with removing obstacles in the sphere of social consciousness. As an ideology, neoliberalism construed the market as the essence of democracy, presenting it as a universal solution to social problems and as a model for the structuring of all social relations. Schools and mainstream media became 'cultural apparatuses', producing mass passivity, conformity and obedience, and transforming citizens into consumers. A space dominated by corporate powers is created, where the creativity of political and responsible citizenship is redefined as a narrow set of consumer choices, at the expense of critical reflexivity (Giroux 2014: 29). Humans are pushed into survivalism as isolated individuals – obedient consumers and labourers, where the logic of savage market instrumentality is dominant. In a process of depoliticisation, many people relegated to sites of terminal exclusion are forced to negotiate their fates alone, held responsible for a society that forces them to bear the weight of problems that are not of their own making and for which they bear no personal blame. Social and environmental public problems are collapsing into the limited and depoliticised register of private issues.

The contemporary process of changes in global civilisation can be grasped with the concept of civilisational formation (Arnason 2009), formed by a specific configuration of global capitalism, and its deformed method of using scientific, technical and technological resources, its conflictual social relations and its contradictory orientation of cultural values – in particular the cult of profit, consumption and domination – which stand against values of human social development, societal solidarity, democratic participation and cooperation. A further part of the crisis configuration is the progressing environmental crisis.

The civilisational formation of global capitalism inherently combines, as a hybrid, forms of organisation, technologies and ideological priorities of both industrialism and post-industrialism, that is, high technology and the environmental plundering of the planet, while capitalism without labour opportunities is combined with a rise in the exploitation of live human labour, and the celebration of the profit of the selfish actor ignores diminishing human dignity in the context of social exclusion, economic growth is grasped not as the creation of conditions for human development and improvements in the quality of life, but rather as an instrument to accumulate increases in short-term profit and to dispossess the weak.

Distrust in the future, in an atmosphere of 'globalised risk society', has also been manifested in massive switches of investments from the 'real' economy to the realm of 'fictitious capital', of 'casino' financial capitalism and its networks drawing on the technical basis of the information and telematics infrastructure.

On the social level, the transformations accompanying the expansion of capitalist civilisation as a global risk society, associated with the penetration of the profit imperative and the financialisation of value judgments into all areas of societal organisation, also engender institutional crises. The question is whether and under what conditions the resultant critique of institutions can result in their transformation. Ulrich Beck showed that, in particular, the economic sphere of social action, privatising technical decisions and the use of scientific knowledge, places the problem of the externalised consequences for society and the biosphere outside of the political sphere. Economic life cannot replace or define its political and cultural frameworks in the long run without this having destructive repercussions for social life (Beck 1999; 2009a). A central problem of the current system is the power asymmetry of economic, political and cultural institutions. Multiple crises with global consequences are an integral manifestation of the crisis of institutional structures underlying contemporary capitalist industrial civilisation, but are various 'faces' of the same global civilisation crisis.

Obviously, the global civilisation crisis will not be overcome through any kind of smooth institutional adaptation, simply on the basis of insight derived from critical analysis; such insight must feed into the political struggle for the transformation of global civilisation.

Critics now often target the concept of a single universal model of global modernisation. The point at issue here is not just some outdated idea imposing a single type of modernity on everyone. What we have here is a more ambitious theoretical model of the structural anatomy of modern society as a comprehensive system of functionally differentiated spheres of social action. One of the problems with it is that the complex division of labour, grasped by the theory of modernisation as an evolutionary advantage, has become a disadvantage: the excessive division of labour and specialisation has resulted, in relative terms, in the closure and blocking of mutual lines of communication between institutionalised social subsystems. Here, Niklas Luhmann, for example, pointed out the growing problems of the communication of subsystems with autonomous communication codes in a situation in which technology, as a functional simplification, creates increasingly new levels of social complexity (Luhmann 1989). We are trying to address the problems of technology with technology – and where there is control, there is also risk (Luhmann 1992). The fundamental problem – the hypertrophy of power on the side of the economic sphere and the ever greater independence of capital power – cannot be resolved by communication, technology or management solutions.

Charles Perrow's works also shed light on issues related to the organisation of the new situation of risk in a technologically globalised capitalist civilisation. He argues that complex sociotechnical systems strive for managerial control of risk by normalising the hazards inherent in their functioning, while at the same time increasingly endangering not only themselves, but also entire societies, regions and continents (Perrow 1999). In other words, the fact of the matter is that, in structures of social action against a backdrop of expanding globalised complexity and the dynamic variability of contexts, partial solutions to problems cannot be found only after they have arisen (ex-post solutions), and problems associated with the repercussions of the instrumental rationalisation of societal life cannot be addressed by technocratic and bureaucratic resources; rather, the point at issue here is the confrontation thereof with broader sociocultural rationality.

In the politics of civilisational transformation, we cannot continue along a technocratic course of trial and error or the treatment of the disease of one technology with another technology. Rather, we need a discussion on the relationship between resources and objectives, in relation to the risks inherent in the conflictual integration of contemporary societies on a global scale. Another necessary ingredient of transformational politics is the critique of domination in relation to the control and use of knowledge – and as such this constitutes a new axis of conflict involving the structural conditions in place for the democratisation of public participation in key decisions of industrial, energetic, commercial, cultural, and so on, innovation concerning the global contexts of our way of life. So far, this decision-making has been subordinate to the interests and objectives of profit and power, and has been regarded as a private area of social action, despite its public, global repercussions.

Normative challenge: civilisation at the crossroads or the great transformation?

Today, in the context of the global crisis of the capitalist industrial civilisation formation, we can, as I have tried to show, not only link up with the idea of civilisation at the crossroads, coined by Radovan Richta and his associates, but also draw on Karl Polanyi's notion of a great transformation, originally applied to the rise of capitalism as a market society. In our context, the term would serve to anticipate another sea change: a set of revolutionary, root-and-branch systemic changes geared towards the establishment of a socially and environmentally sustainable civilisation.

The capitalist project of globalisation in the name of deregulated markets was, to some degree, an attempt to come to grips with the limits of civilisational industrial expansion, encountered on technical, economic, political and ideological levels. These limits were meant to be overcome by the transnationalisation of economic and, in particular, capital processes. This transnationalisation, crossing state and regional borders, entailed, among other things, a rise in transport and communications, resulting in further growth of the global consumption of resources, energy and capital (and in the exploitation of natural and human resources reduced to capital resources). The subordination of states and societies to the need to speed up the accumulation of profits in financialisation processes engendered the rapid growth of social inequalities, the greater polarisation of wealth and poverty, social exclusion, environmental stress and societal segmentation. The process of market globalisation is also accompanied by the loss of accountability, dangerous for democracy (Beck 2009a). In this respect, 'market logic' and political transformations have changed the institutions of the state, government and democracy (Jayasuriya 2006; Sassen 2008: 421). According to William Tabb (2008), the global crisis currently takes four forms: financialisation and financial crises; the crisis of dwindling hegemony affecting the American empire; a crisis connected with creating new centres of power (such as the BRICS); and, finally, the long-term crisis of resource depletion and sustainability of the planetary ecosystem.

Structural and cultural changes, dictated by global trends of flexible industrialisation and post-industrialisation, have resulted in a paradoxical situation: consumption-driven individualism of lifestyles coexists with a gradual slowdown in economic growth as well as widespread unemployment and underemployment, with marginalisation and social exclusion. Social exclusion, in the concrete sense of pauperisation, exploitation and uncertainty, along with worldwide growth in the number of people 'redundant for the system', stands in contrast to the cultural pledges of global consumerist ideology. Against a backdrop of slowing economic growth, trust in the ideology of globalised modernity, in which economic growth was held up as the prime objective and means, has been undermined. Yet at the same time, 'in the name of crisis', we have witnessed the normalising of stagnation associated with policies aimed at dismantling welfare states and at the privatised pilfering of the state and public services. Particularistic class interests are thus promoted over 'collective consumption', intended for the benefit of universal needs and the objectives of socioeconomic reproduction. This is happening in a situation of growing depletion of the planet's natural resources and global climate change, with adverse consequences for the employment of both capital and labour. The crisis linked to the logic of consumerist values reflects the contradictions of contemporary capitalism on social, political and environmental levels.

The moral and social impacts are no less serious. We are witnessing the erosion of social solidarity, diminishing social cohesion, indifference towards public targets, voter passivity and the marginalisation, decline and involuntary exclusion of relatively large swathes of the population. At the same time, political pressures generated by extremism, fundamentalism, and ethnic and terrorist violence are increasing, and this translates into associated intensifying risks of the political destabilisation of the democratic public, the reinforcement of the state's centralised policing power, authoritarian government, censorship, electronic surveillance, top-down patriotism, militarisation (and larger-scale armament) and unilateralism in external policy. States confront new problems resulting from a multicultural situation, breeding racism and xenophobia, without being able to address, on the basis of solidarity and collaboration, the causes, for example, of global migration from poorer to richer parts of the world. States and citizens alike face the impact of flows of information, money, goods and the labour force in the arena of the global interdependence of societies. It often seems that, against a background of capitalist globalisation, processes are at work which the citizens of a nation state cannot influence or control, and which, in many cases, they do not even understand. New differentiations in the social sphere, new forms of stratification and segmentation present citizens and civil societies with new gaps, very hard to legitimise, between globally successful 'winners' and globally unsuccessful 'losers'; national governments and democratic politics are confronted with the ongoing fragmentation and disintegration of domestic national societies and with the intensifying crisis of the legitimacy of government in political, politico-economic and cultural respects.

Social inequalities and environmental stresses compound and engender new risks and conflicts. They cannot be explained simply by the growing complexity of social changes, without considering political factors in the actions of the dominant power-wielding social forces. The hybrid neoliberal model of crisis management politics redefined and challenged growth limits. The aim of deregulation was to enable capital to scale back public spending on social development in a bid to cut costs, entailing the dismantling of the welfare state and the squeezing of people out of paid work, while striving to maintain profit growth. Here, growth limits, viewed as a lack of material resources (raw materials, energy, food and capital), are invoked to justify measures to increase profits and returns. The aim is to preserve the growth of capital gains (and especially short-term rises therein) by reinforcing the social imbalance between capital and labour, in the name of the growth imperative. Conversely, any attempt to tackle this currently deep-seated structural crisis in a different way would soon confront the further question of revolutionary alternatives.

Let us attempt, in the spirit of positive utopia, to outline certain aspects of a political response.

In particular, we need to

1. strategically intensify the struggle for global justice and to initiate a qualitative turn in the development of civilisation towards greater social and environmental sustainability;
2. engage capital in the cooperative – not starkly competitive – creation of resources for the socioeconomic reproduction of human society

and for much broader human civilisational development towards improved socioenvironmental living conditions. In this respect, it is essential to prevent the escape of capital from its point of generation by localising it

3. in the field of policy, contribute to the redefinition of the state, public authority and local government with a view to reinforcing political and politico-economic and environmental responsibility towards the public, and with a view to the participative development of the public sphere of care for the development of human potential and the environment. Civil policy bodies must join forces and exert pressure on public institutions to guarantee the fair distribution of opportunities and provide assistance in risk management, to eliminate negative social and environmental impacts while respecting limits to the growth of reckless and irresponsible profit, and to halt the dangerous deformation of the momentum driving forward civilisational transformations. An important prerequisite for cooperative policy in this respect is the attainment of the state's fiscal autonomy.

At the moment, democratic criticism and politics are confronted with the widespread use of political alibis which essentially blame all political failures in the local and global arena on impersonal, spontaneous, anonymous or global forces, or on the inability of individuals or governments to adapt flexibly to market momentum. The ideologically employed concept of competitiveness or alibistic myths, presenting capitalist 'globalisation' as some kind of external, superior and unopposable force, are intended to conceal the dangerous political and social irresponsibility of institutions, privileged groups and actors wielding decision-making powers. The conflict between the global scale of today's civilisational crisis and the restricted competitive regime, driven by the socially blind imperative of profit maximisation, is intensifying; the crisis of capitalism is structural, aimed at the deprivation of the majority for the greater gain of the minority (Foster 2007: 63). All of this also deepens the crisis of the legitimacy of institutional structures and dominant power interests (Wallerstein 2013).

The individual level of the development of human potential for reflexivity is also important for large-scale civilisational transformation; this can be defined as the ability to perceive one's own social action in broader contexts and against a global background, or as the capacity for the more responsible social action of self-assured actors when confronted with the social and environmental cost of their actions. Various contexts of relative individual autonomy in the face of collective pressure from social groups, classes, families, nations and states come into play here. The quality of the public sphere and public communications, as well as the local and global media used for the communication of information, or alternative forms thereof, also have a significant impact on the reflexivity of individual actors and their participation in the formation of civil society. Media, in the form of global conglomerates, tend to be businesses pursuing commercial interests, whereas the actions of civil associations or movements are generally campaign-based, one-off and temporary. Another problem is democratic representation and the legitimacy of various non-governmental organisations active in the field of global civil society. Reflexive civil action and global engagement are connected, according to Cohen and Kennedy, with a widening of identities under the influence of growing global cohesion and interdependence (Cohen and Kennedy 2000).

The struggle over the nature of civilisational transformation is taking place in a contested global arena. Replacing conflicts with cooperation requires social actors to be willing and able to move beyond their partial and selfish interests, replacing them with the pursuit of common interests. The need for intercultural dialogue and the cultivation of an understanding of others is rapidly increasing. Democratic dissent from below, critical dialogue, conflicts of opinion, cooperation and confrontation between institutionalised and individual, formal and informal actors will result in many risks and tensions, but also in new opportunities for creative innovation, in the transformation of the existing civilisational formation and in the shaping of a socially shared world.

Notes

1. An example of efforts to adapt to risks by means of monetary compensation is insurance, which also entails the naturalisation of risk as a random process purportedly beyond human control. In the contemporary world, such reliance on insurance policies can essentially be regarded as fatalism, i.e. resignation to risks and immorality, in the sense of the abdication of both personal and collective responsibility.
2. The crisis system of financialisation can also be described as 'the mutation of capitalism into a hybrid phase of the monopoly stage of capitalism' (Foster 2007: 1).
3. A total of 74.5 million young people aged between fifteen and twenty-five were unemployed in 2013 and the rate is expected to edge up to 13.2 per cent in 2014 (ibid.: 21).

4. World military expenditure in 2012 was $1.756 billion, representing 2.5 per cent of global gross domestic product (SIPRI 2013)

References

Appelbaum, R. and W. Robinson (eds) (2005) *Critical Globalization Studies*. New York: Routledge.

Arnason, J. P. (2009) *Civilizační analýza*. Translated by various translators. Praha: Filosofia.

Bardi, U. and J. Randers (2014) *Extracted: How the Quest for Mineral Wealth is Plundering the Planet*. White River Junction, VT: Chelsea Green Publishing.

Beck, U. (1999) *World Risk Society*. Cambridge: Polity Press.

Beck, U. (2009a) *World at Risk*. Cambridge: Polity Press.

Beck, U. (2009b) 'Critical theory of the world risk society', *Constellations* 16(1), 10–22.

Camilleri, J. A. (1976) *Civilization in Crisis. Human Prospects in a Changing World*. Cambridge and New York: Cambridge University Press.

Chossudovski, M. (2010) *The Global Economic Crisis, The Great Depression of the 21st Century*. Montreal: Global Research Publishers.

Cohen, R. and P. Kennedy (2000) *Global Sociology*. London: Macmillan.

Foster, J. B. (2007) 'The financialisation of capitalism', *Monthly Review* 58(11), 1–14.

Fumagalli, A. (2011) 'Twenty theses on contemporary capitalism (cognitive biocapitalism)', *Journal of the Theoretical Humanities* 16(3), 7–17.

Fumagalli, A. and S. Lucarelli (2010) *Cognitive Capitalism as a Financial Economy of Production*. Pavia: Quaderni di Universita Pavia.

Giroux, H. (2014) *Violence of Organised Forgetting*. New York: City Lights Publishers.

Held, D. (1995) 'Democracy and international order', in D. Archibugi and D. Held (eds) *Cosmopolitan Democracy. An Agenda for a New World Order*. Cambridge: Polity Press, pp. 96–120.

Helm, D. (2013) *The Carbon Crunch*. New Haven, CT: Yale University Press.

ILO (2013) *ILO Global Employment Trends 2013*. Geneva: International Labour Office.

ILO (2014) *ILO Global Employment Trends 2014. The Risk of a Jobless Recovery*. Geneva: International Labour Office.

IPCC (2013) 'Summary for policymakers', in T. F. Stocker, D. Qin, G.-K. Plattner, M. Tignor, S. K. Allen, J. Boschung, A. Nauels, Y. Xia, V. Bex and P. M. Midgley (eds) *Climate Change 2013: The Physical Science Basis. Contribution of Working Group I to the Fifth Assessment Report of the Intergovernmental Panel on Climate Change*. Cambridge and New York: Cambridge University Press.

IPCC (2014) *Climate Change 2014. Impacts, Adaptation, and Vulnerability. Summary for Policymakers*. Cambridge and New York: Cambridge University Press.

Jayasuriya, K. (2006) *Statecraft, Welfare, and the Politics of Inclusion*. New York: Palgrave.

Kiersley, N. (2011) 'Everyday neoliberalism and the subjectivity of crisis: post-political control in an era of financial turmoil', *Journal of Critical Globalisation Studies* 4, 36.

Luhmann, N. (1898) *Ecological Communication*. Berlin and New York: de Gruyter.

Luhmann, N. (1992) *Risk. Sociological Theory*. Berlin and New York: de Gruyter, pp. 89–90.

Meadows, D. L., J. Randers and W. W. Behrens (1972) *The Limits to Growth*. New York: Universe Books.

Nitzan, J. and S. Bichler (2004) 'Dominant capital and the new wars', *Journal of World-Systems Research* X(2), 255–327.

North, D. (2011) *The Capitalist Crisis and the Return of History*. Oak Parks, MI: Mehring Books.

Perrow, C. (1999) *Normal Accidents. Living with High-Risk Technologies*. Princeton, NJ: Princeton University Press.

Piketty, T. (2014) *Capital in the Twenty-First Century*. Cambridge, MA: Harvard University Press.

Richta, R. (1969) *Civilizace na rozcestí. Společenské důsledky vědeckotechnické revoluce*. Praha: Academia. English trans. M. Šlingová (1969) *Civilisation on the Crossroads. Social and Human Implications of the Scientific and Technological Revolution*. Praha: Svoboda.

Robinson, W. (2011) 'Global capital leviathan', *Radical Philosophy* 165, 1–5.

Roggero, G. (2010) 'Five theses on the common', *Rethinking Marxism: A Journal of Economics, Culture and Society* 22(3), 357–73.

Sassen, S. (2008) *Territory, Authority, Rights: From Medieval to Global Assemblages*. Princeton, NJ: Princeton University Press.

Sassen, S. (2014) *Expulsions: Brutality and Complexity in the Global Economy*. Cambridge, MA: Harvard University Press.

Tabb, W. K. (2008) 'Four crises in the contemporary world capitalist system', *Monthly Review* 60(5), 43–59.

Wallerstein, I. (2013) 'Global turmoil in the middle run', *Commentary* 344, available at www.binghamton.edu/fbc/commentaries/archive-2013/344en.htm

6

Environmental Crisis and Political Revolutions

Richard Šťahel

THE CONFLICTS AND revolutions in North Africa and the Middle East during the last few years have multiple causes; among the main but not always most visible ones, we can surely list excessive use of resources,[1] environmental limits to population growth and consumption, and the resultant long-term inability of these countries to supply their inhabitants with food and drinking water from domestic reserves. Egypt, the world's top wheat importer, is an obvious case in point.

According to Terazono and Saleh (2013: 2), the Egyptian government had to back down in 1977 when riots broke out following a rise in the prices of staple foodstuffs, and since then food subsidies have been a sensitive issue. When the food crisis of 2007–8 made wheat more expensive than ever, many families had to rely on subsidised bread, and army bakeries helped to maintain supply.

The situation worsened in 2010 when, due to the drought and extensive burning of cornfields,[2] Russia banned the export of wheat in order to reserve its supply for its own inhabitants. Wheat prices – and consequently the price of staple food items – increased to such an extent that riots broke out not only in Egypt (Palazzo 2014) but also in other North African countries reliant on its import. These riots destabilised the whole region and in many areas grew into a real Hobbesian war of all against all. The subsequent regime change in Egypt has not improved the situation. The liberalisation of the political system worked in favour of fundamentalists whose leader became the first democratically elected president of Egypt. However, this provoked resistance from the secular opposition supported by the army and so in 2013 the military regime in the country was restored. We might talk, then, of one revolution in 2011 and another in 2013,[3] although the latter could be considered as a counter-revolution (Beránek 2013). The production and sale of oil, which has been the source of foreign currency for the purchase of wheat, is decreasing; therefore, the riots continue. Since 2010, Egypt has spent most of its foreign reserves on importing wheat, which it has not been able to grow because of the lack of suitable farmland and water for irrigation. Because food security and social stability are closely connected, this type of situation, a consequence of overpopulation and overexploitation, in combination with global climate change and the degradation of the environment, may be the future model for revolutions.[4] It is also possible that the lack of food security may be the first step to the collapse of local and regional political and social systems.

The economic crisis of 2007–8 began in Europe and the USA simultaneously. In the Western world, food prices did not increase so sharply as they did in Egypt, and the state social system, including the production and distribution of food, worked much better than it did in North African countries. This may be one of the reasons why the crisis in industrial countries instigated only protests and not revolutionary movements. It is not likely that an environmental and food crisis could initiate political revolution in developed industrial countries.

For this reason, social scientists tend to devote more attention to the economic, social and political aspects of the crisis than to the material, food and environmental ones. However, looking at the bigger picture, it is apparent that the current crisis is not only an economic crisis, nor is it – in view of its connection with the subsequent social and political crises – only a crisis of capitalism. As we face a deepening environmental crisis, we must see it as a crisis of industrial civilisation. The basic imperatives of this civilisation tend to make political and economic elites attempt to overcome such a crisis by further intensive growth in production and consumption.

As a result of population growth, the total consumption of products, services and energy is increasing despite more effective and more environmental technologies and the decrease in economic activity due to the economic crisis. This is in addition to the concentration of greenhouse gases in the atmosphere[5] and the chemical condition of the oceans, the speed of extinction of animal species and plants, deforestation, reduction of arable land and the decrease in fresh water supplies (McLellan 2014). The growth of production and consumption, as well as that of population, always leads to the increased exploitation of natural resources and pollution.[6]

The growth imperative, which is an immanent part of the majority of the systems and institutions of industrial civilisation, can be considered the common denominator of these crisis phenomena. The globalisation process allowed the application of the growth imperative in areas and sectors that were, thirty or forty years ago, arranged on the basis of different imperatives (see Sťahel 2013a). It also eliminated or weakened the influence of the traditional cultural and political tools regulating not only growth but its side-effects too. This perspective enables one to consider the current crisis as a systemic crisis of the industrial civilisation, and to understand the economic, social, political, demographic, food and environmental crises as individual manifestations or aspects of this systemic crisis (see Sťahel 2013b). The question remains whether this crisis can be overcome without political revolutions and armed conflicts.

Habermas's crisis theory

All these phenomena can be interpreted in light of the coherent crisis theory which Jürgen Habermas proposed in the early 1970s in his *Legitimation Crisis* (Habermas 2005).[7] This theory also offers a basis for reflection on the current crisis. As Raymond Plant reminds us, '*Legitimation Crisis* is a research programme, not a final report' (Plant 1982: 346). Several crisis tendencies of capitalism considered by Habermas in the 1970s can, as a consequence of globalisation, be identified today on the level of global industrial civilisation; and this global industrial civilisation[8] is to a great degree determined by capitalist organisational principles.[9] Habermas's approach may therefore be used to analyse the current civilisational crisis.

According to Habermas, 'only when members of a society experience structural alterations as critical for continued existence and feel their social identity threatened can we speak of crises' (Habermas 2005: 3). He based this on the claim that 'social systems have identities and can lose them; historians are capable of differentiating between revolutionary changes of a state or the downfall of an empire, and mere structural alterations' (ibid.: 3). It is an open question, then, whether global industrial civilisation can be perceived as such a social system. Since the scientific and public media discourses work with the term 'civilisational crisis', applying it also to the current global crisis, and many economic, demographic and environmental phenomena are considered in a global context, the answer is tentatively positive.

In general, according to Habermas, 'crisis occurrences owe their objectivity to the fact that they issue from unresolved steering problems' (ibid.: 4). However, Habermas 'distinguishes four social formations: primitive [*vorhochkulturelle*], traditional, capitalist, post-capitalist' (ibid.: 17).[10] Each of them faces different problems of governance, and the failure to manage them, or solve them, can lead to crisis; responses to this crisis can give rise to transformations or to revolutions. According to the internal organisational principle and the scope of the social and system integration of these types of social formation, Habermas distinguishes the types of crises that can occur.

Primitive social formations are organised on the basis of age and gender principles which are institutionalised in a kinship system. The usual sources of social crises are contradictory imperatives in the socio-economic system, but 'no contradictory imperatives follow from this principle of organization' (ibid.: 18). Therefore, such societies, according to Habermas, are mainly affected by external identity crises where 'the usual source of change is demographic growth in connection with ecological factors – above all, interethnic dependency as a result of economic exchange, war, and conquest' (ibid.: 18). He goes on to state that only primitive or archaic social formations face crises caused by external factors; all others face crises that begin internally.

Traditional social formations are created at the civilisational level of development. Their basic 'principle of organization is class domination in the political form' (ibid.: 18). These societies are divided according to class and social status and need to pay attention to justifying and legitimising these divisions because they give rise to internal contradictions. Traditional societies are then threatened by internal identity crises, as Habermas states: 'In traditional societies the type of the crisis that arises proceeds from internal contradictions' (ibid.: 20). Production relations are at the same time political relations; owners of the means of production, primarily the land, are the owners of political power. In other words the political and economic powers are one and the same. According to Habermas, 'in traditional societies, crises appear when, and only when, steering problems cannot be resolved within the possibility space circumscribed by the principle of organization and therefore produce dangers to system integration that threaten the identity of the society' (ibid.: 25).

Liberal-capitalist societies are organised around relations of capital and wage labour. Production relations are differentiated from political relations, from which in turn 'civil society' is also differentiated. The economic system is thus free from the limitations of the socially integrative subsystems, and this allows the state to intensify the dynamics of growth, which means that crises manifest predominantly as economic crises. However, in the end, these crises affect the whole social system. Liberal capitalism is thus affected by systemic crises. 'In liberal-capitalist societies . . . crises become endemic because temporarily unresolved steering problems, which the process of economic growth produces at more or less regular intervals, *as such* endanger social integration' (ibid.: 25). A crisis is then a recurrent phenomenon, a cyclic phenomenon, and in its occurrence certain general signs can be identified. It is not an accidental, one-time occurrence, but is an unwanted consequence of previous growth. 'No previous social formation lived so much in fear and expectation of sudden system change, even though the idea of a temporally condensed transformation – that is, of a revolutionary leap – is oddly in contrast to the form of motion of system crisis as a permanent crisis' (ibid.: 25). The threat of a return of the crisis has become a permanent part of the social and political system, together with revolutionary and counter-revolutionary movements and their conflicts. 'Economic growth takes place through periodically recurring crises because the class structure, transplanted into the economic steering system, has transformed *the contradiction of class interests into a contradiction of system imperatives*' (ibid.: 26). We can therefore talk about a crisis cycle – or cyclic crises – which affects more than the economic subsystem of the society. Moreover, according to Habermas, the economic crisis in liberal-capitalist systems is specific and historically unique in that it is a consequence of contradictions of system imperatives which cannot be structurally solved because their source is the structure of the society which is organised on the basis of a certain rationality. Systems crises then 'have the appearance of natural catastrophes that break forth from the center of a system of purposive rational action' (ibid.: 30). In other words, a crisis arises because the society and its subjects perform strictly 'rationally', that is, under the system imperatives, but these imperatives are contradictory. Finally, Habermas asks whether in organised capitalism the logic of the crisis has preserved or has been changed, that is, if capitalism has 'been fully transformed into a post-capitalist social formation that has overcome the crisis-ridden form of economic growth' (ibid.: 31). Developments in the last decade or more has answered this question – economic growth has been constantly interrupted by acute crises, appearing because economic subjects are trying to achieve the highest possible economic growth in accordance with the basic system imperative.

Organised, or advanced, capitalist social formation (state-regulated capitalism) appeared after World War II as a reaction to the failure of liberal capitalism in the crisis of the 1930s which led to a world conflict. According to Habermas, 'the state intervene[d] in the market as functional gaps developed' (ibid.: 33), in order to at least ease the conflict potential of a system imperative intensified by acute crises. The economic and social politics of Western European countries in the first three decades after World War II can be regarded as a reaction to the phenomenon of economic crisis:

> The structures of advanced capitalism can be understood as reaction formations to endemic crisis. To ward off system crisis, advanced capitalist societies focus all forces of social integration at the point of structurally most probable conflict – in order all the more effectively to keep it latent. (ibid.: 37–8)

Habermas at the same time points out that state intervention in the economic sphere, which, in liberal capitalism, is differentiated from politics, brings new types of problems into organised capitalism. 'Re-coupling the economic system to the political – which in a way repoliticises the relations of production – creates an increased need for legitimation' (ibid.: 36). An effort of the political sphere to ease the conflict potential of cyclic crises, arising as a consequence of unregulated economic growth, leads not only to an increase of the influence of the political system on the economic one, but also to a transfer of steering problems from the economic to the political sphere.

'In the decades since World War II the most advanced capitalist countries have succeeded (the May 1968 events in Paris notwithstanding) in keeping class conflict latent in its decisive areas; in extending the business cycle and transforming periodic phases of capital devaluation into a permanent inflationary crisis with milder business fluctuations' (ibid.: 38). The state has taken the role of a participant and a regulator of the market. It has simultaneously taken a role as a compensator of its negative social, cultural and, later, ecological consequences so as to prevent an outbreak of acute crises. The price we pay is a systematic overload of public budgets in the form of long-term deficits.

Moreover, in the 1970s, Western countries were hit by a number of acute crises, caused by a disruption to the oil supply, which might be termed externally produced crises. Western European countries thus faced a different type of crisis from one their institutions were prepared for. However, Habermas points out:

If governmental crisis management fails, it lags behind program-
matic demands *that it has placed on itself.* The penalty for this failure
is withdrawal of legitimation. Thus, the scope for action contracts
precisely at those moments in which it needs to drastically expand.
(ibid.: 69)

At the same time, it seems that there is no clear difference between
crises whose primary causes are external and those whose causes are
internal. The trustworthiness of the institution of the state as a protec-
tor against crises, as well as the legitimacy of the political elites, has
suffered considerably. As Habermas states, one of the features and conditions of the postwar class compromise was that 'civic privatism – that
is, political abstinence combined with an orientation to career, leisure,
and consumption – promotes the expectation of suitable rewards
within the system (money, leisure time, and security)' (ibid.: 37). By
the end of the 1970s it became clear that the state was, as in the pre-war
period, again unable to provide career and employment opportunities to all and it was certainly not able to provide a steady growth of
consumption. All this happened despite the steady increase in the tax
burden and the broadening areas over which the state was trying to
gain bureaucratic or legislative control. As Raymond Plant reminds us:

[C]apitalism has built up expectations about consumption, and
these have increased pressures on governments to steer the economy
to produce more goods. The non-provision of goods to meet expectations becomes a dysfunctional feature of the market which it has
become a task of government to correct. (Plant 1982: 343)

However, as development in the last decade has clearly shown, governments must also intervene when production is growing faster than
possibilities for the consumption of this production. The support of
consumerism, regardless of its social, cultural and environmental consequences, is a problem for producers as well as governments.

The present typology of crises is based on the neo-Marxist theoretical framework from which Habermas diverged in his later work. But
his study of the 2008 crisis is, in terms and methods, closer to his 1970s
position, when he comments on the tension between capitalism and
democracy in a globalised world, referring to issues such as imperatives
of banks, markets and economy or distribution, regulation and political legitimacy (Habermas 2012).

The return of the acute crisis phenomenon

The process of economic globalisation can be understood as a result of an effort to support further growth of production and consumption, previously limited by resources and capacities of national markets. The result of globalisation in the preceding three decades has been, in the industrially developed countries, expressed in the form of liberalisation and privatisation, not only of productive capacities, but also of infrastructure and public services, including health and welfare systems, education, science and culture. Therefore, we can talk about the dismantling, twilight or progressive reduction of the social state. A considerable number of regulation mechanisms, which were meant to prevent the development of acute crises or to reduce their possible consequences, were eliminated. With regard to the social formation of current industrial civilisation, classical liberal capitalism, as described by Habermas, has in some ways prevailed over the so-called late, or regulated, capitalism of the 1970s. The liberalisation and deregulation (or desocialisation, as Ricoeur (1986) calls it) of the economic-political system in the 1990s, saw the return of acute economic crises. This corresponds to Habermas's characterisation of a crisis affecting liberal capitalism where '[t]he economic crisis results from contradictory system imperatives and threatens social integration. It is, *at the same time*, a social crisis, in which the interests of groups collide and place in question the social integration of the society' (Habermas 2005: 29–30). These words also characterise the crisis of 2008. In the euphoria of 1989, Habermas warned in his essay on the Eastern European revolutions that the fall of the Berlin wall had not solved any of the system problems which had specifically arisen:

> The indifference of a market economy to its external costs, which it off-loads onto the social and natural environment, is sowing the path of a crisis-prone economic growth with the familiar disparities and marginalisations on the inside; with economic backwardness, if not regression, and consequently with barbaric living conditions, cultural expropriation and catastrophic famines in the Third World; not to mention the worldwide risk caused by disrupting the balance of nature. (Habermas 1990: 17)

All these problems are still unsolved and are even more complex in today's global civilisation. Two decades later, reflecting on the 2008 crisis, Habermas pointed out its historical uniqueness when he wrote:

'In autumn 2008, for the first time in the history of capitalism, the backbone of the financial market-driven global economic system could be rescued from the brink of collapse only by the guarantees of the taxpayers' (Habermas 2012: 125). The contradiction in the system imperatives has not disappeared; instead, it has deepened. According to Habermas, it has become obvious that 'capitalism is no longer able to reproduce itself under its own steam' (ibid.: 125), so we can talk not only about a 'system crisis' but also about 'system failure'. We can even suggest that the current steering structures cannot manage the consequent problems of growth, identified in the 1970s by Habermas as the crisis tendencies of the late capitalist system, although they make every effort and use all available means.

The lack of resources for growth became evident before 2008. As Peter Staněk states, growth in production, consumption and profit was, to a great extent, possible only through growth in the indebtedness of individuals, businesses and countries. This indebtedness is one of the main reasons for the current economic crisis (Staněk 2012: 36). Indebtedness, as one of the by-products of the process of the polarisation of income, has been accelerating since the 1970s. The income of most of the population stagnates or even decreases; income of the richest multiplies. Aside from the growth in social tension, this has led to a global decrease in consumption, which could be saturated for a short period of time only by credit expansion (ibid.: 61–2). Despite this, many attempts to overcome the current crisis focus on stimulation of consumption.

The environmental aspect of the crisis

Artificially stimulated consumption also means an acceleration in the exploitation of natural resources and the pollution of the environment, which intensifies the environmental aspect of the crisis. In the 1990s, this connection was pointed out by Ladislav Hohoš when he observed that 'ecologic and economic systems are closely connected and therefore we are confronted with different aspects of one and the same crisis; after all, the degradation of the environment directly endangers economic systems' (Hohoš 1993: 120). Today, even economists admit that the economic damage caused by climate changes and extreme weather, along with the expenses necessitated by the need to adapt the infrastructure to these changes, will intensify the economic, social and political aspects of the crisis (Staněk 2012: 64–5).

As Habermas states, the crisis threatens the identity of social formations. A failure to control a crisis can then lead to a transformational,
or revolutionary, change in the political-economic system. This conclusion can be accepted provided that reflection focuses mainly on the
economic, social and political aspects of the current crisis, that is, on
those aspects whose causes are considered internal. In the words of Ivan
Dubnička: 'History has often confirmed that revolutions and destabilisation of an established system happen in the moment when the extent
of unequally redistributed property (accumulated surplus production)
becomes unacceptable to the majority of the society' (Dubnička 2007:
418). The political-economic system can collapse in the dramatic form
of revolution, in an international or even global conflict or in internal
conflict; however, the form and extent of the current threats show that,
for the crisis of global industrial civilisation, reflection on only the
economic, social and political level is insufficient. It does not take into
consideration the existential threat for the civilisation as a whole. This
threat will be seen in its full extent when reflection on global industrial
civilisation covers material, food and environmental aspects, that is,
aspects whose causes can be classed as mainly external. Habermas
regards these as relevant mainly for archaic societies; at the same time,
however, he identifies them as possible consequent problems of growth
(Habermas 2005: 41–3).[11]

Environmental and demographic threats produce those types of
crisis which, Habermas says, were faced mainly by archaic or traditional
social formations, meaning agrarian or rural societies. Capitalist societies are industrial and urban. In the preceding century, environmental
problems were marginalised or partly resolved by technological development, or by the export of environmentally demanding productions
to distant areas, or by the export of waste to these areas. Demographic
and social problems arising from environmental problems were solved
by mass displacement. The lack of soil and food was solved by territorial (mainly colonial) expansion[12] and by business, which, owing to the
development of transportation and storage technologies, allowed the
import of food and other resources from the other side of the world.[13]
However, this process only put off – in time and space – the realisation
that environmental and demographical crisis tendencies also threaten
the societies of the industrial civilisation and that they have the same
conflict potential as other types of threat.

All aspects of the current crisis (economic, social, political, material,
food, demographic and environmental) have a conflict potential that

has been manifested many times in the past. Due to the growth of population, we can assert that their conflict potential has grown. 'If future populations respond similarly to past populations, then anthropogenic climate change has the potential to substantially increase conflicts around the world, relative to a world without climate change' (Hsiang et al. 2013). The climate changes caused by industrial civilisation will very probably be faster and more extensive than those in the past. The environmental crisis, caused by climate variations or some other cause, will primarily be expressed as a food or humanitarian crisis[14] and can turn into a social or political crisis quite quickly.

Potential solutions for the global crisis must entail internal system changes, for example in a form suggested by James Lovelock according to which we may have to accept certain limits, a system of rationing[15] and compulsory military service, as in periods of war, and, moreover, give up our freedom for a certain time (Lovelock 2006). These changes could resemble Hobbes's limitations of freedom in the name of security or survival. If these were merely short-term limitations, there would be such a significant change of political, economic and legal sub-systems that the identity of the social formation might be under threat. Albert Palazzo states that 'climate change is a further amplification of the coming Revolution of Limits' (Palazzo 2014) at which point the period of growth ends. The signs of 'the age of resource limits' are already appearing and they will bring not only new types of conflict over the diminishing resources, but also another military revolution. Today's military and civil infrastructures and technologies are based mainly on finite resources. The pressure of population growth, along with the growth of consumption expectations, will exacerbate existing contradictions and conflicts in societies and between societies: '[p]reparing for a most hostile world in which war is more common is also a necessity' (ibid.). According to Palazzo, the question is not whether or not the coming Revolution of Limits and climate change will influence economic-political systems, but how these systems will be able to deal with them on the theoretical and practical levels.

Environmental crisis, therefore, can be regarded as a consequence of conflicting system imperatives threatening the system integration. The interests of executive groups collide, and this can result not only in the disintegration of the society, but also in the endangerment of a society's ability to reproduce. This applies not only to the reproduction of the economic-political and cultural systems, but also to the biological reproduction of a society, because the environmental crisis also threatens the ecological conditions of the civilisation's existence. The revolution of limits and climate change require the transformation of the basic imperatives of the economic-political system. The extent of this transformation will be quite revolutionary. Habermas's concept of crisis can thus be applied to the environmental crisis as a display of antagonism between the imperatives of growth and the imperative of sustainability.

The imperative of growth vs the imperative of sustainability

In connection with the imperative of growth in capitalist social formations, Habermas in the 1970s stated that '[e]cological balance designates an absolute limit to growth' (Habermas 2005: 41). Many analyses of the current crisis suggest that the growth of population, production and productivity is moving closer to this absolute limit. As Habermas points out:

> with capital accumulation, economic growth is institutionalised in an unplanned, nature like way, so that no option for self-conscious control of this process exists. Growth imperatives originally followed by capitalism have meanwhile achieved global validity through system competition and worldwide diffusion ... The established mechanisms of growth are forcing an increase in both population and production on a worldwide scale. (ibid.: 41)

These established mechanisms of growth are so characteristic of the capitalist social formation that: '[c]apitalist societies cannot follow imperatives of growth limitation without abandoning their principle of organization' (ibid.: 42). However, if they do not limit growth, the lack of resources will threaten not only their identity but also their forms of social integration and their forms of organised mass loyalty. It will also threaten their basic external requirements of system reproduction and perhaps even life in any human society or the reproduction of the human species. This is the key contradiction and the main reason for the current civilisation crisis.

Habermas suggests that the basic system imperative of capitalism to produce surplus differentiates this social formation from the traditional one, and especially from archaic societies, which are systems in which there is 'no systematic motive for producing more goods than are necessary to satisfy basic needs, even though the state of the productive forces may permit a surplus' (ibid.: 18). We can object that the cause of not producing the surplus is due more to the low productivity of work or to the limited availability of technologies and the few possibilities of storing and conserving the surplus than to an instititional or ideological motive. Ivan Dubnička's hypothesis makes convincing arguments: the production of surplus is the primary evolutionary strategy of homo sapiens and 'does not depend on time and space on the level of cultural development nor its consumption' (Dubnička 2009: 86). This is documented in many cultural rituals for destroying surplus possessions, such as the Native American ritual of potlatch. At the same time, 'the production of surplus, its accumulation and consumption are the main causal phenomena of the global environmental crisis' (Dubnička 2007: 20). The global environmental crisis is, then, a consequence of this human strategy, the application of which, at present, reaches the limits of natural resources and the ability of nature to absorb the pollution created by the production and consumption of surplus. This would support the thesis that environmental crises threaten all kinds of social formations, primarily as a result of population growth, which, in itself, leads to the necessity of a growth in production, and thus to the exploitation of natural resources as well as the pollution of the environment.

The growth of the human population is a key factor which every type of social formation must deal with. Apart from a few short and rare periods in history, Thomas Malthus's perception holds true – a population grows more quickly than its ability to secure enough food (Malthus 1798). For thousands of years the human solution to the pressure of population excess was territorial expansion, that is, colonising uninhabited areas. Populating the world, except for remote islands, was completed in prehistoric times. In most of the newly populated areas, either people were able to produce more food than necessary for the basic reproduction of the human population or they produced other commodities that could be exchanged for food. This helped them survive in times of poor harvest. However, in a good year, it led to population growth, which in turn led to the populating of new areas. Even in ancient times it was the case that territorial expansion was only possible at the expense of other human communities. Indigenous people were driven out or eliminated by more successful societies. For most of history, the ability to keep a high reproduction potential was key to the survival of a society. Societies that were not successful in this almost always became extinct because they were not able to protect themselves. Population growth, then, has been proven to be existential inevitability. On the other hand, this growth itself has created the necessity for territorial expansion as a way of gaining the space needed for life and for the production of food for the growing population.

The imperative of population growth is therefore eventually a prerequisite for reproduction (in competition with other societies – clans and tribes, and states) as well as one for societal sustainability. This makes it a system imperative in archaic and traditional societies. Therefore, in preindustrial societies, the growth of production, especially of agricultural production that often entailed territorial expansion, had already become an imperative. In the long term, territorial expansion was possible only when there was a relatively small world population. By the end of the nineteenth century, territorial expansion was becoming a more difficult way of dealing with population growth and the connected rise in resource needs. The efforts to apply it led to local[16] and global conflicts.

Another possibility of solving the problem of overpopulation consists in innovations of agrotechnologies (creativity, development of productive forces or an ability to learn – Habermas 1975: 297) which, in the twentieth century, led to the intensification and industrialisation of agricultural production. At present, this is the only possibility of increasing food production because there are no unused arable lands, pastures or fisheries. On the contrary, arable land is diminishing because of the expansion of transport, residential and energy infrastructures. Erosion, desert expansion and the rise of sea levels also contribute to this reduction. The expansion of arable land by deforestation disrupts the water circulation of the global ecosystem, which affects its ability to regulate the planet's climate. Intensification and industrialisation of agricultural production has such a devastating impact on the environment that the ability of the civilisation to produce food may at some point be considerably limited or even made impossible, due to climatic changes and the change in the chemistry of the atmosphere and oceans (Lovelock 2010). It will still be possible to increase global food production, but it will be at the expense of biodiversity and the quality of the environment which enables this production, and so in turn at the expense of the possibility to produce food in the future.

Besides the growth of population and production, the basic imperative of each social formation is to secure its own reproduction, including the reproduction of the economic-political system. All living things, not only in the biological sense, but also in the cultural, political and social senses, try to retain their way of life, or at least survive.

This tendency to struggle and fight for survival can be identified in all kinds of social formations and at all levels or stages of development. In fact, the origin of institutions such as clans, tribes or states can be interpreted as a direct consequence of this tendency and as the main reason for legitimising their further existence. This phenomenon might be described as the imperative of sustainability.[17] Even growth can be perceived as a strategy to fulfil this basic imperative. Survival in the biological, cultural and sociopolitical senses is a consequence of the self-preservation instinct. It is also a basic condition for all reproduction and growth. Long-term sustainability is based on early identification of real threats. If the threat is growth (of population, production, consumption, pollution, and so on), its limitation might be a reasonable response. One example would be a limitation of population or consumption growth in favour of sustainability. In ancient times many cultures learned the connection between the possibility of food production and the stability and sustainability of society and its political organisation. As a consequence, very stringent rules were often developed and enforced to impose limits on population growth. These kinds of rules and institutions are also known to have existed in preliterate tribes in limited areas (such as islands or areas of infertile land). By contrast, traditional and capitalist social formations preferred the imperative of growth and territorial and market expansion. Market subjects themselves, mainly companies and corporations fully determined by the growth imperative, often collapse because they are forced to grow at any price. The imperative of sustainability is easily identifiable at the stages of clan, tribe and nation or state organisation, but at the global stage this distinction is still only theoretically conceived. However, in general, one can say that the imperative of sustainability is the first and immanent imperative which is incorporated into all social and cultural institutions.

This imperative is in conflict with the imperative of growth because of the limited resources and limited ability of the environment to absorb the side-effects of the reproduction of numerous more complex and more energy-demanding social formations. The contradiction of the imperative of growth and the imperative of sustainability is found in all social formations; at the civilisation level of development this contradiction of system imperatives intensifies. It is fully manifested in the global society[18] because all the previous ways of overcoming it – territorial expansion, mass emigration and global trade – neither solve nor reduce this contradiction, even temporarily. On the contrary, they deepen it.

At this point, we can try to mediate between Habermas's theory of crisis and the objection outlined above. The growth of population, production and consumption occurs at all stages of pre-capitalist societies, but only capitalism with its unlimited pursuit of profit and its ultimately global reach makes it a central imperative that dominates all institutions and activities. As a result, the growth-oriented dynamism of global industrial civilisation exacerbates crisis trends to such a degree that they can no longer be kept latent (Habermas 2005: 37–8). They explode in the form of acute crises, more and more frequently leading to conflicts and catastrophes. Existing institutions cannot cope with such crises, mainly because they are directly or indirectly aligned with the imperative of growth, and thus with a key factor conducive to crisis (Sayre 2010). This very imperative forces individual and collective subjects to behave in a way that aggravates the environmental crisis. And in global capitalism the imperative of growth has spread not only across all societies but also through all domains of life, including those that were previously not committed to growth of production and profit (such as the educational system, the health and social insurance systems, the prison and security systems and so on). The privatisation and commercialisation of such systems exacerbates not only conflicts within society, but also the conflict between civilisation and the planetary ecosystem, on which humanity depends for survival. The inability to apply knowledge about the limits of growth to the organisation of society confirms Habermas's thesis (see Meadows et al. 1972; 1993): capitalist societies cannot impose controls on the imperative of growth without abandoning their organisational principle (Habermas 2005: 42), and thus acting against their systemic logic. The environmental threat to the existence of civilisation calls for a radical change of course, a revolutionary change to the organisational system of society, but such a change is obstructed by the institutions of global capitalist civilisation and resisted by dominant social forces. The contradiction between basic imperatives thus endangers the sustainability of particular societies as well as that of global industrial civilisation, and the most likely outcome might be the Habermasian scenario of learning from catastrophe (see Habermas 2001: 38–57). But in the case of a global environmental catastrophe, the lesson would be a harder one than those following from all political catastrophes of the twentieth century.

To put it another way, states functioning in the contemporary system of global capitalism seem headed for failure: they will increasingly lack the capacity to prevent crises or mitigate their consequences

(Habermas 2005: 37). Moreover, efforts to bring the risks linked to global environmental crisis under administrative control will – as in the developed capitalist societies that had to deal with economic crises in the 1970s – shift problems to the political sphere. And state failure in the face of environmental crisis will erode the last remnants of legitimacy, left in place after the unsuccessful efforts to manage economic and social crises (ibid.: 65). We are witnessing an unfolding contradiction between systemic imperatives, similar to the one theorised by Habermas. On the one hand, the imperative of growth imposes itself because it helps – in the short term – to solve problems, satisfy demands and keep the system in business. On the other hand, the environmental consequences of global economic growth do not only provoke demands for regulation and limitation; they also raise the question of sustainability in a more fundamental sense, with regard to the biochemical and biophysical preconditions for life on this planet. But limiting regulations would interfere with the supply of consumer goods, career chances and leisure, essential to the post-World War II class compromise.

Conclusion

Industrial civilisation faces threats that take the form of both internally and externally induced crises. In connection with the current situation of the parallel global environmental and economic crises, we might also talk about a system crisis threatening the identity of industrial civilisation. The source of internally induced crises is the system of production and redistribution. The source of externally induced crises is the finite character of resources that are a condition of all production. The solution to economic and social crises through production growth deepens the environmental crisis. The global growth of population leads to the growth of food production; but this production significantly contributes to the deepening of the environmental crisis. Its consequences, mainly in the form of climatic changes, threaten the sustainability of global food production at the current level. Without food security, the stability of the political system is threatened. Two system imperatives collide – growth and the sustainability of the possibility of reproduction. At the same time, this contradiction deepens the conflict potential of the past crisis tendencies present in different social formations. The basic source of conflict is an unequal distribution of limited resources. If resources are depleted or devastated, including the environment

itself, this will endanger the possibilities of production, possibly deepening even further the social and political conflicts which, in the past,
were often precursors of political revolutions.

Notes

1. The sources include drinking water, unpolluted or at least breathable air, living space, working space, space for production of at least basic food and stable climate conditions. The lack of these resources cannot be retrieved, not even by potential technologies that would allow us to mine minerals from interplanetary space and transport them to Earth.
2. At the same time, harvests were annihilated by heavy rains and flooding in Pakistan, where thousands of people died.
3. This development could be interpreted in the framework proposed by S. N. Eisenstadt in his essay on multiple modernities, according to which fundamentalist movements emerged as a part of basic antinomies of modernity not only in non-Western societies. See more in Eisenstadt (2000).
4. As Francesca De Châtel points out, Syria had already faced a environmental and humanitarian crisis, with thousands of internal refugees, a few years before the uprising in March 2011. Rapid population growth (from 3.3 million in 1950 to 21.4 million today) and similar growth of agroproduction led to a depletion of water resources and overexploitation of soil and desertification. The situation was worsened by the drought of 2006–10, forcing Syria to import wheat in 2008 for the first time in fifteen years. 'The humanitarian crisis that followed the 2006–10 drought can thus be seen as the culmination of 50 years of sustained mismanagement of water and land resources, and the dead end of the Syrian government's water and agricultural policies . . . It was the Syrian government's failure to adapt to changing environmental, economic and social realities [which drove] Syrians into the street in protest' (De Châtel 2014: 522). Hundreds of thousands of internally displaced refugees, who had been living for years in tent camps near big Syrian cities, played an important role in the destabilisation of the Syrian regime.
5. Despite the Kyoto Protocol, the goal of which was to reduce greenhouse gas emissions by 5 per cent from their 1990 level, their concentration in the atmosphere has, since the year 2000, increased by 20 per cent. See also IPPC (2013).
6. The devastation of the global environment could be described as a complex of significant quantitative changes in climate, biosphere integrity (earlier biodiversity loss), novel entities (earlier chemical pollution), stratospheric ozone depletion, ocean acidification, biogeochemical flows (linkage between phosphorus and nitrogen cycles), land-system change (deforestation, forest degradation and agricultural practices), freshwater use (overexploitation of water resources) and atmospheric aerosol loading. See Rockström et al. (2009) and Steffen et al. (2011, 2015).
7. *Legimation Crisis* was first published as *Legitimationsprobleme im Spätkapitalismus* in 1973 (Frankfurt am Main: Suhrkamp Verlag) and in its English translation in 1976.
8. I understand the term 'civilisation' in a broad sense that applies to the whole of humanity, as argued by Hrubec (2010).

9. The term 'global capitalism', as used by W. I. Robinson, covers substantial parts of the field analysed by Habermas in the 1970s. And the crisis of global capitalism, as theorised by Robinson (2010, 2012, 2013), is a consequence of the very crisis tendencies identified by Habermas in his *Legitimation Crisis*. The term 'global industrial civilisation' is broader than the term 'global capitalism'. Industrial civilisation is characterised not only by capitalism as its political-economic system but also by globally spread technologies of production and distribution of products and services, as well as transport and communication. On the importance of communication technologies for the extent of civilisation see Toynbee (1976).

10. By the term 'post-capitalist social formation' Habermas means 'state-socialist societies' (Habermas 2005: 17), which are in his view also class societies; the difference is that production means are handled by political elites.

11. However, the French revolution in 1789 could also be interpreted as at least partly the result of external causes, mainly environmental. See Gore (2000). This means that this kind of threat (climate fluctuation) could destabilise more than archaic social formations, as Habermas claims.

12. Following up on T. R. Malthus, J. S. Mill states in his *Principles of Political Economy* that due to the growing population and the need to feed it, Great Britain 'no longer depends on the fertility of her own soil . . . but on the soil of the whole world' (Mill 1994: 114). That is why '[t]his limited source of supply, unless great improvements take place in agriculture, cannot be expected to keep pace with the growing demand of so rapidly increasing a population as that of Great Britain; and if our population and capital continue to increase with their present rapidity, the only mode in which food can continue to be supplied cheaply to the one, is by sending the other abroad to produce it' (ibid.: 115). Not every European country could solve these problems by the 'export of poor' to their colonies and by the import of food and other resources from them. In this connection we need to point out that the Fascist movements in Italy and Germany began to gain the support of the masses shortly after the USA limited immigration in the early 1920s, and these and other countries couldn't reduce their social tension by emigration.

13. Trade accelerates the processes of the division of labour and the deepening of social differences, but it also enables humankind, as a biological species, to circumvent the limits resulting from climate conditions and material resources in specific areas. Humans could then populate and live in areas that have not offered the possibility to produce the sufficient renewable and unrenewable resources necessary for life in human communities. Since prehistoric times, trade has at least helped to reduce the immediate determination of specific natural conditions.

14. The first consequences of floods, earthquakes and tornados are injuries and the loss of homes. Devastated sources of drinking water, food reserves or the loss of harvest come later. If the administration of the affected country is unable to deal with the humanitarian crisis in time, the consequences will probably also influence the stability of the social and political system. Crisis management in Pakistan after the floods in 2010 was not well managed and consequently deepened the political crisis in the country. The response of the Obama administration to Hurricane Sandy in October 2012 influenced many voters in the US presidential elections.

15. When, at the end of October 2012, Hurricane Sandy hit the east of the US and Canada, it killed several dozen people and caused flooding over wide areas and other damage exceeding $50 billion. As a result, the supply system over a wide area collapsed, leading to the temporary rationing of fuel and several other commodities in New York and the restriction of some rights and freedoms. It is clear that Lovelock's vision is more realistic than it would have seemed several years ago.

16. Processes of enclosure and expropriation and the social conflicts caused by them in the past have been described and analysed many times. See the famous Chapter 27 in the first volume of *Capital* (Marx 1999: 366–71). These processes continue today in many ways, not only in developing countries in Latin America and Africa, but also in countries of the former Eastern Bloc, where small landowners have to resist the encroachments of foreign investors or mining corporations. As the resisters emphasise, the surface of the Earth, in its capacity as living space, is the most basic of all resources. Furthermore, this source is finite, or non-renewable, because, in an overpopulated world, it could be obtained only at the expense of other people (communities) or animals.

17. I prefer to use the term 'imperative of sustainability' rather than Jonas's famous concept of 'imperative of responsibility' – act in such a way that the effects of your action are compatible with the permanency of an authentically human life on Earth (Jonas 1985) – because the real aim is sustainability of the conditions for life of humankind and civilisation as well, and responsibility is only a tool that can be used to achieve it.

18. Accordingly it is needed to emphasise the need to spread global education in order to present knowledge about the issues of the global market and global economy in the context of sustainability. One of the main goals of this new approach in education is to lead young people to a sense of global responsibility in global society. See Svitačova and Mravcová 2014: 43–61.

References

De Châtel, F. (2014) 'The role of drought and climate change in the Syrian uprising: untangling the triggers of the revolution', *Middle Eastern Studies* 50(4), 521–35.

Dubnička, I. (2007) *Kultúra a environmentálna kríza (Culture and Environmental Crisis)*. Nitra: UKF v Nitre.

Dubnička, I. (2009) 'Genéza environmentálnej krízy. Pokus o evolucionistickú interpretáciu' (Genesis of environmental crisis. The attempt at evolutionistic interpretation), in I. Dubnička (ed.) *Zborník príspevkov z medzinárodnej konferencie 'Ekofilozofia včera, dnes a zajtra' (Collection of Papers from the International Conference 'Ecophilosophy Yesterday, Today and Tomorrow)*. Nitra: UKF v Nitre, pp. 75–91.

Eisenstadt, S. N. (2000) 'Multiple modernities', *Daedalus* 129(1), 1–29.

Gore, A. (2000) *Earth in the Balance: Ecology and the Human Spirit* (rev. edn). New York: Houghton Mifflin Harcourt.

Habermas, J. (1975) 'Towards a reconstruction of historical materialism', *Theory and Society* 2(3), 287–300.

Habermas, J. (1990) 'What does Socialism mean today? The rectifying revolution and the need for new thinking on the Left', *New Left Review* 183(1), 3–21.

Habermas, J. (2001) *The Postnational Constellation: Political Essays* (trans, ed. and with an introduction by Max Pensky). Cambridge, MA: MIT Press.

Habermas, J. (2005) *Legitimation Crisis* (trans. T. McCarthy). Boston, MA: Beacon Press.

Habermas, J. (2012) *The Crisis of the European Union* (trans. C. Cronin). Cambridge: Polity Press.

Hohoš, L. (1993) 'Ekologická ekonomika ako nová paradigma' ('Ecological economy as a new paradigm'), in *Spory o charakter ekologickej paradigmy* (*Disputes about the Character of Ecological Paradigm*). Bratislava: Filozofický ústav SAV, pp. 115–21.

Hrubec, M. (2010) 'Preconditions of intercultural dialogue on human rights', *Veritas* 55(1), 183–205.

Hsiang, S. M., M. Burke and E. Miguel (2013) 'Quantifying the influence of climate on human conflict', *Science* 341, 1–14.

IPCC (2013) 'Summary for policymakers', in T. F. Stocker, D. Qin, G.-K. Plattner, M. Tignor, S. K. Allen, J. Boschung, A. Nauels, Y. Xia, V. Bex and P. M. Midgley (eds) *Climate Change 2013: The Physical Science Basis. Contribution of Working Group I to the Fifth Assessment Report of the Intergovernmental Panel on Climate Change.* Cambridge and New York: Cambridge University Press.

Jonas, H. (1985) *The Imperative of Responsibility: In Search of an Ethics for the Technological Age.* Chicago, IL: University of Chicago Press.

Lovelock, J. (2006) *The Revenge of Gaia: Earth's Climate Crisis & The Fate of Humanity.* New York: Basic Books.

Lovelock, J. (2010) *The Vanishing Face of Gaia: A Final Warning.* New York: Basic Books.

Malthus, T. R. (1798) 'An essay on the principle of population', available at www.esp.org/books/malthus/population/malthus.pdf

Marx, K. (1999) *Capital.* Oxford: Oxford University Press.

McLellan, R. (ed.) (2014) *Living Planet Report. Species and Spaces, People and Places*, available at http://wwf.panda.org/about_our_earth/all_publications/living_planet_report

Meadows, D. H., D. L. Meadows, J. Randers and W. W. Behrens III (1972) *Limits to Grows: A Report for the Club of Rome's Project on the Predicament of Mankind.* New York: Universe Books.

Meadows, D. H., D. L. Meadows and J. Randers (1993) *Beyond The Limits. Global Collapse or a Sustainable Future.* London: Earthscan Publications Limited.

Mill, J. S. (1994) *Principles of Political Economy.* Oxford: Oxford University Press.

Palazzo, A. (2014) The military revolution of limits and the changing character of war, *Small Wars Journal* available at http://smallwarsjournal.com/jrnl/art/the-military-revolution-of-limits-and-the-changing-character-of-war

Plant, R. (1982) 'Jürgen Habermas and the idea of legitimation crisis', *European Journal of Political Research* 10, 341–52.

Ricoeur, P. (1986) 'Ist "die Krise" ein spezifisch modernes Phänomen?', in K. Michalski (ed.) *Über die Krise.* Stuttgart: Klett-Cotta, pp. 38–63.

Robinson, W. I. (2010) 'The crisis of global capitalism: cyclical, structural, or systemic?', in M. Konings (ed.) *Beyond the Subprime Headlines: Critical Perspectives on the Financial Crisis.* London: Verso.

Robinson, W. I. (2012) 'The "Great Recession" of 2008 and the continuing crisis: a global capitalism perspective', *The International Review of Modern Sociology* 38(2), 169–98.

Robinson, W. I. (2013) 'Global capitalism and its anti-"human face": organic intellectuals and interpretations of the crisis', *Globalization* 10(5), 659–71.

Rockström, J., W. Steffen, K. Noone, Å. Persson, F. S. Chapin III, E. Lambin, T. M. Lenton, M. Scheffer, C. Folke, H. Schellnhuber, B. Nykvist, C. A. De Wit, T. Hughes, S. van der. Leeuw, H. Rodhe, S. Sörlin, P. K. Snyder, R. Costanza, U. Svedin, M. Falkenmark, L. Karlberg, R. W. Corell, V. J. Fabry, J. Hansen, B. Walker, D. Liverman, K. Richardson, P. Crutzen and J. Foley (2009) 'Planetary boundaries: exploring the safe operating space for humanity', *Ecology and Society* 14(2), 32.

Sayre, K. M. (2010) *Unearthed: the Economic Roots of Our Environmental Crisis*. Notre Dame, IN: University of Notre Dame Press.

Sťahel, R. (2013a) 'Globalization and the crisis', in K. Mitterpach and R. Sťahel (eds) *Philosophica 12: Towards a Political Philosophy*. Nitra: UKF, pp. 45–56.

Sťahel, R. (2013b) 'Global crisis and crisis of globalization', *European Journal of Transformation Studies* 1(1), 92–107.

Staněk, P. (2012) *Globálna kríza a jej systémové implikácie* (*Global Crisis and her Systemic Implications*). Bratislava: Ekonomická univerzita.

Steffen, W., Å. Persson, L. Deutsch, J. Zalasiewicz, M. Williams, K. Richardson, C. Crumley, P. Crutzen, C. Folke, L. Gordon, M. Molina, V. Ramanathan, J. Rockström, M. Scheffer, H. J. Schellnhuber and U. Svedin (2011) 'The Anthropocene: from global change to planetary stewardship', *AMBIO* 40(7), 739–61.

Steffen, W., K. Richardson, J. Rockström, S. E. Cornell, I. Fetzer, E. M. Bennett, R. Biggs, S. R. Carpenter, W. de Vries, C. A. de Wit, C. Folke, D. Gerten, J. Heinke, G. M. Mace, L. M. Persson, V. Ramanathan, B. Reyers and S. Sörlin (2015) 'Planetary boundaries: guiding human development on a changing planet', *Science* 347(6223), 1–41.

Svitačová, E. and A. Mravcová (2014) 'Implementation of global development education into the curriculum at the Faculty of Economics and Management, Slovak University of Agriculture', *International Journal of Development Education and Global Learning* 6(2), 43–61.

Terazono, E. and H. Saleh (2013) 'Currency crisis hits Egypt´s wheat supply', *Financial Times* (20 February), 2.

Toynbee, A. (1976) *Mankind and Mother Earth, A Narrative History of the World*. New York: Oxford University Press.

7

Communists and Social Democrats in the 1919 Hungarian Soviet Republic

Gábor Gángó

Introduction

IN THIS CHAPTER I intend to challenge the usual interpretation of the 'Kun regime' (Seton-Watson and Seton-Watson 1981: 365) as merely an import of the Leninist model to Hungary, and Kun himself, as, in Robert Seton-Watson's words, 'Lenin's Magyar lieutenant' (ibid.: 354). That view neglects the regime's inner social basis, its intellectual foundations and the rather wide social support which undoubtedly existed at the beginning of the Soviet Republic, even though it had diminished and then disappeared by the end. The proletarian dictatorship was not just Béla Kun's regime: its basis and its matter, so to speak, was social democracy, and a handful of Communists tried to give form to this matter.[1] The Bolsheviks themselves regarded the Soviet Republic as an unhappily mixed form of government, Communist and socialist.

The consideration of the 1918 bourgeois revolution, led by Count Mihály Károlyi, and the 1919 proletarian one as two phases of one single revolutionary process may be helpful to the proper evaluation of the role played by the Social Democrats in these events. Afraid as Hungarian intellectuals were of unleashing the unknown forces of revolution, they could not get away from the idea that the events were following (and would follow) the inherent logic of the 1789 French revolution. Károlyi's retrospective account is typical on this point. In a speech delivered to parliament in February 1918, he voiced his growing fear of revolutions in Hungary and around the world (Hajdu 1958: 28). After the so-called 'chrysanthemum revolution' at the end of the war, he doubted that the way he had assumed power could be interpreted at all as a revolution. On the other hand, he painted a revolutionary portrait of his peers, describing the Social Democratic leader Zsigmond Kunfi as Danton and the Lower House president and clergyman János

Hock as the abbot Sieyès – so that the arrival of Tibor Szamuely as a Bolshevik Saint-Just, accompanied by a terrorist squad, was perfectly in tune with Károlyi's ideas and fears (Károlyi 1982: 153, 170, 186). Social Democrats shared Károlyi's views on the escalating revolutions. On 8 January 1919, during a meeting of the workers' council, the socialist leader Sándor Garbai proposed the establishment of a pure socialist government. His statement that the history of revolutions in Hungary had not come to an end with the 31 October revolution was applauded (Hajdu 1958: 86). The idea of a necessary radicalisation of the revolution was in accordance with the Communists' faith too. György Lukács expressed the conviction of many after 20 February 1919, in his article '"Law and order" and violence' in the newly founded Communist magazine *International*: 'no revolution,' he wrote, 'has ever stopped halfway' (Lukács 1972: 43). Therefore, the change from a moderate republican system to the ultra-leftist terror of a handful of fanatics was not totally unexpected. One part of the revolutionary leadership feared the terror and the other longed for it but neither could drop the subject and all tried to predict the future. These predictions inevitably influenced the following events.

As to the meaning of the whole process, the proletarian revolution seemed to make sense of the Károlyi revolution. The poet Mihály Babits had greeted the Károlyi revolution in the progressive literary review *The West* with an essay entitled 'In the first moment', in which he raised questions concerning possible interpretations of the events:

> What kind of revolution is this? A bourgeois revolution? A 1848-type revolution of liberty? A nationalist one? Or an anti-nationalist revolution, a red revolution, a socialist, a social one? A Hungarian or a general human one? Or just the first, yet dissimulated, explosion of the Bolshevik anarchy from the bottle of Order? Each party, each class regards it in another way, just like a miracle: and everyone can see it according to their heart! And everyone has different expectations towards it: different results, different tendencies!' (quoted in József 1984: 32)

The pivotal question, therefore, was whether Károlyi's rise to power was a revolution or not. Contemporaries did not take much heed of the events when trying to answer this question. Once Károlyi's change of government was regarded as a revolution, then not to see 21 March as the radicalisation of the same process would have been equivalent to the recognition of the total collapse of the Károlyi revolution. The prospect of being befriended by Bolshevik Russia or establishing radical equality did not, of course, appeal to everybody in the revolutionary camp. The Hungarians were willing to accept Kun's coup as a revolution and did not reject it as a proletarian one, simply because as yet they did not have any knowledge of the practical meaning of the latter.

Social Democrats in the bourgeois coalition government

The November 1918 revolution in Hungary was a bourgeois democratic one fought by proletarians: workers and soldiers from worker and peasant families. The revolution was based on and favourable to the creation of popular organisations. But the popular movements were far too radical and dangerous for the new government from the moment of its establishment.

The coalition government was formed by the Independent (Károlyi) Party, the Radical Democrats and the Social Democrats. After the political honeymoon, which lasted only a couple of days, effective cooperation proved to be impossible. The difficulties caused a breakdown in the inner constitution of these protest parties, unfit for the duties of administration. The right-conservative, nationalist wing of Károlyi's party split from the left wing and the Radicals disappeared: only the Socialists survived in organised shape.

The most prominent figures of the government were Károlyi himself as Prime Minister and Minister of Foreign Affairs and the Radical Oszkár Jászi as Minister for National Minorities. Two Social Democratic ministers, Zsigmond Kunfi and Dezső Bokányi, served in Károlyi's government. After the appointment of the government, Kunfi announced that the Social Democrats would temporarily lay down the arms of class struggle and class hatred. This was enough for them to be condemned as class traitors, limiting themselves to bourgeois democratic political goals. Later, in his recollections, Károlyi reasoned that the neglect of the social character of the 31 October mass movements had had fatal consequences. He liked to think that the timely recognition of the importance of this factor and a corresponding change of governmental policy could have kept Bolshevism at bay.

The radical differences between the programmes of the coalition parties resulted in discord on strategic points and complete administrative gridlock. The programme of the Károlyi party consisted in demanding wider deregulation concerning the constitutional ties between the Hungarian and the Austrian parts of the moribund but still existing dual monarchy, democratic reform and social reform. In addition, they demanded an end to the war and the establishment of a peace that would safeguard Hungary's territorial integrity. With the war over and Austria-Hungary broken, the party could not set any other task than the democratisation of the country.

Oszkár Jászi founded the National Civic Radical Party in early 1914. The programme envisaged land reform, regulating the coexistence of Magyar and non-Magyar nationalities in Hungary, and the introduction of compulsory and free primary education. As a leading theorist of the nationality question, Jászi defended Hungary's territorial integrity on the illusory basis of Wilsonism. The radicals as a political force sank into oblivion together with the Wilsonian illusions and played no role at all during the Soviet Republic (Siklós 1988: 18 sqq.).

In opposition to the other coalition partners, the Social Democrats had extensive past experience in party organisation and possessed a nationwide network. After the early phase of defending workers' interests and rights, Social Democracy developed into a political movement in the first decade of the century. It gained momentum as the Hungarian proletariat increased in number: between 1900 and 1910, the number of enterprises employing more than 500 workers rose from 69 to 134, with the total number of workers increasing from 75,000 to almost double that. In the pre-war years over 100,000 members joined trade unions and about 50,000 the Social Democratic Party (Gábor 1961; Horváth 1974; Siklós 1988: 22 sqq.).

The Social Democrats formed the most powerful element of the non-parliament opposition in the Tisza era. During the war years, between 1916 and 1918, membership increased from 50,000 to 200,000–300,000 and totalled more than 700,000 under the Károlyi government. In the first years of the war, like their German and West European counterparts, Social Democrats supported national militarism. And later, again similarly to German Socialists, they turned their back on the nationalist goals of the cabinets (Schulz 1972: 58 sqq.). In spite of initiating the anti-government Electoral Bloc in June 1917, the Social Democrats returned a couple of months later to their pre-war politics of supporting the government in exchange for more or less empty promises concerning future electoral reform.

The news of the victorious Russian revolutions divided the party membership and opened up the possibility of a fundamental restructuring. As a result, new political leaders, the future coalition partners of Kun in the Soviet Republic, gained dominant positions.

The new party leader was the centrist Zsigmond Kunfi. He was not a man of strong moral fibre. In the critical moments of the Soviet Republic he generally hesitated until he reached a compromise. The existing left-wing faction of the party (Béla Szántó, Béla Vágó and László Rudas) had strengthened its position after the Russian revolution. A new left-wing current also emerged, headed by Jenő Varga, Jenő Hamburger and Jenő Landler. Various platforms of revolutionary socialists, anarcho-syndicalists or radical left-intellectuals, who worked illegally outside the organisation of the Social Democratic Party, grouped under the leadership of Ottó Korvin (Congdon 1991: 21).

During the government crisis in early October 1918, the Social Democrats developed their programme. They published their manifesto 'To the Hungarian people' in the 8 October issue of the socialist organ *The People's Voice*. The manifesto demanded electoral, social and political reforms, the establishment of fundamental human rights and the acknowledgment of the rights of non-Magyar minorities. They called for a new consensual government with the active participation of non-Magyar nationalities, the dissolution of parliament and elections on the basis of universal suffrage and secret ballots, extended to both sexes. The manifesto called for a peace based on Wilsonian principles, and the democratisation of public life. As to social and human rights measures, the socialists demanded freedom of assembly and association, radical land reform, the nationalisation of industrial plants, a fair taxation system, social and welfare institutions for the working class and the war invalids, widows and orphans, and the eight-hour working day (Siklós 1988: 21).

The Social Democrats' congress on 13 October 1918 wholeheartedly supported the programme expressed in the manifesto. Beyond this, following the propositions of the party's right wing, the congress approved of two inconsistent resolutions concerning the possible future allies of the Social Democrats. In the interest of a future coalition government, the congress now consented to the formerly prohibited political alliance with bourgeois parties. In other words, they put national unity before class struggle. On the other hand, however, the Social Democrats stated their intention to restore the ties with non-Magyar Social Democrats, loosened during the war, in order to enforce class solidarity in spite of national differences (Siklós 1988: 25–6).

The propositions of the left-wing Socialists were rejected mainly because of their reckless radicalism. However, these propositions were still a far cry from what actually happened after March 1919. They proposed the abolition of the Upper House, the redistribution of Church estates and the establishment of industrial plants under the cooperative management of white- and blue-collar workers. Their proposition was a characteristic and impracticable mixture of capitalist and cooperatively owned and managed industry. They would not hear of nationalisation except in the case of banks. The only proposal that was reconsidered in 1919 was the idea of solving the housing shortage by prescribing a direct proportion between living space and the number of people occupying that space.

Prime Minister Károlyi endorsed the democratic changes in Hungary solely in the hope of safeguarding the territorial integrity of the country. He reasoned that a democratic government would more easily win the sympathy of the entente. He was mistaken. When the Wilsonian illusion was shattered, Károlyi lost his popularity very quickly (Nagy 1988: 263). At the end of 1918, it became clear that the great powers would not recognise the new Hungarian state. Instead, they saw Hungary as the Bolshevik wolf in sheep's clothing and raised the alarm. On 31 December 1918, the government's newspaper published an article entitled 'Wilson reconciled with the British imperialists' in which it expressed regret over being let down by the messiah Wilson (Raffay 1987: 280). Sándor Garbai's dictum on the eve of the Communist coup about the necessity of turning eastwards expressed the general mood rather than shaped it: 'we must find a new orientation in order to obtain from the East what had been denied to us by the West' (quoted in Hajdu 1988: 367).

The left's road to power

Béla Kun, together with the future leader of the terror groups during the Soviet Republic, Tibor Szamuely, was a prisoner-of-war in Russia during World War I. After the victory of the Russian October revolution, hundreds of Magyars joined the Bolshevik Party, and tens of thousands joined the Red Army as volunteer 'Internationalists'. Once the armistice was signed, Magyar prisoners began to come home via the southern Polish region Galicia (Gábor 1974; Borsányi 1979; Krammer 1983; Pastor 1983; Siklós 1988: 28).

Soon after, on 17 November 1918, Kun arrived in Budapest to start his political fight – not against the bourgeoisie but against the Social

Democrats. Instead of building up a new party and challenging them, Kun's strategy consisted in winning over the left-wing Social Democrats, or forcing the whole party to the left. The first issue of the *Red News* on 7 December 1918, together with Kun's pamphlets *What do the Communists Want?* and *Who will Pay for the War?*, was put at the service of Kun's plan. At that time, the future leaders of the Soviet Republic were at each other's throats. The *Red News* incessantly fulminated against József Pogány, Péter Ágoston and Sándor Garbai. The Social Democratic organ *The People's Voice* was caught in a troubling situation: it could not attack Kun personally because of his earlier merits in the Social Democratic movement; all they could do was reprimand the Communists for their attacks. The Communists were always finding fault with the Social Democratic Party, mostly for its reconciliation with the bourgeois order. They made it plain that they did not want any alliance against capitalism: they would do the work alone and sacrifice the social democrats if necessary. On the one hand, Kun never explicitly cut off communication with the Social Democrats but, on the other, he drove them into situations which reflected badly on them on account of their bourgeois coalition partners. The most demagogic and most successful of his actions was egging on proletarian tenants to not pay their rents to the landlords, and when the Social Democratic members of the government had to take action to maintain the legal order it presented them in a bad light (Petrák 1969).

The story of the foundation of the Communist Party in Hungary is a narrative forged and polished by the people involved rather than a historical account of what actually happened. The truth, as David Kettler commented on György Lukács's refusal to speak about the foundation of the Hungarian Communist Party in the late 1960s, 'will simply never be known' (Lukács and Kettler 2012: 44).

The Hungarian Communist Party is reported to have been founded in Moscow on 4 November 1918, while 24 November 1919 is the reported date of the 'second' foundation of the Communist Party in Budapest (Siklós 1988: 128 sqq.). The story of the increasing number of party members should rather be seen as a hagiographic tradition than as an account of the real course of events: first the Russian prisoners-of-war joined, then the left-wing Social Democrats, then Szamuely, then the 'Engineers', then the 'Ethical group' that is, György Lukács and his friends. Lukács and his friends, who were accepted by Kun despite the reservations of the other leaders as well as those of rank-and-file members, joined the party in the December. With regard to the sub-sequent Soviet Republic, this story highlights the diverse elements entering into the making of 'proletarian' power: the Communists and Social Democrats (as governing parties), the liquidators (the organis-ers of violence), the engineers (as leaders of the economy) and finally the 'ethical group' (as leaders of the cultural policy). The historical order also says something about the impact of the various groups. The 'Russians' came first because they provided the programme and they were the closest to the sources of Bolshevism.

Kun's strategy proved to be the winning one. The more the Communists censured the Social Democrats during the winter months for their opportunism, the more readily the Social Democrats believed that they could not govern without the Communists. On the one hand, they were conscious that the Communists were indispensable partners in military matters; on the other, they were increasingly irritated by the ruthless criticism of the Communists in political matters.

Before 21 March 1919, Kun saw clearly that the time was not ripe for revolution in Hungary. He was waiting for the outbreak of the proletar-ian revolution in Germany and kept assuring Lenin that Communists in Hungary would never be satisfied with less than a full-scale revolu-tion (Hajdu 1989: 143 sq.). Kun's tactic consisted in relentless criticism of everything the government (and especially the Social Democrats in government) did, and in wild promises to the proletariat.

Kun, while he was still in Russia, formulated a Bolshevik response to the Social Democrats' position concerning the future of the country in an article entitled 'The judgement of the Bolsheviks' published on 23 October 1918 in the prisoner-of-war organ *Social Revolution* (Siklós 1988: 29). He argued that the victory of the Russian revolution boosted the prospects of a possible socialist revolution in Hungary too. The Social Democrats' programme, on the contrary, was in his view nothing more than political opportunism. They not only neglected the eventuality of a proletarian revolution but also turned a blind eye to the demands of the democratic transition.

As the vivid debates about the feasibility of a socialist order between October 1918 and March 1919 show, the socialists and the Communists were preparing a bid for power. Their preparations were secret, and there were no plans for an armed uprising. The transition of power was arranged behind Károlyi's back. Later, Kun commented that power had fallen into the Communists' lap (Johancsik 2010). This remark also supports the theory that their coming to power was by no means the outcome of their preparations but rather of their being ready and able to seize the opportunity as it arose.

The only chance of survival for the Károlyi government would have been support received from the entente. By early 1919 the so-called Vix memorandum (that is, an ultimatum of the Paris peace conference to the government of Hungary handed over by Lieutenant-Colonel Fernand Vix, the leader of the French military mission in Hungary) made it clear that it was an unattainable dream.

The genesis of the memorandum is closely connected to the military operations continuing in Eastern Europe after the November 1918 armistice. By the end of February 1919, under Marshal Ferdinand Foch's command, an all-out offensive was in preparation against Soviet Russia. This would have required an unprecedentedly long united front from Finland to the Crimea. In order to establish an appropriate railway communication between the Czechoslovakian and Romanian armies, the demarcation line between the Romanians and the Hungarians had to be pushed westwards.

The military experts of the Council of Ten therefore drew up plans, on 26 February 1919, for a new demarcation line between Hungary and Romania. According to these plans, Hungarian cities such as Debrecen and Szeged would no longer have been under the control of the Hungarian government. The over-ambitious plan of invading Russia was abandoned soon after but the new demarcation lines remained in force.

The content of the Vix ultimatum, that is, the new demarcation lines, was presented to the Hungarians a month later than scheduled. There were several reasons for the delay. First of all, when General Louis Franchet d'Esperey, the Allied commander on the ground in the Balkans, realised that the intention of the great powers was to let Romania occupy Transylvania, he contrived a scheme to gain the necessary time for the Romanian army to create a military fait accompli. Second, the reversal of fortune on the Odessa front brought the hastily planned offensive to an end. The French and White troops lost ground against the Russian Red Army in the south of Ukraine. In the new situation, rumours about the emergence of Bolshevism in Hungary and the eventual cooperation between Hungarians and Russians could move the French to grant Romania new concessions. Consequently, French Prime Minister Georges Clemenceau issued an order on 14 March 1918 in which the Hungarian government was ordered to establish the new demarcation lines with a wide neutral zone. Lieutenant-Colonel

Vix gave Károlyi this ultimatum six days later, on 20 March 1919, in Budapest with the instruction that it had to be carried out within thirty-six hours. This course of action revealed the true colours of the entente and made it obvious that Károlyi's foreign politics would suffer defeat.

At the point when the Vix memorandum arrived, Károlyi's credibility was also a thing of the past with regard to domestic policies. In this sense, the memorandum was not the principal cause of the government's collapse (Ormos 1990: 161 sqq.). Loath to accept the considerable territorial losses demanded by the Vix ultimatum, Károlyi and his Prime Minister, Dénes Berinkey (who replaced Károlyi on 19 January 1919, when the latter became temporary President of the Republic), resigned the next day. They handed over power to the only remaining organised political force, the Social Democrats. The Social Democrats' conduct towards the Communists was influenced by the desire to improve relations with Soviet Russia. They embarked on this new task by releasing the recently arrested Communist leaders. Not only were they set free but they were also given leading positions in the newly-formed cabinet. The Hungarian Soviet Republic was proclaimed on 21 March 1919. Lieutenant-Colonel Vix left for Belgrade two days later (Pastor 1988: 259).

The Social Democrats participating in the new cabinet were not the same as those who had been part of the Károlyi government: the former were left-radicals while the latter had been moderate. Even these left-wing Social Democrats, who agreed with the fundamental aims of Bolshevism, rejected the anti-democratic, even terroristic methods the Bolsheviks used to reach their goals. Bolshevik methods were a distinctive feature of the Communists. Nevertheless, the Social Democrats played a crucial role since theirs was the only political party able to reorganise the army. The head of government was Sándor Garbai, a Social Democrat, while the People's Commissar for Foreign Affairs was Béla Kun.

The council system

The difference between the councils founded before 21 March 1919 and those founded after that date may not be obvious at first sight; nonetheless it is a fundamental one. While the first councils in Hungary were organised by politically aware members of the lower classes, those coming after 21 March 1919 were imposed upon the lower classes by the Communist elite. The Communists, when naming the organs of the new power councils – just like in Russia – were consciously exploiting the democratic reputation of the existing councils and cautiously disguising their real intentions, at least for the time being (Hajdu 1958).

In Hungary, the Social Democratic Party was hostile to the organisation of Soviets for two reasons: first, because they did not want to upset the applecart and second, because any rival organisation in the workers' movement would have threatened their advantageous position. Thus, the Soviets were supported mainly by the illegal Revolutionary Socialists. The first organisations, following the Russian example, were brought into being in early 1918.

The soldiers' council was founded on 25 October 1919. As it had no real power, none of the established political parties took it seriously or wanted to rub shoulders with its leaders (Siklós 1988: 60). Neither were they encouraged to carry out their plan for an armed seizure of power. Their allies, out of necessity, were the Revolutionary Socialists and the left-wing Social Democrats. In the factories, the workers' councils were founded after 31 October 1918. In the countryside, the councils, varying in their aims and composition, intended to control or even replace the waning state power.

Therefore, the advent of the Soviet Republic was warmly welcomed by that part of the population which had supported the idea of councils. The council elections in early April 1919 mostly returned the already functioning deputies. The soldiers' councils, however, behaved differently and became a buffer between the army and the state power which effectively hindered the government from controlling the army. The Bolsheviks, together with the Social Democrats, wanted to be rid of the troublesome and meddling soldiers' councils and decided to reduce them to insignificance. As a first step, József Pogány, a former war reporter of *The People's Voice*, was appointed as their head. Then, on 14 April 1919, the Military People's Commissariat took their place.

As to the workers' councils, the Social Democratic Party expected them to run out of enthusiasm soon and disappear, as has happened in Austria and Germany. In the meantime, the leaders wanted to keep the councils under their thumb, which was easily done because the members of the councils were identical to the rank-and-file of the Social Democratic Party. Consequently, the councils adopted a more moderate political stance than the rest of the workers. This way the Communists were thwarted in their attempt to take control of the councils by the Social Democrats who by late 1918 were already 'inside'. The Communists did not take offence because they were also aiming to eliminate the councils. Because of that, they decided to isolate them as Social Democratic councils. As a result, the revolutionary forces established the Soviet Republic without the participation of the Soviets. They were incorporated into the political system only in the aftermath of 21 March 1919.

The Revolutionary Governing Council, presided over by the Social Democrat Sándor Garbai, held the executive power. The branches of administration were distributed among People's Commissars (before 4 April and after 14 June also Deputy People's Commissars). In some cases there were several commissars to a ministry, and this was a reason for incessant rivalry between Communists and Social Democrats. Out of the thirty-three members of the Revolutionary Governing Council, fourteen were Communists, seventeen were Social Democrats and there were two 'experts.'

The most public face of proletarian dictatorship was Béla Kun who was personally in charge of the international image of the Soviet Republic. He had strong views on the essential character of Bolshevism: before anything else, it was anti-Social-Democratism. He described it as the content that was thrown out of the Social Democratic boat 'floating on the waters of accommodation and opportunism' (Kun 1985: 98), that is, revolutionary Marxism – 'a scientific politics based on economic and social laws for the liberation of the proletariat' (ibid.: 98). In contrast to the humanist People's Commissar for Culture, Zsigmond Kunfi, Kun did not believe in an overall 'inter-class' morality. As he said: 'Capitalism has its own class morality that has to be opposed with the proletariat's own morality. Let Comrade Kunfi call it Machiavellism, I say that *I know only that morality which corresponds to the proletariat's class interests*' (quoted in Lukács 1987a: 509, editorial note).

The National Meeting of the Councils was opened on 14 June 1919, and was made up of representatives sent by the local councils. Essentially, however, the congress was a failure. Since Communists and Social Democrats disagreed on fundamental things, they could not define a common political direction. On 24 June 1919, the Central Executive Committee elected the new, more exclusive government with thirteen members. Kun and Garbai could maintain their posts but several extremists, Béla Vágó and Szamuely among them, were sent away on new missions, far from the central power, in a newly created Tcheka-like organisation, to fight the counter-revolutionaries.

The first congress of the united party took place on 12 June 1919 on Kun's initiative. The congress was a considerable defeat for the Communists on a symbolic as well as political level. Kun wanted to call the party the Communist Party in Hungary, but this proposal was strongly opposed by the Social Democrats. In the end, the title of the Communist-Socialist Workers' Party of Hungary was chosen as a compromise substitute for the name Socialist Party originally given to the unified party on 21 March 1919. Socialist council republics in Germany and Austria were the left-wing extremes of a bourgeois democratic parliamentary upheaval that allowed an eventual right-wing shift within the system. Communism, however, made any return to the parliamentary order possible only by counter-revolution. While discussions around the party's name resulted in compromise, in personal issues the Social Democratic offensive was victorious: the only Communist to remain in the leadership was Kun.

Thus, from mid-April to mid-June the revolution went to the left; from mid-June to the counter-revolutionary attempts two weeks later, it shifted to the right and thereafter it turned to terrorism (Romsics 1988). Kun's measures against the counter-revolutionaries were regarded by the Social Democrats as too much, by Ottó Korvin and his colleagues as too little. On 15 July 1919, they reorganised the dismissed Lenin boys, and the new wave of terror, previously applied exclusively in court-martials, was launched systematically with the approval of the government (Gratz 1935: 125 sqq.).

On the day of the collapse, Kun did nothing for the survival of the party or for the escape of the compromised leaders. His agreement to the establishment of a pure trade unionist (that is, Social Democratic) government was not only politically doubtful but also a tactically fatal decision. Relying on Kun's approval, local leaders of the Soviet Republic evaluated this turn of events as a right-wing transformation of the government, not as a complete political collapse. Accordingly, they remained at their posts to be exposed to the rage and revenge of the counter-revolutionaries.

In his last telegram to Lenin, Kun blamed the military collapse and the anti-revolutionary behaviour of the workers for the breakdown of the Hungarian Soviet Republic. He finished his letter with the comforting thought that 'every fight for the preservation of the genuine but watered-down dictatorship would have been in vain' (quoted in Borsányi 1979: 198). He wanted to find an adequate formulation of the essence of the political system he governed as a People's Commissar: the dictatorship was 'genuine' (that is, Bolshevik and not Social

Democratic in essence) but 'watered-down' (that is, its spirit diluted in lukewarm Social Democracy).

The party basis of the Hungarian Soviet Republic

The Communist Party and the Social Democratic Party united on 21 March 1919, and the newly formed organisation became the Socialist Party of Hungary. It may seem a nondescript choice but it did actually say a lot about the new formation. First, it carried the message that the two Left parties were united, instead of fighting for power. Second, it made clear the fact that the Social Democrats had renounced the most important attribute of their party by leaving out any democratic idea and substituting 'socialist' for 'social'. The Social Democrats left behind parliamentary politics and embraced the socialisation of the means of production. Third, it indicated that the Communists had decided to present themselves as the legal heirs of the Hungarian workers' movement, and that they had not broken with its values and traditions. In contrast to the Russian Bolshevik movement, candidates for membership were accepted without probation.

Before 26 April 1919, the Social Democrats never wanted to call it a day, but by the time of the congress they felt that the values and traditions of their own party were being destroyed by the Communists while their resources were being used up by the same Communists. They regretted having been too conciliatory at the critical moment of the seizure of power. With regard to their mass of support among the proletarians, both parties had good reasons to worry: the Communists did not have their own organisation, while the Social Democrats' membership grew to 1.5 million through the influx of non-proletarian trade unionists by the time of the congress. Here we should note the exemplary case of the journalists' trade union, which openly took a stand against the dictatorship.

The Social Democrats and the Communists held each other in contempt. The Socialists despised the new-born Communists, while the Communists disdained the discredited Socialists. The general loathing had a generational aspect, too. The Social Democrats, aged forty to fifty, were the 'elderly', the Communist leaders, aged between twenty-five and thirty-five, counted as adults and the young workers were regarded as the hope for a brighter future. The coalition partners, Social Democrats and Communists, divided the proletarian class between them. While skilled workers had been organised for decades by the Social Democratic Party, the newly recruited supporters of the Communist Party generally led a precarious existence. Evidently, this stratification generated tension between Socialist and Communist workers.

The quantitative disproportion between the two parties rendered impossible the enforcement of Communist policies on a majority basis. Their union meant that the Communists turned the well-built Social Democratic organisational system to their own advantage, and thus acquired an instrument of party politics which they had not had sufficient time to develop, while the Social Democrats adhered, in theory, to the Communist political programme. The ideological dominance of the Communists was neutralised by the fact that masses of rightists joined the united party.

In general, the leaders of the Hungarian Soviet Republic wanted to emulate the Russian political system. But when it came to the details, there were many differences. This was no surprise: even the Communists did not know what was going on in Russia and so imitating the Russian model in any great detail would have been a senseless objective.

The general programme of the substitution of the old state with the dictatorship of the proletariat was laid down in Lenin's *State and Revolution*. As for the political system, with regard to the regulation of the suffrage, the Hungarian Soviet Republic imitated the Russian constitution, as Kun had already declared before March 1919. The Russian pattern was followed in the from-below election system of the Soviets, the establishment of the People's Commissariats and the creation of the People's Commissars' Council as the supreme executive organ. The Central Executive Committee and the National Soviet Congress had their Russian counterparts, too. One of the main differences consisted in the role the workers' councils played. The workers' councils in the plants and factories did not assume management functions in Hungary and their – in Kun's eyes temporary – controlling function worked only to a limited extent.

Another difference between the Russian and the Hungarian Soviet Republics concerns the role of the party. While Leninism endowed the party with the role of vanguard, this solution was impossible in Hungary because of the complete overlapping of the party and the trade unions. The Hungarian Communists tried to interpret this difference as Hungary's advantage over Russia, since, as Lukács wrote, the proletariat established its dictatorship in Hungary 'without a fratricidal struggle' (Lukács 1987b: 104) and through a direct collective decision. Kun said in an interview that the Hungarian political system was harsher than the Russian one. Thus, it seems that the Hungarian Communists did not conceive their task as merely copying Russia: in a sense, they rather wanted to outdo the model. They spread the rumour widely that Kun's Bolshevism was decisive for the political order in Hungary, but that the entente, not they themselves, was responsible for the presentation of this Bolshevism as an imitation of Russia. The Soviet Republic's economy was a war economy but not a war Communism (like in Russia): the Hungarian Bolsheviks introduced compulsory work, but restrictions on private commerce and finance were less complete than in Russia, and the regime abstained from comprehensive and brutal food requisition. Unsurprisingly, Lenin had a poor opinion of the Soviet Republic's domestic policy: he urged the emulation of the Russian model of the nationalisation and distribution of land to landless farmers and peasants. He was also disappointed that power was not taken exclusively by the Communists, and that after the fusion with the Social Democrats, the party's name did not include the word 'Communist'.

Economic policy

The particular way of organising socialist production was the reason why workers' councils in Hungary did not function in the same way as in Soviet Russia (Péteri 1979, 1988). The economic policy of the Soviet Republic materialised as a compromise between the doctrinaire Social Democratic theory, Béla Kun's Leninism and the technocratic utopia of left-wing engineers. It was characterised first of all by the economic rationalisation of social needs and the overwhelming predominance of organisational and institutional elements at the expense of financial policy, the banking system, market processes and even political aspects. On the macroeconomic level, the Bolsheviks believed themselves able to overcome the country's economic backwardness by imitating capitalist monopolies. The shortage of raw material and the narrowness of the resources were undoubtedly strong arguments for the restrictions imposed on the market economy. Evidently, the complete nationalisation of the economy could not be achieved. Nonetheless, the Communists had enough time to create a wide nationalised sector which consisted of at least 4,000–5,000 enterprises.

From the possible forms of non-capitalist ownership, the leaders of the Hungarian Soviet Republic chose one close to state socialism. In

Hungarian usage, 'nationalisation' meant state ownership and 'socialisation' meant the nationalisation of institutions that should have been
socialised according to the Russian pattern.

As Lenin saw it, there was no royal road for a socialist transformation of the economy. The Hungarian proletarian dictatorship chose
the way of state socialism, partly because that could allow the existing
state capitalist framework of the economy to be exploited. The manifesto 'To Everyone!' clearly stated this intention of the government.
It imposed a very tight limit (twenty employees) above which each
and every enterprise was nationalised. Not only was the limit much
tighter than in Russia (fifty employees), but it was not respected by the
authorities. The Hungarian Bolsheviks reasoned that since they took
power 'more easily' than their Russian comrades and the working class
was more organised and more 'conscious' than it was over there, they
could advance towards their goal, complete socialism, 'more quickly'.
They knew that the appropriation of service enterprises with one or two
employees was neither rational nor politically desirable but, even so, it
was their practice.

In theory, management was shared between the political commissar and the workers' councils. One of the tasks of the councils
consisted in classifying the workers according to their qualification
and implementing a wage increase (up to 100 per cent) according to
class criteria. Qualified workers (old Social Democrats in general) were
short-changed in favour of the unqualified labourers who were more
devoted supporters of the Communists because they obtained a bigger
wage increase. This generated tensions everywhere.

In the atmosphere of general crisis during the last days of World
War I, the workers' council of the Weiss-Manfréd Works in Csepel was
created on 30 October 1918. The councils generally demanded control
over the management and a say in the redistribution of incomes.
These demands were accompanied by traditional social claims: the
suppression of abuses in connection with military management, wage
increases, social insurance and efforts to eliminate unemployment.

The workers' hopes were not fulfilled by the Soviet Republic.
Industry was directed by the People's Commissariat for Production,
later by Department III of the National Economic Council. There was
no love lost between the new economic leadership and the industrial
intellectuals who had long possessed a particular 'engineer consciousness' (Péteri 1988: 140–1) and anti-capitalist vision. A production commissar was employed in every plant; he represented 'the' proletariat

and transmitted the orders and requirements of the centralised economic administration. Given that the commissars were not supposed
to interfere in professional matters, the system was in conformity
with the general aim to build a centralised bureaucratic industrial
system. However, the workers' councils, the truly democratic management organs that were created spontaneously and given prominence
during the Károlyi revolution, were seen as a potential threat by the
Revolutionary Governing Council.

The Revolutionary Governing Council acted accordingly. It swiftly
tackled the political and economic problem posed by the workers'
councils. The key political issue from its viewpoint was that the mandate
of the workers' councils interfered with the production commissar's
role. Therefore the workers' councils were discarded as management
organs of enterprises. The role they occupied during the winter months
of 1918–19 was now fulfilled by a political commissar. The new function of the councils was to maintain and strengthen proletarian labour
discipline, as the Governing Council decreed on 26 March 1919. So Kun
succeeded in pushing the workers' councils into a marginal position.

The emerging Jewish technical intelligentsia came to accept the
Communists' state socialist political programme which was easily rec-
oncilable with their own technocratic vision. Many of them joined the
Communist Party. However, Communists and engineers were merely
ships that passed in the night, and their alliance did not prove to be a
strong one during the Soviet Republic. When the institution of commissars was established by the centralised bureaucracy, the engineers'
organisations were incorporated into the National Economic Council
just like the workers' councils had been before into the trade unions.
Friends and foes of the Communists were treated alike. Neither engineers nor workers had a leading position in the Economic Council.

Though the capital city of Budapest was an industrial centre,
Hungary as a whole remained at that time an agrarian country. The
agricultural policy of the Hungarian Soviet Republic proved to be
disastrous. Its leaders did not keep their promise to distribute land to
the agrarian proletariat. This was not only because of a lack of time, but
also because of a lack of will. This strategy of the Communists alienated
the widest social stratum from the cause of the proletarian dictatorship.

On 3 April 1919, the Governing Council decreed the socialisation
of medium-sized and large landed property, specified later as landed
estates over seventy-five acres. The decree, however, prohibited the
redistribution of land to the landless; instead, it prescribed the estab-

lishment of agricultural cooperatives and state farms. This measure affected the richer farmers very negatively, and aroused their suspicion concerning the Hungarian Soviet Republic. Small landowners could still retain possession of their land but certain government decrees served as an eye-opener for them. To complete the marginalisation of the agricultural classes, they were also excluded from the cultural project of the Soviet Republic.

The proletarian dictatorship's cultural policy

The area of education and culture had a central place in the Soviet Republic because here the nominal proletarian rule could be transformed into real possession of power. As Lukács (1987c) wrote, the proletariat could come into possession of those segments of social life from which they were previously excluded.

The educational reform was an odd mixture of ideological elements and the intention to fulfil demands formulated decades ago. The Soviet Republic launched a great offensive against churches and religious sentiment in Hungary (Gratz 1935: 115). To evade the otherwise inevitable conflict between the bourgeois curriculum and the exigencies of the new regime, the educational commissariat decided not to award the baccalaureate in 1919. Waiting for the start of the new academic year, teachers were ordered to participate in a Marxist indoctrination course. Many professors in universities were dismissed and substituted by those who seemed to be more inclined to agree with the ideological training of teachers. The Marx-Engels Workers' University opened in May 1919 with faculties for natural and social sciences. The students, numbering 75 to 120, were recruited from the ranks of the proletariat. The Research Institute of Historical Materialism opened on 7 July 1919 (József 1984).

The plans for educational reform seemed more coherent than they actually were because the Communists and the Social Democrats shared some basic ideas: for example, they unanimously wished to abolish the old class privileges in education. But there was some disagreement on the reasons for doing this: while the Communists wanted to create a 'new human being', the Social Democrats did not share the anthropological optimism of their coalition partner. The Social Democratic cultural political commissar Zsigmond Kunfi highlighted in his speech 'Proletarian culture, proletarian art' on 19 April 1919 the importance of endowing the proletariat with the intellectual weapons necessary for class struggle.

The controversy between Communists and Socialists was much more manifest with regard to cultural issues. Lukács wanted to get rid of the cultural institutions of the old regime (Jászi 1989: 147). On 26 March 1919, he fired a number of professors from the University of Budapest, and in doing so he also settled accounts with those who had played an eminent role in the rejection of his *Habilitation* thesis some years earlier (Congdon 1983: 156 sqq.; 1991: 36 sqq.). On 30 March 1919, he banned the activity of the most renowned literary society in Hungary, the Kisfaludy Society, the nineteenth-century flagship of the national language and culture. Two weeks later, the Hungarian Academy of Sciences had fallen victim to his unrelenting anger.

During their very first meeting on 22 March 1919, the Revolutionary Governing Council established the Press Directory which immediately banned more than 250 newspapers and magazines. People's Commissar Kunfi was dismayed by such a restriction of press freedom and the uniformity of the remaining press organs. He saw clearly that the press was losing its credit because of its servility. He also recognised the problem caused by the inability of the official organs (*The People's Voice* and *Red News*) to carry weight with the agrarian masses. Surely they were not trying very hard, as they did not even inform the farmers about the land decrees. Backed by Jenő Varga, Kunfi urged differentiation and more flexibility concerning press issues. Kun and Lukács, however, remained intransigent. On 14 May 1919, the bourgeois newspapers, reviews and magazines were prohibited, and the People's Commissariat for Public Education prescribed the subject matter of the editorials for the remaining ones. Among the thirty or so surviving newspapers, the most important ones were the official organs of the unified party, the morning paper *The People's Voice* and the evening paper *Red News*. However, the shortage of printing paper democratically decimated both Communist and bourgeois newspapers.

The Communists' concept of culture clashed with that of the Social Democrats; while the former were obsessed with the relation of violence to culture, the latter focused on the conceptual problem of the culture of the masses.

The culture of the masses, according to Lukács's core concept, was not a mass culture. Others, however, perceived more clearly the taste and intellectual level of the proletarian masses which, in their opinion, were more receptive to the products of mass culture. Accordingly, they tried to captivate the proletariat through thematically and ideologically updated popular novels. Curiously, the right-wing Social Democrats advocating 'consumable' literature and Lukács stubbornly champion-ing the case of classic literature fell upon the same scapegoat. Lajos Kassák, together with his collaborators in their review *Today*, proposed a third way to win the masses over: the avant-garde literature which held the promise of a meaningful form language. They supposed this form language would meet expectations by being consumable without being banal or kitschy. Instead of doing their homework, the Social Democrats and Lukács ignored the real theoretical problem and attacked Kassák. The Social Democrats mocked the comic miscon-ceptions of *Today* poetry while Lukács simply could not tolerate the 'unpleasant fellow' (Lukács 1983: 62) and overlooked Kassák's literary achievement.

The relation of the proletarian dictatorship to its culture was best formulated by Zsigmond Kunfi, who pointed out the paradox that violence in the interest of culture's liberation is in itself hostile to culture. Kunfi's report to the General Assembly of the Party on 13 June 1919 did not corroborate the theses about the benign influence of the dictatorship on cultural production. Instead, they were in harmony with Béla Bartók's disappointment with the lamentable conditions of creative work. He maintained that in the field of intellectual life, culture, science, literature and the arts, there is no place for any vio-lence since they can exist only in the atmosphere of freedom. The artists and writers were threatened and paralysed by the regime's violence in political and economic matters. Therefore, Kunfi received with very little enthusiasm and much more scepticism Kun's proposal to turn to violence in resolving the problems of culture (József 1978: II, 257). Kun consequently saw the People's Commissar for Culture as an obstacle to the victory of proletarian culture.

Communists and Social Democrats in Lukács's *History and Class Consciousness*

After the defeat of the revolution, the fight between Communists and Social Democrats continued in emigration, in Béla Kun's polemi-cal writings as well as in Lukács's *History and Class Consciousness*. In his Austrian emigration, Béla Kun composed his pamphlet *From Revolution – to Revolution* which blamed the Social Democrats for the failure of the Soviet Republic. Its weakness – as Lenin remarked – consisted in the complete lack of empirical evidence for the argument. Lukács's *History and Class Consciousness* (1923) and *Lenin* (1924) are much more renowned retrospective accounts of theoretical lessons of the events of 1918–19 in Hungary.

The goal of *History and Class Consciousness* is to justify the revolutionary praxis of orthodox – or Communist – Marxism, as opposed to Social Democratic opportunism, by the methodology of Marxism as a complete view of history. To achieve this goal, Lukács's theory has two main pillars. The first is the distinction between 'real' and 'psychological' class consciousness. The second is the endowment of this 'real' consciousness – or, as regarded historically, this process of consciousness – with a reality better founded than empirical reality. The conclusion of the book links epistemological optimism to ontological hope, prophesying that 'every step in the direction of true knowledge is at the same time a step towards converting that knowledge into practical reality' (Lukács 1971: 339).

Hence, revolutions in their process possess more truth than in their factuality: as Lukács wrote, 'the *developing tendencies of history constitute a higher reality than the empirical "facts"*' (ibid.: 181). The Social Democrats' inability to change their perspective originates in their way of thinking; they give priority to facts and not to processes (ibid.: 196). The Social Democratic stance, according to Lukács, is an amalgam of 'economic fatalism and ethical utopianism' (ibid.: 196). As a consequence, 'the proletariat will be drawn on to the territory of the bourgeoisie and naturally the bourgeoisie will maintain its superiority' (ibid.: 196). Seen from this rigid point of view, Kunfi's 'humanism' in 1919 proves to be nothing but the confirmation of this basically bourgeois attitude.

Lukács, who never tired of criticising Social Democratic opportunism, vented his anger in pure Marxist manner, stating that opportunism is nothing else but a way of acting which derives discouraging consequences not from dialectics but from the actual situation because it '*mistakes the actual, psychological state of consciousness of proletarians for the class consciousness of the proletariat*' (ibid.: 74). Hence, Lukács formulated in *History and Class Consciousness* a Jacobin solution: the separation of the *conscience de tous* from the *conscience générale*. However, the general consciousness of the proletariat is not a mere fiction, as its existence is proven by the recent revolutions and their principal institutions, the revolutionary workers' councils. The latter were eventually corrupted by Social Democracy, but the dominant idea behind them is clear: forming the class consciousness of the proletariat. This consciousness, according to Lukács, is also manifest in the painful self-deprecations following these revolutionary attempts. In this sense, Lukács's book can also be perceived as an outcome of collective soul-searching after the failure of the 1919 Hungarian revolution.

For Lukács, the lesson of the Hungarian Soviet Republic as a historical experiment with concessions made to the Social Democrats was that these concessions had undermined the belief in the legality of the dictatorship among members of society. Another, worse consequence of these concessions was the failure of the economic transformation. As for culture, Lukács regretfully noted that the economic and political class consciousness is generally not accompanied by an adequate cultural class consciousness which often remains nothing but 'the self-criticism of capitalism – carried out here by the proletariat' (ibid.: 79).

Lukács had no doubt at all that the French revolution and the Hungarian Soviet Republic were two elements of a single process: in his eyes, 1919 was historically as important as any of the great historic events from the collapse of the Roman Empire to the Great War itself. In the foreword to his *Lenin*, Lukács characterised Ottó Korvin as the ascetical type of the revolutionaries, a Robespierre or Saint-Just type. Similarly, the appendix written in 1969 described Lenin's non-ascetical personality as a *tertium datur* between Danton and Robespierre.

History and Class Consciousness and *Lenin* complement each other: the subject matter of the former is Marxism as a 'total' philosophy of history while that of the latter is Leninism as a revolutionary theory.

In opposition to the standpoint of a vulgar (Social Democratic) Marxist who regards the defeated revolutions as 'mistakes' and victorious revolutions as temporary achievements, historical materialism is, in Lukács's view, real Marxism that believes in the actuality of proletarian revolution in world history. The 'actuality' of the revolution does not refer to its everyday feasibility but rather to the constant consideration of its historical horizon. In harmony with Rosa Luxemburg, Lukács held that from the point of view of the philosophy of history, no revolution can come 'too early'; its actuality, in this sense, has nothing to do with the fact that from the point of view of assuming and retaining power, it comes necessarily always too early. The problems and questions of the organisation were of secondary importance: that is, the fusion of the two workers' parties in Hungary and the renouncing of the name 'Communist' has no significance with regard to the essence of the revolution.

As for the diminishing social basis of the revolution, in *Lenin* he also blamed the hesitant attitude of the Social Democrats. The characterisation Lukács gave to the bourgeois and proletarian revolutions in general clearly mirrors his experiences in Hungary in 1918–19. According to the 'opportunists' (that is, the Social Democrats) the bourgeois revolutions must be supported by the proletariat if they advocate some of the demands of the fourth estate. As a consequence, the proletariat gives up its class aims. Lukács, however, found a perspicuous Hegelian formulation to link the proletarian revolution to the bourgeois one:

> For the real revolution is the dialectical transformation of the bourgeois revolution into the proletarian revolution . . . [T]he bourgeoisie's recourse to counter-revolution indicates not only its hostility towards the proletariat, but at the same time the renunciation of its own revolutionary traditions. *It abandons the inheritance of its revolutionary past to the proletariat.* From now on the proletariat is the only class capable of taking the bourgeois revolution to its logical conclusion . . . Thus, the proletarian revolution now means at one and the same time the realization and the suppression of the bourgeois revolution. (Lukács 1970: 48–9)

Conclusion

The Hungarian Social Democrats' position was so peculiar in 1918–19 that they could taste, in rapid succession, the politics of opportunism as well as of revolutionary radicalism. Unfortunately, the real outcome of the Hungarian Soviet Republic was that intellectuals ceased to seek social ideals, the working class stopped believing in the feasibility of self-management and collective action, and the agrarian population appealed for help to right-wing populists against the agrarian oligarchy that came back after the exit of the Communists. The political platform that suffered the greatest loss of credibility during the defeated 1918–19 revolutions in Hungary was not Soviet-type Communism or Bolshevik strategy, even less the politics of the old conservative elite. It was Social Democracy. As a partner in both coalition governments, the Social Democratic Party had its share in the responsibility for the failure of both revolutions.

Notes

1. In recent Hungarian scholarship, see Varga 2010: 542 sqq.; Hajdu 2004: 392–3; Varga 1999: 124 sqq.; Erényi et al. 1990: 308.

References

Borsányi, G. (1979) *Kun Béla: Politikai életrajz* (*Béla Kun: A Political Biography*). Budapest: Kossuth.

Congdon, L. (1983) *The Young Lukács*. Chapel Hill, NC and London: The University of North Carolina Press.

Congdon, L. (1991) *Exile and Social Thought. Hungarian Intellectuals in Germany and Austria, 1919–1933*. Princeton, NJ: Princeton University Press.

Erényi, T., J. Kende and L. Varga (1990) *A szociáldemokrácia története Magyarországon, 1868–1919* (*A History of Social Democracy in Hungary, 1868–1919*). Budapest: Politikatörténeti Intézet.

Gábor, S. (1961) *A két munkáspárt egyesülése 1919-ben* (*The Unification of the Workers' Parties in 1919*). Budapest: Kossuth.

Gábor, S. (1974) *Szamuely Tibor*. Budapest: Akadémiai.

Gratz, G. (1935) *A forradalmak kora 1918–1920* (*The Era of Revolutions 1918–1920*). Budapest: Magyar Szemle Társaság.

Hajdu, T. (1958) *Tanácsok Magyarországon 1918–1919-ben* (*Councils in Hungary in 1918–1919*). Budapest: Kossuth.

Hajdu, T. (1988) 'Plans of strategic cooperation between the Russian and Hungarian Red Armies', in P. Pastor (ed.) *War and Society in East Central Europe, Vol. XX, Revolutions and Interventions in Hungary and Its Neighbor States, 1918–1919*. Boulder, CO: Columbia University Press, pp. 367–75.

Hajdu, T. (1989) *Közép-Európa forradalmai 1917–1921* (*Revolutions in Central Europe 1917–1921*). Budapest: Gondolat.

Hajdu, T. (2004) 'Demokrácia és diktatúra válaszútján 1919-ben és 1945 után' ('On the crossroads of democracy and dictatorship in 1919 and after 1945'), in I. Feitl, G. Földes and L. Hubai (eds) *Útkeresések: a magyar szociáldemokrácia tegnap és ma* (*In Search of the Right Path: Hungarian Social Democracy Yesterday and Today*). Budapest: Napvilág, pp. 391–4.

Horváth, Z. (1974) *Magyar századforduló. A második reformnemzedék története (1896–1914)* (*Hungarian Fin-de-siècle. A History of the Second Generation of Reforms (1896–1914)*). Budapest: Gondolat.

Jászi, O. (1989 [1920]) *Magyar kálvária – magyar föltámadás. A két forradalom értelme, jelentősége és tanulságai* (*Hungarian Calvary – Hungarian Resurrection. Meaning, Significance and Lesson of Both Revolutions*). Budapest: Magyar Hírlap Könyvek.

Johancsik, J. (2010) *Magyarország külpolitikája 1918–1999* (*Foreign Policy of Hungary 1918–1999*). Budapest: L'Harmattan – Zsigmond Király Főiskola.

József, F. (ed.) (1978) *Büszke tettek ideje. Válogatás az 1918-as polgári demokratikus forradalom irodalmából* (*Time of Proud Deeds. Selections from the Literature of the Bourgeois Democratic Revolution of 1918*), vols 1–2. Budapest: Akadémiai.

József, F. (1984) *Értelmiség és forradalom. Kultúra, sajtó és irodalom a Magyar Tanácsköztársaságban* (*Intellectuals and Revolution. Culture, Press and Literature in the Hungarian Soviet Republic*). Budapest: Kossuth.

Károlyi, M. (1982) *Hit, illúziók nélkül* (*Faith Without Illusions*) (trans. G. Litván). Budapest: Európa.

Krammer, A. (1983) 'Soviet propaganda among German and Austro-Hungarian prisoners of war in Russia, 1917–1921', in S. R. Williamson and P. Pastor (eds) *Essays*

On World War I: Origins and Prisoners of War. New York: Brooklyn College Press, pp. 239–64.

Kun, B. (1985) 'Lenin', in É. Moharos (ed.) *Válogatott cikkek és beszédek (Selected Articles and Speeches).* Budapest: Kossuth, pp. 92–9.

Lukács, G. (1970) *Lenin. A Study on the Unity of his Thought* (trans. N. Jacobs, from Lukács, G. (1924) *Lenin. Studie über den Zusammenhang seiner Gedanken.* Wien: Verlag der Arbeiterbuchhandlung). London: New Left Books.

Lukács, G. (1971) *History and Class Consciousness. Studies in Marxist Dialectics* (trans. R. Livingstone, from Lukács, G. (1923) *Geschichte und Klassenbewusstsein.* Berlin: Malik Verlag, 1923). London: Merlin.

Lukács, G. (1972) '"Law and order" and violence', in *Tactics and Ethics. Political Essays 1919–1929* (trans. M. McColgan, ed. R. Livingstone). New York, Evanston, San Francisco and London: Harper & Row, pp. 41–7.

Lukács, G. (1983) 'Record of a life: Georg Lukács in conversation about his life', in I. Eörsi (ed.) *Record of a Life: An Autobiographical Sketch* (trans. R. Livingstone). London: Verso, pp. 26–142.

Lukács, G. (1987a) *Forradalomban. Cikkek, tanulmányok 1918–1919 (Revolution. Articles, Essays 1918–1919)* (ed. M. Mesterházi and F. L. Lendvai). Budapest: Magvető.

Lukács, G. (1987b) 'A proletáregység helyreállításának elméleti jelentősége' ('The theoretical significance of the restoration of proletarian unity'), in Lukács, *Forradalomban. Cikkek, tanulmányok 1918–1919*, pp. 96–104.

Lukács, G. (1987c) 'A kultúra tényleges birtokbavétele' ('The real appropriation of culture'), in Lukács, *Forradalomban. Cikkek, tanulmányok 1918–1919*, pp. 111–13.

Lukács, G. and D. Kettler (2012) 'Briefwechsel und Dokumente, Introduction by David Kettler', in F. Benseler and R. Dannemann (eds) *Lukács 2012/2013. Jahrbuch der Internationalen Georg-Lukács-Gesellschaft.* Bielefeld: Aisthesis, pp. 23–64.

Nagy, Z. (1988) 'The Hungarian Soviet Republic and the Paris Peace Conference, 1918–1919', in P. Pastor, *War and Society in East Central Europe, Vol. XX, Revolutions and Interventions in Hungary and Its Neighbor States, 1918–1919.* Boulder, CO: Columbia University Press. pp. 261–75.

Ormos, M. (1990) *From Padua to the Trianon, 1918–1920* (trans. M. Uszkay). Budapest: Akadémiai.

Pastor, P. (1983) Hungarian Prisoners of War in Russia During the Revolution and Civil War. In: Williamson et al. 1983. pp. 149–62.

Pastor, P. (1988a) 'The French military mission in Hungary, 1918–1919', in P. Pastor (ed.) *War and Society in East Central Europe, Vol. XX, Revolutions and Interventions in Hungary and Its Neighbor States, 1918–1919.* Boulder, CO: Columbia University Press, pp. 251–60.

Péteri, G. (1979) *A Magyar Tanácsköztársaság ipaririányítási rendszere (Industrial Management of the Hungarian Soviet Republic).* Budapest: Közgazdasági és Jogi.

Péteri, G. (1988) 'Engineer Utopia: on the position of the technostructure in Hungary's war Communism, 1919', in P. Pastor (ed.) *War and Society in East Central Europe, Vol. XX, Revolutions and Interventions in Hungary and Its Neighbor States, 1918–1919.* Boulder, CO: Columbia University Press, pp. 139–56.

Petrák, K. (1969) *Az első magyar munkáshatalom szociálpolitikája, 1919 (Social Policy of the First Hungarian Workers' Rule, 1919).* Budapest: Táncsics.

Raffay, E. (1987) *Erdély 1918-1919-ben* (*Transylvania in 1918–1919*). Szeged: JATE.

Romsics, I. (1988) 'The social basis of the Communist revolution and of the counterrevolutions in Hungary', in P. Pastor (ed.) *War and Society in East Central Europe, Vol. XX, Revolutions and Interventions in Hungary and Its Neighbor States, 1918–1919.* Boulder, CO: Columbia University Press, pp. 157–67.

Schulz, G. (1972) *Revolutions and Peace Treaties 1917–1920* (trans. M. Jackson). London: Methuen & Co.

Seton-Watson, H. and C. Seton-Watson (1981) *The Making of a New Europe. R. W. Seton-Watson and the last years of Austria-Hungary.* Seattle, WA: University of Washington Press.

Siklós, A. (1988) *Revolution in Hungary and the Dissolution of the Multinational State 1918* (trans. Z. Béres). Budapest: Akadémiai.

Varga, L. (ed.) (1999) *A magyar szociáldemokrácia kézikönyve* (*A Manual of Hungarian Social Democracy*). Budapest: Napvilág.

Varga, L. (2010) *Háború, forradalom, szociáldemokrácia Magyarországon: 1914. július – 1919. március* (*War, Revolution, Social Democracy in Hungary: July 1914 – March 1919*). Budapest: Napvilág.

8

Can Political Participation Become Dangerous for Democracy? Participatory Experiences in Brazil and the Reactions Against Them

Emil A. Sobottka

Brazil: a recent and weak democracy

IN BRAZIL, POLITICAL participation is a recent phenomenon, overcoming a long tradition of apathy among the population with regard to politics. Although a National Health Council was created in 1930 and some national conferences on specific issues, in which citizens participated directly, had been held since 1941, these were local experiences, with sporadic activities and few people involved. In the late 1970s, still under the military dictatorship (1964–85), social movements and some organisations like churches and professional bodies began to demand what they called a 'right to participate' in the control of the state and the decision-making processes of public policy. Although their demand was unsuccessful at that time, popular councils were created in some cities. These experiences of voluntary participation were generally parallel, external and opposed to state agencies. In many segments of society, however, there was a growing desire to have more voice and influence in public affairs, even if the concepts were very different about how this right would be implemented.

A landmark for these aspirations was a national health conference that took place in 1986, soon after the return to democracy. It emphatically recommended the creation of a national health assistance system, with the direct participation of government agents, health care professionals and users of the new system. The implementation of this recommendation was the embryo of a new participation space called the public policy council. The Federal Constitution from 1988 created many different instruments to involve stakeholders directly in the formulation and management of specific policies by foreseeing direct participation in them. It paved the way for claims of power-sharing in many different areas, totalling around thirty articles that encouraged experiments in participatory public management. In addition to these policy councils, conferences continued to be held, and in 2001 mandatory participation in the masterplans of cities, expanding the formal channels of participation, was introduced.

Probably the best known mode of participation is participatory budgeting. It was first implemented in Porto Alegre in 1990 and quickly expanded to involve around 170 cities in Brazil (Ribeiro Torres and Grazia 2003). Although it is often associated with the Workers' Party, participatory budgeting was implemented by local governments from various political currents. In many other countries there have been similar experiences. This mode is usually more informal, and more open to voluntary participation of citizens then the public policy councils. But when it comes to the scope, it is more limited: it is focused specifically on the issue of public budgets (Sobottka et al. 2005).

When analysed with a historical perspective, however, Brazil is still a recent democracy. The record of alternating periods of dictatorship and of regularly elected officials during more than a century of its republican life, as well as of several restrictions like the late inclusion of women in the electoral system, the banning of political parties and the ban on illiterate people taking part in elections lead most analysts to consider only the most recent period, after the end of military dictatorship and the introduction of the 1988 constitution, a democratic one.

Seen from a strictly political-electoral perspective, some previous periods already contained important elements of democratic life. In the long period between the proclamation of the republic in 1889 and the coup that brought Getulio Vargas to power in 1930, elections were fairly regular. During that period oligarchies of São Paulo, driven by the coffee wealth, and Minas Gerais, mainly sustained by the production of milk, alternated in the presidency, leading to what scholars have often called a 'coffee with milk republic'. In the states there were also elections, even if local oligarchies controlled them, with voting rights restricted to men with high incomes.

Ironically, it was during the authoritarian government of Vargas (1930–45) that women acquired the active and passive right to vote; but they had to wait for the end of his administration to be able to effectively exercise this right. Despite limitations such as the prohibition of the Communist Party, in the two decades that followed the Vargas government elections were held regularly and elected officials could carry out their mandates. The country saw large demonstrations of urban workers in favour of improvements in their living conditions and the mobilisation of various segments of the rural population, with different requirements according to their relationship to the land: land reform and the legalisation of the possession of public land and labour rights. The middle class was also mobilised and pushed for deep reforms in various aspects of public life, particularly universal free public education.

This flirtation with democratic life was abruptly interrupted by the military coup of 1964. There followed twenty-one years of dictatorship, initially with intense repression, followed by a long phase of limited moves towards democracy, strictly controlled by those in power. Measures such as the end of censorship, a general amnesty – including the military themselves – the end of imposed bipartisanship and the gradual introduction of elections at subnational levels were accompanied by demonstrations in favour of the end of the dictatorship and the return of democracy.

In 1985, a civilian president took office. He was still elected under the rules implemented by the military regime. Over the next two years there followed a constituent process with intense mobilisations and polarised disputes by two suprapartisan fronts formed ad hoc. One was composed mainly of parliamentarians from left-leaning parties and was supported by a broad spectrum of social movements; it defended, in general terms, a constitution that would prioritise welfare and the expansion of citizens' rights. The other front was formed by conservative and liberal parliamentarians, supported by, among others, traditional regional leaders as well as those involved in agrobusiness and large enterprises, both domestic and foreign. The resulting constitution came into force in September 1988 and reflects in many ways this tension: it greatly enhances citizens' rights and state responsibilities and expands the possibilities of political participation, but it also protects private property, including the latifundia, almost unrestrictedly, and obstructs policies that would affect established privileges.

Since 1989, direct elections for the presidency of the republic have occurred regularly, their outcome has been respected at all levels of government and political parties with very different ideological orientations have alternated in power.

Despite now having lived for a quarter of century under democratic government, Brazil continues to face the need to implement reforms that would make its democracy stronger. One area where necessary reforms are blocked is politics. Political parties and institutions have proved very resistant to renewing the corresponding legislation despite long-established problems: the financing of election campaigns that makes politicians hostages of their sponsors; the proliferation of tiny parties that sometimes act more as an exchange currency than as a representation of social sectors; the need to form majority coalitions to be able to govern, which is done by the distribution of positions and plots on the public budget, among others (Limongi and Figueiredo 1998).

In addition, Brazil still remains a deeply unequal society (Sobottka 2009). In the Human Development Index of the United Nations, Brazil is currently in 73th place, due in particular to the low mean schooling level of 7.2 years. The Gini coefficient for income distribution is currently 0.547 and reflects the fact that 10 per cent of the wealthiest people share 43 per cent of the national income, while 10 per cent of the poorest people have to survive on 1.1 per cent. Such data is a reflection, even today, of past policies such as the deliberate concentration of income by the military regime. The creed at that time was that 'first, the cake must grow, and then it can be distributed'. The leaders of the regime were convinced that in order to make the economy grow faster, wealth should be forwarded to those who would reinvest it. Because social groups with low income would spend additional income on consumer goods rather than savings, it would make more sense to reduce their share. In this manner, costs would be reduced and more resources would be released for investments.

But current policies also contribute to this inequality. One such example is the difference between the amount spent on public-sector employees' retirement schemes and that spent on broader social policy, the *Bolsa Família* programme: for each dollar invested in the *Bolsa Família*, $620 is spent on the pensions of public servants (Sobottka 2012). While 89 per cent of the housing deficit affects people with an income under a threefold minimum wage and only 4.1 per cent affects people with more than a fivefold minimum wage, in recent years only 27 per cent of public investment in social housing has benefited the first group, while 38 per cent has benefited the second.

Some authors, such as Marcelo Neves (2006), have argued that inequality is so deep in Brazil that it is possible to speak about two different levels of citizenship. On the one hand, there are overintegrated people: for them, citizenship is a set of rights and privileges, but they are almost immune to the corresponding duties and sanctions. On the other, there is a kind of infra-citizenship for people who experience the controlling, repressive side of the state and have scant access even to fundamental rights. It is easy to believe in Neves's thesis, given the systematic violation of the constitutional principle of equality among citizens and clear differences in treatment in public policy, access to different retirement systems and networks of corruption. A clear division into 'classes' is, for example, explicit in the fact that the Brazilian Criminal Procedure Code (Decree-Law No. 3689, art. 296) affords, for a number of occupants and former occupants of official public positions, members of the armed forces, ministers and all people with a college degree, the right to special prisons. Thus, there is a social apartheid even among those who have placed themselves outside the law in some regard.

A recent episode involving a judge and a traffic enforcement agent illustrates very well the differences between the rights of citizens in Brazil. In 2011, the traffic officer Luciana Silva Tamburini, during a routine check in Rio de Janeiro, stopped a vehicle that had no licence plate. The driver of the car did not have his mandatory driving licence on him. João Carlos de Souza Correa, the driver, presented himself as a judge and claimed that he should be released to continue his journey. The agent admits that her first reaction was to tell him that he might be a 'judge, but not God'. The driver was insulted, told the traffic officer she was under arrest and processed her because she had offended 'the judicial function he represents for society' (Barcelos 2014). Now, three years later, the judge has still not been punished, but the traffic officer was ordered to pay him compensation for 'moral damages'. This same judge, according to reports in the newspaper that reported this story, had previously been involved in similar serious episodes. According to reports, he approved the appropriation of an entire neighbourhood in the resort town of Buzios by a friend of his and, in 2007, forced a cruise ship captain to open the duty-free shop outside business hours so he could shop there.

The complete reversal of roles between the defender of the rules and the transgressor in this episode reveals a dark facet of democracy in Brazil: the radical inequality of different 'classes' of citizens before the law. So Brazilian democracy is not only recent; it is still weak and needs to be improved.

Participation, civil society, democracy . . . same words, different meanings

To say that in daily politics or in the social sciences words have an ambiguous sense is a truism; it is like raining on wet ground. My purpose here is not to explore this issue. But to better understand the political disputes regarding participation, it is necessary to devote some attention to the meanings of certain key words in the debate that are in dispute (Dagnino and Tatagiba 2007; Dagnino 2004). The purpose of the brief description that follows here is not to define concepts, but to emphasise significant differences that are hidden behind similar words.

The oppression of the military regime contributed to unify many sectors that often designated themselves as civil society in the fight for democracy. In successive local and regional elections the support for the official party clearly diminished, and the only legal opposition party continued to broaden its base. In those circumstances the concept of civil society began to be used more often to designate this wide range of opponents of the regime. It may have been appropriate to present themselves as *the* civil society while confronting a military regime, but in fact this designation simply referred to an ad hoc group that was opposed to the government and was looking for a transition to democracy. This was its only common goal.

In the 1980s, social movements had an ambiguous discourse about a possibly leading role of civil society in political life and as a producer of public services. For some sectors of the broadly leftist movement, collaboration would be strategic while others still understood themselves as a counterpoint to the state.

Due to the creation of several institutional spaces of participation in the 1988 Constitution, during the presidency of Fernando Henrique Cardoso (1995–2002), of liberal orientation, and especially during the government of Lula da Silva (2003–10), who emerged from the struggles of social movements, the relationship between society and the state has deeply changed. Social movements, NGOs and militant intellectuals, who, suspicious of or even opposed to the state, for many years fought for democratisation, were now assuming responsibilities within the state. This position weakened many movements and organisations, depriving them of their leaders, who had now a dual affiliation and had to take into account the government policy.

To better accommodate this situation, the concept of civil society was revived, not as a theoretical concept that allowed close analysis, but rather as a strategic way to justify the new situation. It was no longer possible to emphasise the duality between society and state; now it was convenient to point out the homogeneity of the social field. The movements had not seen themselves as part of the state, but as society's active presence in the institutional spaces and as controllers (Vera and

Lavalle 2012). The responsibility now was to assure the long-desired rights and policies. The belief was that organised civil society was now participating in the full realisation of democracy (Nogueira 2004). Civil society had acquired a sense that could be seen as close to that which Cohen and Arato (1992) had defended when reinterpreting Habermas. For these authors, new rights, values, institutions and identities lead to a new role of the organised substrate of society. It gives greater value to the public sphere, to acting in a horizon marked by communicative rationality and a collaborative spirit in relationship to the state and the market.

Focusing on the question of participation in the perspective of the relationship between various social movements, leftist political parties and militant groups, Teixeira (2013) highlights a significant change in meaning since the 1970s, when participation became a claim. According to the author, in the period before 1990, when the first directly elected president after redemocratisation took office and the Workers' Party won the first elections in major cities, participation was mainly conceived as *emancipation*. The left-wing political utopias were strongly influenced by liberation theology, basic ecclesiastic communities and social movements of popular education and of resistance to the dictatorial regime. Even if there was no unified conception, the state was strongly associated with the dominant interests, and the struggle against the regime was conceived simultaneously as a struggle for redistribution of wealth, equality, social justice; in a word, for socialism. In many cities, popular councils were organised with the purpose of building an independent parallel power that would critically observe public policies without having any formal relation with the state agencies (cf. Sader 1995).

When the Workers' Party was confronted with the responsibility of governing several major cities, the meaning of participation that came to prevail was that of *deliberation*. The main idea was no longer to split up the power of the state acting from outside, but to change the state from the inside, to dispute the power of the state from within and through political institutions and their contradictions. The local government was willing to share power with social movements and with classical non-governmental organisations that supported the party. In return, members of these movements and organisations would help to legitimate the government's policies. In some cases they took up posts in local and regional governments, without abandoning the original organisations, thereby assuming a dual affiliation. Thus, the expectation was that the bourgeois state could be gradually appropriated by popular participation. Priorities of the state, which until then clearly favoured the ruling minorities, should now be reversed: higher public investment and more attention of the state should be directed to city neighbourhoods with few public services and benefit the poorest members of the population. This was the context that gave rise to public consultations on the budget in cities such as Porto Alegre, which would be gradually consolidated in the form of participatory budgeting (Sobottka et al., 2005).

Finally, at the beginning of the first decade of this century a third semantic element for participation was gaining acceptance: participation as *listening*, as a form of collaboration in the public sphere without deliberative binding for the officials. In the country, the neoliberal orientation in public policies predominated in those years, nongovernmental organisations were burdened with the fulfilment of the tasks delegated by governments and social movements had lost much of their force. On the other hand, initiatives such as the World Social Forum and many local and regional experiences of participation improved the mood of those who were committed to a more substantive democracy, with broad social rights of citizenship.

Many militants may not have realised at that moment that the political party that had done most to boost the experiences of participation was now desperate to take the responsibility to govern at the national level, although for this it had to give up many of its precepts hitherto regarded as very important (cf. Sobottka 2006). Thus, they paid no attention, for example, to the fact that in 2002 the government programme of the Workers' Party, almost 100 pages long, made only one vague reference to participation. It seems that the dimensions that participation was taking and the amplitude of the expectations generated were scaring its main sponsor; this fear led to the effort to reduce its significance from co-governance and co-deliberation to simple consultation or listening.

For the vast majority of militants from social movements of that time, electoral democracy was not a value in itself; it was an intermediate objective to reach autonomy (Moisés 2010). To a certain extent, the liberal idea of the rule of the individual by himself as an expression of freedom, equality with all others and self-determination (cf. Kant 1891) guided the aspirations of these sectors of the population. But their reserves towards formal democracy, which was seen as only in service of the dominant bourgeoisie, led them to qualify this democracy more specifically. On the one hand it was qualified as substantive democracy, signalling that it should include the materiality of a wide range of rights, far beyond the regular elections and some liberties. On the other hand, the autonomy was seen as something collective, a popular sovereignty. But the people, and therefore the people's power, did not refer to the entire population of the country, nor even to all of its citizens; it referred to what Dussel (1988) designated as all the organised poor, opposed to the imperial centre of exploitation, the national bourgeoisie and the state bureaucracy.

This view contrasts sharply with the conception which sees it as only the task of citizens to elect the ruler in institutional arrangements in which political parties – and increasingly also individuals – compete for the authorisation to rule. Even if we accept the very restrictive Schumpeterian conception of democracy as a market for preferences (Schumpeter 2010), the difficulty pointed out in formal representative democracy is that voters cast their votes without having real choices; as Bobbio (1984) says, elites are applying themselves and imposing themselves as those who will decide on behalf of the community. The citizens have no chance to participate directly and continuously in governmental concrete decisions, forming a scenario like the one described by Przeworski (2010): a new monster in which we have democracy without effective citizenship.

During the last two decades, when participation became more and more a reality, this class-oriented conception gradually gave way to a more agonistic understanding of democracy. Policy-making became more and more a matter of entering into dispute with opponents in various areas, including the state organisations, the definition of the common objectives and, in particular, public resources.

Diverse experiences of participation

As mentioned previously, in addition to a weak tradition of direct involvement of citizens in daily public affairs, Brazil has few long-distance channels of participation (Avritzer 2008; Dagnino and Tatagiba 2007; Abers et al. 2014). From the 1980s onwards, several others were created. This section will briefly present the most important among them.

National conferences

The first two national conferences planned were in health and education, through Law 378/37, which came into force in January 1937, together with the creation of the Ministry of Education and Health. Its goal was to 'facilitate to the federal government the knowledge of activities related to education and health' and to 'guide it in implementing the local services'. Originally only national and regional administrative authorities of the respective areas were foreseen as participants. Only the health conference flourished; the national conference on education was held for the first time only seventy-three years later, in 2010. For the health conference, participation was gradually extended, involving citizens alongside government representatives (Cavalcanti et al. 2012; Rolim et al. 2013).

National conferences currently consist of a long process that begins with meetings in municipalities, open to the public. After a second stage at state level, a major national meeting is held. At each stage suggestions are collected and discussed and are taken to the next stage by the ad hoc elected representatives. The suggestions that go through all the stages are then presented to the authority, and may or may not be accepted (Faria et al. 2012). According to Pogrebinschi (2014), until 2002, forty-two national conferences were held, half of them under the government of Fernando Henrique Cardoso. Under the Workers' Party, another forty conferences were held, and so both the number and the themes of national conferences have been expanded considerably.

Public policy councils

Although the first public policy council for health care was created more than eighty years ago, in its current form this type of participation was developed by social movements and leftist organisations during the military regime in order to dispute power and to control the resources and activities of public agencies. Historical examples such as the Paris Commune and the workers' councils of Turin and Yugoslavia served as inspiration for some of its creators (Gohn 2006). There was no clear place for them in the legal system, so some were informal bodies for popular struggle, while others were created by local governments as a way of welcoming movements and their demands in public policy.

The new constitution provided fifteen such policy councils; they received a place in the legal system as collegiate structures, as mediators of the relationship between society and the state (Sipioni and Silva 2013). Some are only advisory bodies, while others have deliberative power. Common to all of them is the role of social control of government activities. Their composition should be 'paritarian', although interpretations vary as to how this parity should specifically be defined. In two areas, health and social assistance, the councils have considerable power. They also, however, have strong influence in areas such as education, child welfare and culture. Today thirty such councils exist at federal level. There are more than 540 distributed among the 26 states and more than 27,000 of them in the 5,570 municipalities (IBGE 2009; 2014), involving at least 5 million participants. To a large extent this high number has to do with the fact that if the federal government wishes to transfer resources to specific areas then there must be a functioning policy council in the respective state or municipality.

In the debate on the councils there are several controversial issues (Silva and Tatagiba 2012; Ronconi et al. 2011). First, there is the question of whether they should be advisory or deliberative, and thus whether the manager of the corresponding policy must implement the decisions or can take them purely as guidance. Another polemic issue is parity: does it refer to the poles of government and society or are there other groups to be considered, such as professionals? Even a numerical parity is often unbalanced by the difference in resources, levels of information and educational background between government representatives and professionals when compared with independent citizens or social movements. The multiplicity of councils, the scarcity of resources and the competition between them for funds are also serious problems. These issues will certainly not find a definitive solution in the near future.

Participatory budgeting

In Brazil the public budget is composed of a set of laws originating from the executive branch of government. Early in the mandate a multiannual plan for the entire term is prepared and sent to parliament. Also annually, it prepares a budget directive law, which contains the outline of the next annual budget. Once approved by parliament, the executive establishes the budget project itself, which is then submitted to parliament. There is very little scope for parliament to make changes to the budget on its own initiative.

Usually the budgeting project is based on demands of the various government agencies, respecting legal provisions and policy priorities. As almost all Brazilian governments are coalitions, the priorities of the related parties that govern specific areas (ministries, departments and so on) are mirrored in the budget claims. Most politically articulated sectors use these procedures to ensure their priorities are included, often through lobbying and political patronage (Sobottka 2004).

Participatory budgeting is a direct consultation with the people of the respective jurisdiction during the preparation of the budget draft. There is no legal provision for this consultation and its legitimacy and mobilising force relies heavily on the commitment of the authorities to effectively respect the suggested priorities, including them in the budget draft and turning them into public policy (Sintomer et al. 2012). The wide acceptance of the participatory budget is mainly due to this informal commitment of the rulers – and some electoral defeats of the Workers' Party, especially in cities, are related to the recent breaking of this commitment.

This way of consulting the population has two major implications that can be highlighted here. First, people who previously had little or no interest in politics and the management of the city or state realised how they could become protagonists in the definition of their collective destiny. They began to think more in political terms, to pay attention and to understand how priorities in public investment and expenditure are created and that this has implications for their own lives. It was a stunning political lesson. Another implication, at least for democracy, is that the historical practice of patronage and prioritisation of invest-ments just for the benefit of those most able to sponsor their own lobby sectors suffered a major setback. Through participatory budgeting, citi-zens in general – and many citizens previously marginalised in political affairs – caused a significant change in spending priorities and invest-ments, making public policy more beneficial to the entire population. Teixeira (2013) considers it the most innovative democratic experience of the last few decades in Brazil, but there is no provision for it in the legal framework. So participatory budgeting occurs only where the government decides to implement it.

On the other hand, the implementation of the participatory budget has also had negative effects, which in Porto Alegre are very clear. Direct participation can become individualised and withdraw move-ments and organisations from the public policy planning. A blatant symbolic appropriation of participatory budgeting as a mark of one political party also occurred there. It was presented like an exclusive creation of this party and not as the result of a long struggle of a broad front. It is not possible to state categorically that the current demobilisation was exclusively the result of these two factors, but it does smack of a somewhat Pyrrhic victory.

In a brief comparison between these three modes of participation it is clear that the policy councils are less open to popular participation. They emphasise the organised sectors of society, while participatory budgeting and national conferences are extensive consultations; they mobilise society and local governments on a particular topic. At the same time, conferences are very delimited processes, with a beginning, middle and end, and the results of budgeting processes depend on the bureaucratic transformation that fit citizens' suggestions into budget items (Lüchmann 2007; 2008). National conferences and participatory budgeting are generally open forms of free entry and participation of citizens; they have their own way of generating representation, usually referring to the number of participants in local meetings. The policy councils, on the other hand, are institutionalised spaces of power-sharing. They have their legal provision established by law and are usually constituted by the head of local, regional or national government, with mixed representation of civil society and government.

During Lula da Silva's two terms, the political debate on participation was centred mainly on questions about the quality and balance of participation through multiple channels and on how effective this participation is in influencing public policy (Abers et al. 2014). More recently, a new question has occupied the centre of concerns, both of the government and of the movements and organisations that wanted to make better use of democratic spaces. The large number of subjects, the frequency of activities and the great geographic dispersion have increased the need to think in terms of a system or a more rationalised coordination of the channels and modes of participation. This has led to a new and controversial initiative of the national government: the creation of a national policy on social participation.

The national policy on social participation: too much democracy?

After a long discussion within the federal government, and pressures from many bodies linked to social movements, in May 2014 the presidency created the national policy on social participation 'with the objective of strengthening and promoting the mechanisms and channels for democratic dialogue and joint action between the federal government and civil society'. The corresponding decree prescribed that 'in the formulation, implementation, monitoring and evaluation of programs and policies and the improvement of public management' it would be required to allow social participation 'as a civil right and expression of the autonomy' of citizens and civil society (Decree No. 8243, 23 May, 2014, art. 1 and 3). In addition to improving 'representative, participatory and direct democracy' and to 'enhance the relationship of the federal government with civil society', the new policy has as its goal to consolidate 'the social participation as a method of government' articulating the different channels of existing participation.

The nine participation mechanisms mentioned include the policy councils and the national conferences. Although the decree did not mention the participatory budget, this policy should also 'develop mechanisms for social participation in the stages of planning and budget cycle'. The decree does not create new channels, and explicitly excludes the possibility of increasing costs and creating new paid positions. It considers the participation 'a provision of relevant public service', so it is forbidden to pay for it. Despite being a federal decree, it also encourages participation at regional and local levels of government. As a decree of the executive branch, this policy does not require approval by the national congress. Its jurisdiction is limited to setting operating rules or running institutional arrangements already provided by law.

There are certainly many reasons why the government has decided to implement this policy, a major one of which was the promise of June 2013 made by President Dilma to the protesters to implement democratising reforms. Those movements were relatively diffuse, and even today there are doubts among scholars about how best to interpret them (Gohn 2014). But in the heat of confrontation, the federal government promised reforms, including the convening of a new constituent commission. Participation policy is an attenuated and delayed response to these movements.

The consent of citizens is generally considered in political theory as crucial for the legitimacy of democratic institutions. But it is also well known that these political institutions – and specially those who govern through them – have to deal with dissent. In democratic states of law, especially through the perspective of constitutional patriotism, a broader conformity with the constitution and the general institutional arrangements can be assumed. But the more the focus turns to details, the more dissent becomes visible. The attempt to create a general policy on social participation is such a 'detail' where dissent emerged.

The reactions contrary to this policy erupted like little volcanoes everywhere. The reactions of the mainstream media, on social networks and in everyday conversation were passionate. In parliament leaders were mobilised and promised to 'take down' this policy, even if it did not depend on their approval. Here I cannot reproduce fairly the whole range of events that took place. I will restrict myself to reactions from the three largest newspapers and from one of the most widely read columnists, Reinaldo Azevedo, who probably represents primarily the right wing of public opinion.

One of the recurring criticisms is that the policy of participation would create mechanisms to diminish the importance or even to abolish the function of parliament. Jungblut (2014), in *O Globo*, mentions the former president of the Supreme Court saying that 'there is a risk of weakening the legislative power as representation of society and as discussion forum of the major topics. This ends up leaving the legislative on the corner.' The issue of representation as exclusive and sufficient or as just one important method of democracy is always a controversial issue. Proponents of participation policy not only argue that the Brazilian constitution explicitly provides for the representative as well as for the direct form as modes of democracy; they also ask why other spaces with very great power to influence people's lives are inaccessible to parliament and citizens in general, like the central bank and the regulatory agencies. Against these dubious islands of technocracy the critics of participation are silent (Pogrebinschi 2014).

The same *O Globo* article, as well as articles in many other publications, also expresses the fear that some measures provided could paralyse government agencies, for example, the requirement that all measures should undergo some type of consultation with civil society and that the result of all policies should be evaluated by a participatory forum and reported to civil society.

In an editorial entitled 'Regime change by decree', the biggest conservative newspaper *O Estado de São Paulo* (29 May 2014)[1] accused the government of trying to 'change the constitutional order' with 'a set of illegal atrocities' – even though it may sound like an answer to the diffuse concerns of the streets from 2013. The editor was convinced that 'the subliminal message in this whole story is that the legislative is dispensable'. For the editor, 'social participation in a representative democracy occurs through elected representatives in Congress, legitimately elected'. Because she disagrees with the Brazilian representative system, according to the article, the president would seek to establish 'another source of power: direct participation'. Because people who do not participate in social movements – this is what the text reduces civil society to – would now be discriminated against, the new policy is harming the basic principle of democratic equality of 'one person, one vote'.

While these criticisms remain in the field of a debate about conceptions of democracy, a wider and noisier range of demonstrations assumed the contours of an ideological struggle. This can clearly be seen in the language and the associations used by protesters, as cited below.

In an article entitled 'Dilma decided to extinguish democracy by decree. It is a coup!' Reinaldo Azevedo warns his readers: 'Right now your rights are being stolen, undermined, diminished'. Unless you are a member of any of those social movements 'who opted for cruelty as a form of political expression' in order to 'install in the country the PT dictatorship by decree'. For Azevedo, the decree establishing the national policy on social participation is 'an outrageously unconstitutional text, which affronts the basis of equality before the law, undermines the principle of democratic representation and creates a category of aristocrats with powers above those of other citizens: the members of "social movements"'. He sees direct participation as 'a guardianship system'. As a result of the involvement of civil society as defined in the decree, the text has 'created . . . two categories of Brazilians: those who have the right to participate in public life and those who don't'.

The question whether the text is constitutional or not may have different interpretations. As previously stated, the Brazilian Constitution has many references to direct participation, so the policy is not unconstitutional, as suggested, only because it encourages direct participation. Also curious is the statement that rights were being taken from the citizens. The fact that the decree explicitly encourages the participation of citizens, social movements and civil society is seen as a cleavage, as discrimination and exclusion of the citizens represented by the supposed readers.

In another text, the author becomes more explicitly ideological, and evokes various characters associated commonly in the current Brazilian press as extremely authoritarian and undemocratic. He says, therefore, that the government 'is trying to consolidate a Soviet-style commissioner', and that '[w]ith this decree, the PT wants to finally make the elections obsolete. The text [of the decree] follows the best standard of the Venezuelan dictatorship and protodictatorships of Bolivia, Ecuador and Nicaragua'. Social participation policy would be a 'Bolivarian burst of Dilma Rousseff, who submits, albeit obliquely, the decisions of the federal government to popular councils'. The author says it is a 'Communo-Fascist decree' that 'delivers part of the federal administration to "social movements", a process of etatization of civil society'. The decree would be 'the boldness of authoritarianism tempered by stupidity'.

Two other statements are also interesting enough to be mentioned here. Olivier da Silva Ferreira, a professor in two major Brazilian universities, says that 'borrowing a phrase from Hayek, we can say that Decree 8243 opens wide the doors to the road to serfdom'.[2] This term already indicates where the author gets his bearings from in the discussion: from neoliberalism and the cold war context.

The journalist Helio Viana Dias reproduces a series of arguments already contained in other texts, brought together under the title 'Presidential Decree No. 8243 or the Sovietisation of Brazil by PT'.[3] Some interesting associations however have to be highlighted. The text was published by an organisation called 'Agency good press', that claims to be 'guided by the ideal evoked by the cross of our logo'. That this cross wants to display a pre-conciliar Catholicism is reflected in its design, and has been reinforced by the laudatory comments made by the organisation Tradition, Family and Property (Tradição, Familia e Propriedade), a well-known supporter of conservative Roman Catholicism, which in the 1930s enthusiastically backed the attempt to implement Fascism in Brazil. Originally the article featured some pictures of various Brazilian social movements, especially the Landless Labourers' Movement (Movimento dos Trabalhadores Sem Terra, MST), with many banners and posters. In November 2014, the same text was reprinted with illustrations borrowed from Soviet propaganda at the time of Lenin.

So in the struggle around the politics of participation the arguments of opponents have come from different conceptions of democracy as well as from an overt, almost insane, insistence on associating this policy with images of authoritarianism and dictatorship. The latter are expressions of a strong fear that the deep structures of inequality and social discrimination in the country could be significantly modified. And fear, as we know, is a very irrational counsellor.

Looking back over the last decades, one can see that democracy has undoubtedly been deepened in Brazil. New forms of relationship between citizens and the state have been attempted – with success – at the various levels of government and in the treatment of a variety of public issues. But severe difficulties in the political representative system still subsist. Substantial changes in social inequality remain in the realm of utopia. It is not surprising, then, that social movements, supported by non-governmental organisations and by militant intellectuals, are still active and are demanding more public policies, more justice and more democracy. Many members of such movements took to the streets in June 2013 when the ostentatious treatment and the amount of public spending in favour of an international agency of sport were disclosed. It contrasted too much with the daily suffering of the people and the scarcity of resources invested in regular public policies. The novelty, however, in Brazil's political scene today is that those who favour less democracy and who fear direct political participation are also demonstrating in the streets, through the media and in many other public spaces. Fear and hope are face to face in today's Brazilian democracy.

Notes

1. http://opiniao.estadao.com.br/noticias/geral,mudanca-de-regime-por-decreto-imp-,1173
2. www.viomundo.com.br/politica/o-debate-sobre-o-decreto-8-243-caminho-da-servidao-ou-medo-do-povo.html
3. www.abim.inf.br/o-decreto-presidencial-no-8-243-ou-a-sovietizacao-do-brasil-pelo-pt

References

Abers, R., L. Serafim and L. Tatagiba (2014) 'Repertórios de interação estado-socie-dade em um estado heterogêneo: a experiência na Era Lula', *Dados* 57, 325–57.

Avritzer, L. (2008) 'Instituições participativas e desenho institucional: algumas con-siderações sobre a variação da participação no Brasil democrático', *Opinião Pública* 14(1), 43–64.

Barcelos, A. (2014) 'TJ Mantém condenação de fiscal que barrou juiz', *Folha de São Paulo* (13 November), C5.

Bobbio, N. (1984) *The Future of Democracy*. Minneapolis, MN: University of Minnesota Press.

Cavalcanti, M. de L., M. H. Cabral and L. R. Antunes (2012) 'Participação em saúde: uma sistematização de artigos publicados em periódicos brasileiros 1988/2005', *Ciência e Saúde Coletiva* 17(7), 1813–23.

Cohen, J. and A. Arato (1992) *Civil Society and Political Theory*. Cambridge, MA: MIT Press.

Dagnino, E. (2004) 'Sociedad civil, participação e cidadania: de que estamos falando?', in D. Mato (ed.) *Políticas de ciudadanía y sociedad civil en tiempos de globalización*. Caracas: Faces, pp. 95–110.

Dagnino, E. and L. Tatagiba (eds) (2007) *Democracia, sociedade civil e participação*. Chapecó: Argos.

Dussel, E. (1988) *Filosofia ética de la liberación*, vol. 3. Buenos Aires: La Aurora.

Faria, C. F., V. P. Silva and I. L. Lins (2012) 'Conferências de políticas públicas: um sistema integrado de participação e deliberação?', *Revista Brasileira de Ciência Política* 7, 249–84.

Gohn, M. da G. (2006) 'Conselhos gestores e gestão pública', *Ciências Sociais Unisinos* 41(1), 5–11.

Gohn, M. da G. (2014) *As manifestações de junho de 2013 e os movimentos sociais*. Petrópolis: Vozes.

IBGE (2009) *Pesquisa de informações básicas municipais: perfil dos municípios brasileiros 2009*. Rio de Janeiro: IBGE, available at www.ibge.gov.br/home/estatistica/economia

IBGE (2014) *Pesquisa de informações básicas municipais: perfil dos municípios brasileiros 2013*. Rio de Janeiro: IBGE, available at ftp.ibge.gov.br/Perfil_Municipios/2013/munic2013.pdf

Jungblut, C. (2014) 'Decreto do governo federal cria conselhos populares sobre grandes temas', *O Globo* (29 May).

Kant, I. (1891) *Kant's Principles of Politics*. Edinburgh: T. & T. Clarck.

Limongi, F. and A. Figueiredo (1998) 'Bases institucionais do presidencialismo de coalizão', *Lua Nova* 44, 81–215.

Lüchmnann, L. H. H. (2007) 'A representação no interior das experiências de participação', *Lua Nova* 70, 139–70.

Lüchmann, L. H. H. (2008) 'Participação e representação nos conselhos gestores e no orçamento participativo', *Caderno CRH* 21(52), 87–97.

Moisés, J. Á. (2010) 'Os significados da democracia segundo os brasileiros', *Opinião Pública* 16(2), 269–309.

Neves, M. (2006) *Entre Têmis e Leviatã: uma relação difícil*. São Paulo: Martins Fontes.

Nogueira, M. A. (2004) *Um estado para a sociedade civil*. São Paulo: Cortez.

Pogrebinschi, T. (2014) 'Novo decreto: não há representação sem participação', *Carta Capital* (16 June).

Przeworski, A. (2010) *Democracy and the Limits of Self-Government*. Cambridge: Cambridge University Press.

Ribeiro Torres, A. C. and G. de Grazia (eds) (2003) *Experiências de orçamento participativo no Brasil: período de 1997 a 2000*. Petrópolis: Vozes.

Rolim, L. B., R. Cruz and K. J. Jesus (2013) 'Participação popular e o controle social como diretriz do SUS: uma revisão narrativa', *Saúde em Debate* 37(96), 139–47.

Ronconi, L., E. Debetir and C. de C. Mattia (2011) 'Gestores de políticas públicas: potenciais espaços para a coprodução dos serviços públicos', *Contabilidade, Gestão e Governança* 14(3), 46–50.

Sader, E. (1995) *Quando novos personagens entram em cena*. São Paulo: Paz e Terra.

Schumpeter, J. A. (2010) *Capitalism, Socialism and Democracy*. London: Routledge.

Silva, C. and L. Tatagiba (2012) 'Os conselhos gestores sob o crivo da política: balanços e perspectivas', *Serviço Social & Sociedade* 109, 68–92.

Sintomer, Y., C. Herzberg and A. Röcke (2012) 'Modelos transnacionais de participação cidadã: o caso do orçamento participativo', *Sociologias* 14(30), 70–116.

Sipioni, M. E. and M. A. Silva (2013) 'Reflexões e interpretações sobre a participação e a representação em conselhos gestores de políticas públicas', *Revista de Sociologia e Política* 21(46), 147–58.

Sobottka, E. A. (2004) 'Orçamento participativo: conciliando direitos sociais de cidadania e legitimidade de governo', *Civitas* 4(1), 95–109.

Sobottka, E. A. (2006) 'The responsibility of governing and the changes in the Workers' Party of Brazil', *International Journal of Action Research* 2(1), 54–77.

Sobottka, E. A. (2009) 'Armut und Armutsfolgen in Ländern der peripheren Moderne', in L. Wagner and R. Lutz (eds) *Internationale Perspektiven Sozialer Arbeit: Dimensionen, Themen, Organisationen* (2nd edn). Wiesbaden: VS Verlag, pp. 137–53.

Sobottka, E. A. (2012) 'Políticas sociales en el gobierno Lula da Silva: la persistencia de la desigualdad', in F. de J. Pérez Cruz (ed.) *América Latina en tiempos de Bicentenario*. Habana: Editorial Ciencias Sociales, pp. 196–220.

Sobottka, E. A, G. Saavedra and V. da L. Rosa (2005) 'Legitimação e democratização no orçamento público estadual', in D. R. Streck, E. Eggert and E. A. Sobottka (eds) *Dizer a sua palavra: educação cidadã, pesquisa participante e orçamento público*. Pelotas: Seiva, pp. 55–84.

Teixeira, A. C. C. (2013) 'Para além do voto: uma narrativa sobre a democracia participativa no Brasil – 1975–2010', PhD thesis, University of Campinas (Unicamp), São Paulo.

Vera, E. I. and A. G. Lavalle (2012) 'Arquitetura da participação e controles democráticos no Brasil e no México', *Novos Estudos* 92, 105–21.

9

Hidden Revolutionary Processes in 1990s India?

Jiří Krejčík

Introduction

THE YEAR 2014 was an especially turbulent one on the Indian political scene. From the Aam Aadmi Party's forty-nine-day rule in the
Delhi State Assembly to the landslide victory of the Bharatiya Janata
Party (BJP) in the general elections in May, routines of the political
system have been broken and its patterns overturned. By capturing the
public imagination and creating a new voting bloc, the Hindu nationalist BJP managed to become the first political party since 1984 to secure a
clear parliamentary majority with 31 per cent of the vote and 282 out of
543 seats in the Lok Sabha. Ideologically, the success of the BJP is even
more important: it marks the end of Nehruvian secularism and socialism as the founding principles of an independent democratic India,
and their replacement with the more exclusive concepts of cultural
nationalism and economic neoliberalism.

The aim of this chapter is not to analyse the immediate causes of
the BJP's electoral success, but rather to explore the conditions which
enabled Narendra Modi to grab power in such a triumphant way. Can
we interpret his achievement not only as a victory of a well-elaborated
political campaign but also as a result of deeper transformational
processes in Indian society which have taken place during the last
two decades? In this chapter we shall explore the mutually reinforcing processes of economic neoliberalisation, cultural nationalism and
low-caste assertion which occurred in Indian politics in the early 1990s.
Although none of them has brought a true revolutionary change in
organisational structures, could we consider them as a trigger of the
rearrangement of Indian polity and society, crowned by the recent electoral successes of Narendra Modi's BJP? Is it even possible to perceive
these processes through the lens of the Gramscian concept of passive

revolution, declared inapplicable by Sudipta Kaviraj in his classic essay almost thirty years ago?

Multiple revolutions

Since independence, India has gone through several transformational processes which have altered the social order in truly revolutionary ways and have been described in various terms in Indian historiography. *Green revolution* is the first of these, referring to the changes that took place in Indian agriculture during the 1960s. These years saw an unprecedented increase in food production through the introduction of high-yielding varieties of seeds and the application of modern agricultural techniques such as chemical fertilisers and irrigation. In combination with land reforms, this led to a restructuring of power relations in rural areas and an assertion of the lower peasant castes and classes. The structural impact of the *white revolution*, on the other hand, was comparably less powerful. Still, the dairy development programme of the 1970s–1990s which linked consumers with milk producers' cooperatives throughout the country, made India the largest milk producer in the world. *Total revolution*, on the other hand, was a wholly political project. Initiated in Bihar in 1974, it began as a student movement against misrule and corruption but soon found its leader in the veteran Gandhian socialist Jayaprakash Narayan. Although the movement adopted revolutionary rhetoric, it remained ideologically vague, without creating a vision of an alternative system. In the end, Jayaprakash's total revolution led only to political chaos and even attracted extremist organisations, especially the Rashtriya Swayamsevak Sangh of the Hindu nationalist volunteers. The last of the series of transformational processes with a revolutionary designation is the *silent revolution*. Coined by the French political scientist Christophe Jaffrelot, the term was used to describe the assertion of the formerly silent majority of lower castes in northern India in the 1980s and 1990s (Jaffrelot 2003); this can be perceived as a sequel to the former green revolution.

Passive revolution: failure in India?

For our purposes, however, the notion of passive revolution will be the most important one. The term originated with Vincenzo Cuoco, the Neapolitan conservative thinker of the early stages of the *Risorgimento*.

Cuoco used it to describe the lack of mass participation in the Neapolitan revolution of 1799, advocating such 'passive revolutions' as preferable to violent ones involving the popular masses, such as the French model (Gramsci 1971). However, the concept became famous only after World War II thanks to the works of Italian Marxist scholar Antonio Gramsci. In his famous *Prison Notebooks*, the expression is used with slightly different connotations: passive revolution means a social transformation which takes place beneath the surface of society, in situations where the progressive class cannot advance openly but the class struggle continues despite the surface stability of the regime.[1]

In the Gramscian concept of passive revolution, the political and institutional structures are transformed slowly and gradually without strong social processes. Thus, we can consider the passive revolution as a form of 'revolution from above', conducted by the state and emergent bourgeois class without a national-popular base. In Gramsci's sense, passive revolution serves as a condition of modern state formation. At the same time, however, there is a second process linked to the passive revolution (Morton 2010). In line with Gramsci's theories of the cultural hegemony in society, the process has more to do with the reaction of the dominant classes to the rebellions of the popular masses and some parts of the popular demands (Gramsci 2007). Thus, it is not a revolutionary social group that would 'lead' other groups, but the dominant class or even the state that 'leads' the group that should have been the 'leading' one in order to establish the institutions of capitalism or to expand capitalism as a mode of production (Gramsci 1971).

If transposed to India,[2] Mahatma Gandhi could be considered the first naive theorist of the passive revolution with religious overtones. After independence, the second attempt to conduct a passive revolution was made by the political elites led by Prime Minister Jawaharlal Nehru. The main features of this concept were the autonomy of the state from the bourgeoisie and the landed elites, secured by its control of heavy industry, mining, transport, communications and other strategic sectors, and its protectionist regime discouraging the entry of foreign capital. In reality, power had to be shared between the dominant classes because none of them had the ability to exercise hegemony on its own. In fact, the ruling bloc in India contained three distinct social groups: bourgeoisie, landed elites (which were replaced by the class of capitalist farmers after the green revolution) and bureaucratic managerial elite. Within Nehruvian socialism and developmental planning, all the interests of these groups were finely balanced for a long time.

In the course of time, however, conflicts emerged between the bourgeois, bureaucratic and urban segment on the one hand and regional bourgeois interests and agrarian propertied classes on the other. Indira Gandhi solved the electoral crisis by populist moves, playing regionalisms and communities against each other and hoping to benefit from their double insecurity. In the long run, however, the decline of political ideology undermined the basis of Indian nationalism and ideas of democratic secularism. According to the classic essay by Sudipta Kaviraj (1988), this emerging structural crisis marks the failure of the passive revolution in India. Kaviraj's essay is indeed a brilliant analysis of the Indian political system of the first forty years after independence. Written in 1987 and published in 1988, however, it could not foresee what would come in the following years. The crisis mentioned and analysed by Kaviraj escalated into three abrupt systemic changes which occurred at the beginning of the last decade of the twentieth century and transformed the framework of class dominance in such a way that the conditions for a new passive revolution could be created.

Mandal affair: caste enters politics

The first of these seminal changes occurred in 1989, when the Janata Dal government under the prime ministership of V. P. Singh announced that it would reserve 27 per cent of government jobs and places in public universities for so-called Other Backward Classes (OBCs).[3] This step, following the recommendations of the Mandal Commission from 1979, can be perceived not only as an attempt to economically and socially empower the backward, but also as a part of a political game, as several of the communities included in the OBC list constituted important vote banks for Janata Dal, and the reservation could consolidate their caste coalition. Thus, the decision to implement the Mandal Commission recommendations can be also understood as a response of Janata Dal to Congress identity politics in the 1980s and as a political attempt to split the vote bank of the formerly dominant Congress Party.

The implementation of the Mandal Commission's recommendations led to violent resistance in many parts of India, including a series of self-immolations by high-caste students. But more importantly, it led to the rehabilitation of caste as a primary identity in independent India and to the 'Mandalisation' of Indian politics, with caste as an important cleavage.

Caste not only continues to be a significant feature of Indian society, but is also becoming an important pattern of group mobilisation on the political scene, as all Indian political parties, including Communists, start to mobilise the electorate on a caste basis. The 'master cleavage' (Yadav 1996) between social groups may differ across the states, and the continuing regionalisation of Indian politics has led to situations where one social group or caste may vote for different parties in different states.

It would be a huge oversimplification, however, to consider caste politics as something very new in the Indian political discourse. In fact, caste as a ready-made identity has been present in Indian politics since independence (Kothari 1970). Its assertion through the 'silent revolution' is linked to the peasant movement of the 1960s, leading to land reforms and rural development which benefited the upper backward castes, such as Yadavs, Kurmis and Koeris, and led to their conflict with upper-caste landlords. It was only after the 1989 measures, however, that the economically strong lower castes could finally take advantage of their position, even on the level of politics, and transform their economic capital into a social one. The process of the secularisation of caste, consisting of its de-ritualisation and politicisation, gradually led to the emergence of a new middle class, associated with ownership of certain economic assets instead of the traditional caste hierarchy (see Sheth 1999).

Babri Masjid: conservative forces strike back

The reaction of the upper and intermediate sections of Indian society followed almost immediately, represented politically by the Bharatiya Janata Party as the champion of the prevalently urban upper castes and classes linked to Brahmin orthodoxy and to the Hindutva ideology.[4] Backed by the affiliated Hindu nationalist organisations such as Rashtriya Swayamsevak Sangh (RSS) and Vishva Hindu Parishad (VHP), the BJP started to consolidate its electorate on a religious basis, claiming to support the construction of the Ram temple instead of Babri Masjid in Ayodhya. As the key initiative of the *Ramjanmabhoomi* campaign, the *rath yatra* (chariot march) was launched in autumn 1990 in Somnath by the BJP. It was to be undertaken across nine states and would culminate at Ayodhya on 30 October 1990, the proposed day for the construction of the new Ram temple by the VHP.

Both of these processes, sometimes referred to as the Mandal-

Mandir combination, symbolically intersected on 23 October 1990. On that day, Lal Krishna Advani, leader of the BJP and conductor of the *rath yatra*, was arrested in Bihar by then chief minister Lalu Prasad Yadav during his political campaign. Advani's detention on his tour can be considered a symbolic act, as a leader of a party representing predominantly upper castes and invoking communal sentiments was stopped by a champion of lower castes, himself an OBC. The incident not only caused the fall of V. P. Singh's government, dependent on the support of BJP; put in a broader context, it also revealed the assertions of the rural lower castes on the one hand, and the urban upper and intermediate castes on the other.

Although the *rath yatra* was stopped before reaching its destination, the VHP activists continued to agitate for the construction of the temple for more than two years. As a result of this campaign, the Babri mosque was demolished on 6 December 1992 by violent Hindu mobs organised chiefly by the VHP and RSS volunteers. The operation lasted about six hours, but both the central and state government witnessed the action helplessly. The story goes that the Prime Minister, Narasimha Rao, was just taking a nap and nobody would want to disturb him. In reality, the Congress party apparently wanted to make use of the demolition to discredit the BJP and to dismantle the political power of its opponent (see Van der Veer 1996: 254).

Obviously, the assertion of religious communities did not happen all of a sudden. Analogously to the reinforcement of caste identities, it was a response to a long-lasting conflict, further boosted by Congress populism in the 1980s. Departing from its original secular ideals, Congress started not only to appease separate religious communities by ad hoc concessions, but even to play the regional and communal sentiments against one another, seeking to gain votes as a single party capable of achieving stability after temporary chaos (see Manor 1997: 119). These tactics can be seen best in Congress's approach to the Shah Bano case, which resulted in the implementation of The Muslim Women (Protection on Rights of Divorce) Act in 1986,[5] or in opening the disputed Babri Masjid in Ayodhya for Hindus in the same year.

The dynamics of the political assertion of the broader Hindu community was similar to that of the rise of the bloc of backward castes: while the latter was a result of the enrichment and empowerment of a section of the traditional farming Shudra castes, the BJP constituted a party of the growing urban elite. The confrontation of interest between the upper and intermediate castes on the one hand and the lower castes on the other one had also a substantive impact on the growing caste violence at the beginning of the 1990s. In the long run, it led to the rise of caste-based and regional parties and overall fragmentation of the Indian party system.

Failure of revolutionary politics

While the middle classes managed to grasp their opportunity and articulate their demands through revitalised or newly emerged political parties, the impact of left-wing politics on contemporary Indian political discourse remained fairly limited. Notwithstanding the fact that the classical Marxist discourse considers caste-focused analysis as a deviation from class analysis, leaderships of the well-established Communist parties have mainly come from the upper Brahmin caste with its standard hereditary privileges. Together with the notion of a unitary Indian state and reluctance to engage in identity politics, these conditions led to their virtual support of the status quo and in the end to ineffective politics. In the states of Kerala and West Bengal, where Communist parties constituted state power for many years, they did not even manage to dismantle the economic power of capitalist enterprise. Instead, they continued the system of market economy with state subsidies for the major Indian and foreign companies, which eventually led to the antagonism of the workers and peasants and a miserable defeat of the Communist parties in the West Bengal assembly elections in 2011.

On the other hand, the Maoist groups which emerged after the split of the original Communist Party of India in the 1960s remained underground throughout the years. Denouncing parliamentary politics and engaging in armed struggle, the so-called Naxalite movement has spread into less developed areas of rural southern and eastern India, such as Jharkhand, Chhattisgarh, Odisha and Andhra Pradesh and evolved into several fairly organised formations with their own distinct political programmes. Unlike in Nepal, where the Maoists have formulated a much wider understanding of their people's democratic revolution and after signing a peace accord with the Nepalese government even managed to win regular parliamentary election, the Naxalites' support basis still remains restricted to the poor rural areas and their ideological formulation is still not adequately developed on the issue of class-caste-gender relationship (see Mohanty 2006).

Economic liberalisation: Hindutva unleashed

Both the abovementioned trends and their intertwining with political issues were further reinforced by the third important transformative process which took place at the beginning of the 1990s. In 1991, the Congress government started selling public enterprises in order to reduce the fiscal deficit. In the following years, the state opened the formerly controlled sectors to private capital, adhering to the neoliberal mantra of the four Ds: deflate, devalue, denationalise and deregulate. The dismantling of the licence regime and greater entry of foreign capital has led not only to a rapid economic growth through the last two decades, but also to a change in the very composition of the capitalist class. The former dominance of a few 'monopoly' houses protected by the licences was replaced by many more competitors and much greater mobility.

This economic transition, however, often goes along with emphasis on 'Hindu' cultural and religious identity and growing communal tensions. Quite surprisingly, the BJP soon emerged as the main champion of this combination of neoliberal approach to economics with social conservatism. After securing power in the centre in 1998–9, it took up the liberalising policies initiated by the Congress. Some of the states, such as Gujarat where the BJP has been permanently in power since 1998, have been accentuated as an example of cultural Hindu nationalism intertwined with economical neoliberalism.

This alliance, in which BJP as the Hindu nationalist party fully supports economic liberalisation, may seem paradoxical, as its party ideology is associated with Deendayal Upadhyaya's concept of 'integral humanism',[6] largely drawing on Gandhian thought.[7] However, as Radhika Desai points out, the Hindu nationalism works in the same way as the other cultural nationalisms: it is structured around the culture of the economically dominant classes of the society – in this case the 'Hindu' bourgeoisie and formerly privileged priest and trader castes which felt deprived by reservations and economic restrictions imposed by the Indian state. This reduction allows formulating all problems as threats to the 'nation' from more or less demonised minorities (see Desai 1999).

Rise of a new dominant class?

As noted earlier, there is often a tendency to overlook the fact that the ethno-religious conflict might have deeper historical and economic roots in Indian society. Among scholars, the organisational skills of Hindutva are often overrated and support for the BJP attributed almost exclusively to the mobilisational activity of the related Sangh Parivar organisations. In this instrumentalist perspective, conflict is seen as a result of an 'elite conspiracy' using religion to promote factionalism for electoral and economic gains (see Basu 1996). The rise of Hindutva, however, cannot be seen in isolation. Along with the decline of Congress and the rise of the regional parties, it is only one of the three political consequences of the gradual shift towards market-driven economy and the fragmentation of Indian polity on the caste/ community basis.

The political system, however, is only an illustration of the broader structure and system of society as a whole. Analysing the two decades after the turbulent changes which took place at the beginning of the 1990s, we can note two distinctive trends. First, there is a shift in the balance of relative power between the corporate capitalist class and the landed elites, leading to the ascendancy of the former. This dominance, however, was not achieved through the mechanism of electoral mobilisation (which used to be the source of the political power of the landed elites before the silent revolution), but through competition on the newly opened field of a liberalised market. In addition, the relation between the state and the dominant classes has been redefined. The autonomy of the state and its interventionist activities have significantly weakened, as there is a strong ideological tendency among the urban middle classes to view the state apparatus as ridden with corruption, inefficiency and populism. On the other hand, there is a much greater social acceptance of the professionalism and commitment to growth and efficiency of the corporate capitalist sector. The urban middle class, once playing a crucial role in creating and running the autonomous developmental state of the passive revolution, appears now to have come under the moral-political sway of the bourgeoisie (Chatterjee 2008).

In the past two decades, the Indian middle class has gradually expanded and nowadays constitutes around one-quarter of the Indian population.[8] This demographic shift is significant also in electoral politics, as the middle-class voters are more likely to support a free market without state regulations and subsidies, irrespective of their caste. Both of these mutually reinforcing processes broaden the power base of the contemporary capitalists and make Indian society more susceptible to the new round of the passive revolution. In this process, Hindutva is to serve as a ready-made ideology not only to unify predominantly Hindu propertied upper-caste formations, but also to spread to the expanding middle class.

The direct reach of corporate capitalism, however, is still limited only to the domain of *civil society*. In the Indian condition, civil society is restricted almost solely to the urban middle classes and represents the domain of capitalist hegemony. But apart from this, there is a much broader domain of *political society* which includes large sections of the rural population and the urban poor. These people have the formal status of citizens and can exercise their franchise as an instrument of political struggle, but they do not have the same access to the organs of the state as the middle classes do. They make their claims on government, and in turn are governed, not within the framework of constitutional rights and laws, but rather through temporary arrangements arrived at through direct political negotiations. On the other hand, this unorganised subaltern domain of political society is not under the moral and political leadership of the capitalist class (see Chatterjee 2004).

With the continuing rapid growth of the Indian economy, the hegemonic hold of corporate capital over the domain of civil society is likely to continue, with the BJP as its political agent. Moreover, as the middle classes are still expected to grow in numbers in the following years, the significance of civil society in India will also steadily grow. This will inevitably cause new tensions originating from on the one side the accumulation of capital by the swelling middle classes and on the other the small primary producers such as peasants and artisans who are losing their means of production and are likely to be marginalised in the neoliberal order.

Catching the 'Modi wave'

To analyse the unprecedented success of Narendra Modi's BJP in the 2014 Lok Sabha elections, we must first avoid the temptation to interpret the landslide victory as a result of the first-past-the-post electoral system or the personal magic of one charismatic leader. Instead, we should rather ask whether Modi was not simply able to tap into the moods of society and articulate the wishes of a sizeable portion of the electorate. After all, the BJP managed to build an unprecedented coalition of social groups: in addition to its traditional base of the upper-caste social conservatives and economically better-off OBCs, it received considerable support from the scheduled tribes (STs) and scheduled castes (SCs). In total, the BJP received more votes from STs and SCs than the Congress, which has never happened before.[9]

Obviously, there has been a clear rightward shift of the ideological centre of gravity in Indian politics. Apart from the neoliberal approach to the role of state in the economy, the arrival of Narendra Modi popularised the public expression of religiosity as a legitimate political action and made the ethnic and religious nationalisms more acceptable. This process was further reinforced by the abject performance of the Congress-led United Progressive Alliance (UPA) government during its term. Massive corruption at the highest levels and inability to deliver on its promises undermined the trust in the state. The feeling that the state could not actually serve the public had a particularly great impact on the traditional Congress vote bank of the marginalised sections of society. Many amongst the poor, who traditionally support the Congress, simply perceived Modi as a better administrator. The anti-corruption emphasis resounded so loudly across society that it became an integral part of the distinctive class culture among the urban middle classes and manifested its strength during the Anna Hazare movement in 2011.

However, as we look back to pre-election times, the major cleavages of the 2014 election emerged not only around the themes of corruption, development and good governance. Just as important was the conflict between civil and political society, projected as a struggle between the BJP and the Aam Aadmi Party (AAP), winner of the recent Delhi legislative assembly elections.[10] In this perception, the BJP was considered as a party of privileged middle classes, using modernist rhetoric of development and occasional references to Hindu mythology to attract support from both social conservatives and the economic right. On the other hand, the AAP was perceived as a representative of the underprivileged lower strata of the society, evoking more traditionalist grassroots solutions as Gandhian self-rule or the total revolution of Jayprakash Narayan.

As the elections showed, it was in fact the AAP that engaged in 'elite conspiracy': the party and its programme were almost entirely orchestrated by intellectuals who gradually lost their social basis and were not to capture the broader public imagination. The AAP projected itself as the sole heir of the Anna Hazare movement but, in reality, Anna's supporters were recruited mainly from the privileged middle class. The famous sit-in public demonstrations of 2011 were even often co-organised by the RSS cadres. Referring to the heritage of the anti-corruption movement of the 1970s, Arvind Kejriwal and other AAP leaders repeated the mistakes of Jayaprakash Narayan, as they did not challenge the system as such and provided only a techno-cratic solution to the problem of corruption (which itself, after all, can be read as a middle-class concern; see Teltumbde 2014). On the other hand, Hindutva successfully made the step from privileged elites to the masses, using the notion of development to bridge both the material and ideological divides in the Indian society and presenting Narendra Modi as the main architect of Gujarat economic growth.[11]

Being sworn in as Prime Minister on 26 May 2014, only a day before the fiftieth anniversary of Jawaharlal Nehru's death, Narendra Modi symbolically ended the Nehruvian era in terms of public imagina-tion. By transforming the ideas of the first Prime Minister in his own creative way, Modi has sought to replace the Nehruvian world with his own alternative vision and gradually force out the ideals of social-ism and secularism. This approach can be perfectly illustrated by the omnipresent notion of development: while the Nehruvian concept of planning refers to the central government and has undoubtedly restrictive associations, Modi's development sounds more open, spon-taneous and liberal. Development is presented as an inclusive process available to everyone irrespective of ethnicity, caste or religion. In other words, Modi promises the members of *political* society that they will be included in *civil* society through the vehicles of develop-ment and better governance. Along with development, there is Modi's strong bias against Delhi (considered as a white, colonial and English-speaking city) which goes hand in hand with his obsessive promotion of the alternative cult of Sardar Patel instead of the Nehruvian one (see Vishvanathan 2014). All these efforts aim at presenting Modi as a spokesman of the new dominant section of the society: the rapidly growing urban middle classes outside the capital, which have ascended to the higher levels of Indian society during the last two decades.

Conclusion

For Sudipta Kaviraj, the passive revolution did not succeed in India because the ruling Indian National Congress, ideologically drawing on Nehruvian socialism, was not able to resolve the emerging challenges of regionalism and communalism. Failing to provide political stability, it began to adopt undemocratic and pre-capitalist responses on vital issues. Its collapse, however, prepared the ground for a new form of passive revolution. The new capitalist class, unleashed by the neoliberal economic reforms, has acquired a moral and political hegemony over civil society, consisting principally of the urban middle classes. Its dominance within the state structure derives from the virtual consensus among all major political parties about the priorities of rapid economic growth led by private investment, both domestic and foreign.

In this chapter, we have sketched three important systemic transformations which took place at the beginning of the 1990s and created the necessary pre-requisites for such passive revolution: the Mandal affair, leading to the assertion of the rural lower castes; the Babri Masjid case, symbolising the rise of the urban upper castes; and the liberalisation of the economy, which allowed both of these sections of society to merge in the new Indian middle class. Although they unquestionably affected all spheres of Indian society in the following years, the abrupt incursions of caste, class and community into the political sphere did not generate an immediate, truly revolutionary process. All of them naturally overlapped with political struggles, but in terms of electoral outcomes, they have been producing only a continuous fragmentation of the party system and remained latent on the central level for more than two decades. The arrival of Narendra Modi, however, indicates a momentous change in the distribution of power between the dominant social groups in India and a possible start of the new form of passive revolution.

Yet, a final question remains: if the capitalist class emerging in the globalising Indian landscape is labelled as the conveyor of the newly ignited Gramscian passive revolution, how can we dub the game-changing procedures of the last two decades which prepared the conditions for the fresh revolutionary process to come? Can we speak of a *hidden revolution*?

Notes

1. In fact, Gramsci is not very precise on this point and thus allows multiple interpretations. See Morton (2007).
2. In the 1980s, a group of scholars inspired by Gramsci's work emerged in South Asia. Contrary to traditional historiography, the Subaltern Studies Group, led by Ranajit Guha, explored the political role of the lower classes and socially marginalised groups – rather than that of the social and economic elites – in the history of South Asia.
3. For various approaches to identify the OBCs, see Galanter (1978).
4. The concept of Hindutva was first used in 1923 by Vinayak Damodar Savarkar, describing Hinduism as an ethnic, cultural and political identity. Borrowing the European Romantic concept of the nation, Savarkar extends the concept of 'Hindu' beyond religion to a term of cultural nationalism. See Savarkar (1923).
5. For more detailed account of the Shah Bano case, see Mody (1987).
6. Deendayal Upadhyaya (1916–68) served as a long-time General Secretary of the Bharatiya Jana Sangh, the forerunner of the present day Bharatiya Janata Party. In 1965, his 'Integral Humanism' programme was adopted as the official doctrine of the party. Appropriating some significant elements of the Gandhian discourse, such as insistence upon religious and moral values in politics and aspiration to develop an indigenous economic model preserving Hindu values, the concept of integral humanism was used to downplay the original aggressive Hindu communal overtone of the Jana Sangh ideology.
7. There were several tensions within Hindutva over its approach to *swadeshi* (national self-reliance) versus globalisation: even after 1991 RSS protested against foreign and multinational products, while at the same time there were fears in the BJP that the Congress would now win over the traditional Sangh Parivar constituency, consisting of small traders and industrialists. As a compromise, the economic policy of the BJP had to be reformulated in a more *swadeshi*-oriented way. This renewed statement enabled the BJP to criticise the Congress for opening the Indian economy to the West on the one hand, and promoting the idea of capitalist growth and free market within India on the other. For more details, see Hansen (1998).
8. For methods of identifying the middle class, see Sridharan (2004); and for a more detailed account Fernandes (2006).
9. For more analysis, see Chhibber and Verma (2014).
10. AAP rule in Delhi lasted for only forty-nine days, with Chief Minister Arvind Kejriwal resigning after a lack of support for the anti-corruption Jan Lokpal Bill. However, in the following assembly elections in February 2015, the AAP managed to win an unprecedented sixty-seven seats out of seventy, proving that its appeal both towards urban poor and middle class remains strong.
11. Some analysts, however, argue that Gujarat was economically ahead of the rest of India as early as the 1990s, well before the arrival of Narendra Modi whose leadership has not significantly contributed to Gujarat's growth rate in the 2000s. See, for example, Ghatak and Roy (2014); Kalaiyarasan (2014).

References

Basu, A. (1996) 'Mass movement or elite conspiracy?', in D. Ludden (ed.) *Contesting the Nation: Religion, Community and the Politics of Democracy*. Philadelphia, PA: University of Pennsylvania Press, pp. 55–80.

Chatterjee, P. (2004) *The Politics of the Governed: Reflections on Political Society in Most of the World*. New York: Columbia University Press.

Chatterjee, P. (2008) 'Democracy and economic transformation in India', *Economic and Political Weekly* 43(16), 53–62.

Chhibber, P. and R. Verma (2014) 'The BJP's 2014 "Modi Wave": an ideological consolidation of the right', *Economic and Political Weekly* 46(39), 50–6.

Desai, R. (1999) 'Culturalism and contemporary right: Indian bourgeoisie and political Hindutva', *Economic and Political Weekly* 34(1), 695–712.

Fernandes, L. (2006) *India's New Middle Class: Democratic Politics in an Era of Economic Reform*. Minneapolis, MN: University of Minnesota Press.

Galanter, M. (1978) 'Who are the other backward classes? An introduction to a constitutional puzzle', *Economic and Political Weekly* 13(43–4), 1812–28.

Ghatak, M. and S. Roy (2014) 'Did Gujarat's growth rate accelerate under Modi?', *Economic and Political Weekly* 46(15), 12–15.

Gramsci, A. (1971) *Selections from the Prison Notebooks of Antonio Gramsci* (ed. Q. Hoare and G. N. Smith). London: Lawrence and Wishart.

Gramsci, A. (2007) *Prison Notebooks*, vol. 3 (ed. and trans. J. A. Buttigieg). New York: Columbia University.

Hansen, T. B. (1998) 'The ethics of Hindutva and the spirit of capitalism', in C. Jaffrelot and T. B. Hansen (eds) *The BJP and the Compulsion of Politics in India*. New Delhi: Oxford University Press, pp. 291–314.

Jaffrelot, C. (2003) *India's Silent Revolution. The Rise of the Low Castes in North Indian Politics*. Delhi: Permanent Black.

Kalaiyarasan, A. (2014) 'A comparison of developmental outcomes in Gujarat and Tamil Nadu', *Economic and Political Weekly* 46(15), 55–63.

Kaviraj, S. (1988) 'A critique of the passive revolution', *Economic and Political Weekly* 23(45–7), 2429–44.

Kothari, R. (ed.) (1970) *Caste in Indian Politics*. London: Sangam.

Manor, J. (1997) 'Parties and the party system', in P. Chatterjee (ed.) *State and Politics in India*. Delhi: Oxford University Press, p. 119.

Mody, N. B. (1987) 'The press in India: the Shah Bano judgment and its aftermath', *Asian Survey* 27(8), 935–53.

Mohanty, M. (2006) 'Challenges of revolutionary violence. The Naxalite movement in perspective', *Economic and Political Weekly* 41(29), 3163–8.

Morton, A. D. (2007) *Unravelling Gramsci: Hegemony and Passive Revolution in the Global Political Economy*. London: Pluto Books.

Morton, A. D. (2010) 'The continuum of passive revolution', *Capital & Class* 34(3), 315–42.

Savarkar, V. D. (1923) *Hindutva: Who is a Hindu?* Delhi: Bharati Sahitya Sadan.

Sheth, D. L. (1999) 'Secularisation of caste and making of new middle class', *Economic and Political Weekly* 34(34–5), 2502–10.

Sridharan, E. (2004) 'The growth and sectoral composition of India's middle class: its impact on the politics of economic liberalisation', *India Review* 3(4), 405–28.

Vishvanathan, S. (2014) 'Narendra Modi's symbolic war', *Economic and Political Weekly* 46(22), 10–13.

Yadav, Y. (1996) 'Reconfiguration in Indian politics: state assembly elections 1993–1995', *Economic and Political Weekly* 31(2–3), 95–104.

10

Matching Reforms of Political and Economic Systems of China

Wei Xiaoping

Problems of economic and political transition

CHINA'S SOCIALIST ECONOMIC reform began in 1978. Its history can be divided into three stages. The first lasted from 1978 to 1992, and was mainly characterised by the introduction of a system of contract responsibility system, as well as the use of monetary incentives. The second can be dated from 1992 to 2001; its chief characteristic was the introduction of a market system, regulating the productive activity of enterprises through market information. The third stage began in 2001, and is still in progress; its defining feature was the joining of the World Trade Organisation (WTO) and a more general linking up with the trends of globalisation. The logic of China's socialist economic reform necessitated the move from the first to the second stage, that is the replacement of hierarchic central planning by central planning combined with the market. At the same time the principle of allocation has been changed from allocation according to contribution to a combination of this rule with allocation on the basis of inputs to production (including capital). In connection with these two changes, the problem of social security has become more acute.

The transformation of productive ownership

The problem of public ownership was already apparent at the first stage of the reform, and as soon as the new system of contract responsibility was set up, the problem of property rights arose both in rural and urban areas. After the beginning of the second stage, that is from 1992 onwards, China's economic development was faster than in the first stage due to the activation of markets; however, the market system caused serious difficulties for public property (that is, the state-owned and collective-owned enterprises); simple monetary incentives, which could serve as lubricants for the first stage of reform, did not work, or even thwarted their original purpose in the second stage. Monetary incentive motivation, combined with contract responsibility, is limited by unclear property rights.

In rural areas, where property rights to land belong to collectives, family contract responsibility has – in some contexts and in different areas – been slowly replaced by sub-contract procedures and concentrated in the hands of a few families. This is one way for peasants to deal with collective property rights and the limits they impose on contract. Another way is that ongoing urbanisation has claimed land on the outskirts of cities and enabled peasants to demand compensation. At the same time, labour migration from the countryside to cities, temporary or permanent, has continued. Many migrants become semi-peasants, working in the city, and this has in many ways changed the relationship between the labour force and its working conditions. In some rural areas, new forms of collective organisation have developed; in order to improve the productive conditions and to enlarge the scale of production beyond the family limit, peasants have joined forces. But this is not the dominant trend.

The urban population has expanded in two ways: through migration into old but still growing cities, and through local urbanisation. In the first case, the moving of whole families tends to take a long time; in the meantime, there are many problems with family life, the education of children, medical care, pensions and so on. These migrants are in a weak position, not only economically but also politically.

The urbanising trends, in both abovementioned versions, change the old relationship between peasants and the land, either terminated by compensation through money and a job or interrupted through subletting. In a very few cases, families leaving their farmland become employers, but most remain workers, migrant or re-settled, and there is consequently a sharp contrast between rich and poor.

In urban areas, non-public enterprise has developed normally in three ways: foreign capital investment in state-owned as well as in private enterprises, often through joint ventures; the emergence of domestic private enterprises, both urban and rural; and through the transfer of state property into private hands, either on the stock market or through direct privatisation.

The previously stable relationship between workers and the means of production has now been replaced by labour contracts, and workers have thus become employees rather than members of a collective, in public as well as private enterprises.

The question for the enterprises is this: who are the masters/owners of state property now? The appointment of state property supervisors, supposed to guarantee increasing value of state property, can be seen as the government's answer to this question. In any case, there are no serious conflicts between employers and employees because there are no employers in the real sense represented by private enterprises.

More recently, since state enterprises entered the stock market, their own workers can hold shares in their stock; in this way they again become, in a sense, masters in their own house. This is a new relationship between workers and the means of production. While the situation in private enterprises is different, and conflicts of interest between employers and employees exist, workers are normally at a disadvantage when conflicts break out. Therefore labour courts and labour laws have been developed to deal with new conflicts between employers and employees. Compared to trade unions, they have a more formal political function. Trade unions can play a role in the defence of workers' interests when there are conflicts. But in the present situation, especially in private business, the leader of the trade union is generally also the leader of the party organisation, as well as a major shareholder of the business.

The transformation of the principle of distribution

Before the economic reform, the predominance of public ownership was – theoretically – a guarantee of the socialist principle of allocation according to contribution (reward allocation), but in practice this principle was replaced by an excessive egalitarianism, that is, no matter what and how much you did, you got almost the same reward.

After the economic reform, the existence and development of non-public ownership was bound to change the traditional socialist allocation principle, from the form of allocation according to contribution to the form of allocation according to contribution combined with allocation according to the productive element. In his report at the 16th Communist Party National Conference in 2002, Jiang Zhemin said:

> To set up the principle of allocation according to the contribution of productive element which includes labour, capital, technique and management, is to complete the principle of allocation according

to contribution as the main allocation principle, while combining it with different principle of allocation.[1]

Whether we can put labour and capital on the same level as elements of production is another, more theoretical question; what Jiang Zhemin said in 2002 expresses the party's practical policy towards non-public ownership.

Market competition, motivation through monetary incentives and the distributive regulation of natural resources ensured economic efficiency during a certain period, but what about the long term? In this chapter I will not discuss the possibility of economic or financial crisis; what I will concentrate on instead is the problem of the relationship between the economic and the political system in the process of socialist transition.

In fact, the change of socialist distributive principles has increased differences in income; moreover, the higher income differences can be transformed into capital and produce profit, which in turn will further increase the same disparity. Generally speaking, there are two main factors that result in these differences in income: one is the law of winners and losers on the market, even in the conditions of a socialist market system, and the other is the change of socialist allocation principles to meet the new reality of multiple ownerships. After China joined the WTO, its market system was more directly affected by the demands of world standards, and state-owned property would have to face the challenge of world competition. Even state banks have to face the competition of private banks.

In this kind of situation, social classes (officially called social layers) are unavoidably produced through legal processes; this highlights the problems of security which had been more latent under the regime of public ownership.

New social security policies replace traditional relationships

Along with the transformation of public ownership into multiple ownership, with public ownership still a dominant sector, and the transformation of allocation according to contribution into a system that combines contribution and investment, in the city, workers have been transformed from members (in theory, masters) of collectives into a labour force exposed to the market. The traditional stable relations between workers and publicly owned enterprises, including housing, medical treatment, pensions and so on, have been terminated. A new social security system has to take care of these as well as of problems arising in connection with employment.

In the countryside, the separation of peasants from their farmland has continued, partly due to the abovementioned urbanising trends, partly also to the development of productive force in the countryside: more machines are used there, and the redundant labour force has to leave the land. Here, too, a new social security system is being introduced to cope with the situation.

The principle of political reform should be different from that of economic reform

Multiple ownership, together with the change of allocation principles, has led to growing income differences and the formation of different interest groups, otherwise known as different social layers, all of which unavoidably challenge the model of the political system that corresponded to comprehensive property ownership, its unitary principle of distributive and its vision of a united society. How could the political system be reformed to match the reformed economic system? The reform of political system is much more difficult than the reform of the economic system. On the one hand, it is hard to construct a political system to match the reformed economic system with its multiple ownership, market competition and different social layers; on the other hand, how could a single party represent the interests of all those groups, and keep a balance between them? Both these problems are now regarded as parts of a process of political democratisation concerning society as a whole and unfolding from below as well as from above. The primary idea of political reform is to deal with a functional problem: enhancing efficiency.

After the beginning of the historical transition, our traditional political system could not match the efficiency demands of the reformed market economic system, and this was bound to cause delays. On top of these functional problems, there is a more fundamental and less well understood problem that has to do with the essence of the party. What has been done until now is mainly related to the first problem.

If we say that the course of China's economic reform can be divided into different stages, the same applies to China's political reform, but in a different way. The first stage dealt mainly with functional problems, the second stage – yet to begin in earnest – will have to deal with the essential one. Before the reform, the economic system of China's socialism was one of public ownership, including both state and collective property; its political system was the dictatorship of the proletariat, but now it is called the dictatorship of people's democracy, led by the Communist Party of China.

The state system consists of three parts: the members of the People's Delegate Committee (in Western terms, a representative assembly); the State Council (in Western terms, the government); and the People's Court and People's Procuratorate. The members of the People's Delegate Committee are legislators, supposedly elected by the whole people and representing its interests. The State Council is the highest administrative department; the People's Court and People's Procuratorate are responsible to the People's Delegate Committee. Highly centralised public ownership was well matched by highly centralised planning, controlled by the central authorities (that is, the combination of the Party and the government).

In the traditional political system, there was no clear distinction between the Party and the government, and the highly centralised political power arranged everything from top to bottom, such as the quantity and price of production, the salaries of government officials and workers, housing allocation, education and so on. This kind of political system could not deal with the reformed economic system: the quantity and price of production are now regulated by the market; workers' incomes depend on economic results; and housing is put into the market and increasingly privatised.

In order to match the demands of market economy, two changes are being implemented. One way is to separate the functions of the party from those of the government; the other is to limit the power of the government, and to shift some of its power from above to below – to the enterprise. The idea that the government and the party should be separated was to some extent put into practice even in the first stage of the reform. In this spirit attempts were made to reduce the intervention of the party in economic affairs and to enhance the role of the government, and thus to stimulate economic activity and to meet the efficiency demands of the reformed economic system, especially with regard to competition on the market, and also to the world economic system in the era of globalisation.

State enterprise (public ownership) in the leading areas enabled and required government to perform micro-regulation, but in the meantime, the private sector has become more and more autonomous and therefore demands more say in economic management. Their voices in the economic sphere are different, but both are supposed to be represented by the Communist Party.

Apart from increasing economic efficiency, the steps taken to separate party and government were supposed to limit corruption. But serious political corruption is more a matter of the essential than the functional problems.

The political reforms now face a great challenge: how to deal with the essential problem?

The existence of multiple ownership and different interest groups has created a new situation with a new spectrum of opinions. Those who would prefer a Western-type political system with multiple parties are now questioning the Chinese model of single-party leadership; problems of political legality and constitutional reform have been discussed by some scholars. Even if we go back to Karl Marx and assume a definite relationship between the Party and the class that it represents, there are now different social layers (even if we do not call them classes); how can the Communist Party represent and defend the different interests of these groups? That brings us to the essential problem of the political system, more complicated than the functional one.

We can analyse it from two points of view: first, there is the structural discrepancy between the pluralism of interest groups and the one-party regime, and the lack of channels to express the demands of these groups. Second, the essential problem can be seen as a matter of systemic disruption: how can this kind of political system prevent dominant economic forces from intruding into or interfering with the political sphere, which in turn can adversely affect the economic one? On a more personal level, the political elite can reap economic benefits. All these trends are conducive to corruption and to the aggravation of social differences.

The stated Communist Party policies of building a harmonious society and enhancing social cohesion are a practical response to the problems caused by all this differentiation of interest groups and their conflicts; attempts at functional reform can also be seen as an anti-corruption strategy aimed at limiting the incursions of political power into the economic sphere.

Besides the problems of representation and systemic interference, the new and growing social differences rooted in the economic sector can also have adverse effects on the political sector. Political elites will not want to be left behind by economic ones; thus the temptation to use public positions to benefit powerful individuals will increase. That is one reason why political corruption is so difficult to deal with and continues to spread from below as well as from above.

Income difference based on capital investment may be compared to income difference due to political advantages as well as to cultural ones; both the latter phenomena preceded multiple ownership. But the point is that they have grown rapidly since it increased much more quickly after the introduction of multiple ownership. Those who possess political or cultural capital (the latter based on good education) also have a strong voice in dominating the policies of re-allocation; incomes outside the domain of fixed and transparent salaries become the main source of revenue for those active in political and cultural sectors, and this is difficult to measure.

All these trends have led to demands for political reform, but the messages from different interest groups are very varied. Corruption is a common target for all of them, but the elites of the private sector are mainly looking for more political rights to match and to protect their growing economic power; the preferences of people on the lower levels of society are very different. The two different voices roughly correspond to the contrast between right and left in Chinese politics.

Generally speaking, political reform is becoming more and more important to both ordinary people (divided as they are into interest groups) and the party leadership. If we adopt a Marxian approach, the task is either to redefine the relationship between the party and the different social layers (or classes) or to realign the political system with new social realities. What in fact is going on is a re-labelling of businessmen as workers, and of other new forces in a similar way. This may be seen as a practical response to emerging problems. But short-term policy is one thing, theoretical understanding of the situation is another.

Could we reform the political system on the basis of the same principles as the reform of the economic system?

The principle of economic reform is clear – although it cannot be used as a slogan, it is to change the relationship between subjects and objects in the economic area, through policies of monetary stimulation and contract responsibility, relying on people's self-interest. But in the actual market economic situation, these changes in relationship have led to conflicts between social subjects.

It is clear that the principle of economic reform cannot be used for political reform. There we are dealing with relationships between different subjects in the public sphere, even if they are subject-object relationships. Marx does not clearly distinguish these two spheres; he explains political relations as based on economic relations, while Habermas distinguishes the two through the concepts of instrumental action and communicative action, corresponding to instrumental rationality and communicative rationality. Concentrating his attention on the difference of instrumental action, unfolding between subject and object, and communicative action, unfolding between subjects, to some extent he has neglected the inter-penetrating relationship between the two dimensions.

This inter-penetrating double relationship shows us that these two kinds of relationship cannot be separated in concrete social contexts; to that extent, it is understandable that Marx does not criticise capitalism from the point of view of political democracy but has to enter into the workings of the economic system. By the same token, although it is true that the political system cannot be reformed in parallel with the economic one, it has to respond to the problems of the latter.

Due to the essence of the political system, the principle of political reform is different from that of economic reform. If we say that the principle of economic reform is based on the self-interest of subjects, which can be understood on very different levels, from individuals to province, the principle of political reform is supposed to be based on public interest. But the political actors are individuals, acting in the general situation of social differences; without an adequate political system, public interest is easily to be replaced by self-interest drawing on political privilege.

It is clear that the political system cannot be reformed according to the same principle as the reform of the economic system. The essential role of the political system is to manage and express the voices of society as a whole. If the principle of self-interest intrudes into the political system, this will unavoidably lead to serious corruption and further increase social differences, for the benefit of those who enjoy advantages based on power.

The aim of political reform is, on the one hand, to limit the scope for people in power to use their privilege to pursue their own interests or other particular ones; and to guarantee that they will be responsible for the whole society (serve the people, as Mao said). On the other hand it should provide a channel for most people to make their voices heard as much as possible; as Jürgen Habermas suggested, most of all it should provide a discursive channel for different groups of people, including different social layers that are inevitably forming in the present situation.

Facing the essential problem of the political system, and wanting to avoid the politics of permanent flux, as experienced during the cultural revolution in the second half of the 1960s, many people increasingly favour the kind of political system that would combine more limited supervision with more openness and be more transparent to society. More freedom for mass media is necessary for the second purpose.

The Western model of democracy, with its multi-party system, is admired and advocated by those who identify with the right wing of the Chinese political spectrum, while it is criticised by many others (both Chinese and Western scholars) as a mere bourgeois democracy based on a class-divided social system that maximises monetary motivation. Under this kind of social system, the people who dominate the economic situation also play a dominant role in political affairs.

Due to a lack of clear ideas about how China could further continue its political reform, the process has now been slowing. Strong demands for political reform have, however, grown stronger, from ordinary people as well as from the central leadership. This is a reaction against not only corruption but also rapidly increasing social differences, which in turn can both hamper economic development and threaten the stability of society. Obviously, compared to economic reform, further reform of the political system is more important and more complicated.

Even so, since the end of the last century a certain process of political reform has been under way in certain domains. In the rural areas, at the basic level, people have tried to elect their own leaders. Political reform may be following the same trajectory as economic reform: starting in rural areas, and then moving into urban areas. In the cities, the system of officialdom has now, in some units and to some extent, been changed from nomination by the government to a system of public competition through self-nomination and equal assessment. These steps have only dealt with the process of assuming power, while still not touching the essential problem of understanding the relationship between the party and the different social layers, as well as between the party and the government.

The principles for essential political reform, which are supposed to match both the socialist market economy and the new situation of existing different social layers, could be as follows. There should be rules to guarantee equal political rights for all citizens, regardless of their economic position, especially preventing the translation of economic advantage into political advantage; and to make public media more open and create more transparency, because this is a kind of effective supervision. No matter how people otherwise understand the essential problems of the political system, these basic principles cannot be neglected.

Prospects

China's socialist economic reform is to some extent connected to globalising trends, which have already turned out to be a historical transition. No matter what the future outcome of this transition will be, the incoherence of the reformed economic system and the only partly reformed political system has become evident. What will the further course of political reform be? This is of concern not only to the Chinese people, but also to many Western leftist scholars, especially those who are committed to socialist or Communist causes. The prospects of China's historical transition depend on how we can guarantee first, that the economic reform will still move in a socialist direction, and second, that political reform will match economic reform.

As for the first point, the prospects of China's socialist economic reform depend on how far we can implement socialist distributive justice and achieve some kind of social equality under the conditions of multiple ownership with a market system, and develop an effective social security system, in order to guarantee that every person's living standard will be, to some extent, raised along with the development of the national economy. This could result in a new kind of socialist political system, on a transformed economic basis.

Regarding the second point, the main concerns of China's socialist reform depend on how the political system is to be reformed, and whether a new model of a democratic political system could be set up, which might function more efficiently with the market economic system, and also match the new situation of the existence of different social layers. What is more important is that a new model of socialist democratic political system should encourage and enable more people to be active in political affairs, in the condition of a socialist market economy.

The problem with Western political models is that they are vitiated by their economic background. Those who dominate the economic sphere also become dominant in the political sector, and the regime known as democracy cannot escape monetary hegemony. But as has been seen, the traditional socialist model of a political system cannot match the reformed economic situation. A new democratic model is needed and urgently expected.

Note

1. Jiang Zhemin, Report of the 16th CPC national delegation conference, 8 November 2002, People's Publishing House, p. 28.

Notes on the Contributors

Johann P. Arnason is a sociologist and philosopher, and Emeritus Professor of Sociology at La Trobe University, Melbourne, and was until 2015 Professor at the Faculty of Human Studies, Charles University, Prague. His research interests centre on historical sociology, with particular emphasis on the comparative analysis of civilisations.

Vladimíra Dvořáková is a political scientist and historian, and Professor at the Department of Political Science in the School of International Relations, University of Economics, Prague. She analyses transitions to democracy and models of democracy, and previously studied Latin America. She was Head of the Department of Political Science at the University of Economics, President of the Czech Political Science Association and Vice-President of the International Political Science Association.

Gábor Gángó is a philosopher and a historian of ideas in the Institute of Philosophy at the Hungarian Academy of Sciences, Budapest. He is also Professor at the University of Miskolc. He has conducted research into Kant, Fichte, Lukacs, Benjamin, the history of Hungary and Weimar Germany, and cultural critique of capitalism.

Jerry Harris is a historian and political scientist, and Secretary of the Global Studies Association of North America as well as a member of the International Executive Board of the Network for the Critical Study of Global Capitalism. He organises annual conferences of global studies in the USA. He has pursued research in global and transnational capitalism, and economic, political and social conflicts.

Marek Hrubec is a philosopher and a social and political theorist, and Director of the Centre of Global Studies in the Institute of Philosophy at the Czech Academy of Sciences in Prague. He also teaches at Charles

University in Prague. He focuses on critical theory, social and political justice, recognition, development, global capitalism, and social and political changes in the macro-regional and global contexts.

Jan Keller is a sociologist, and Professor in the School of Social Studies at the University of Ostrava, Czech Republic. Since 2014, he has been a Member of the European Parliament (political group S&D). He is also a commentator for the Czech daily *Právo*. He deals with issues of the welfare state, ecology, theory of organisation and modernisation, and sociological theory.

Jiří Krejčík is an Indologist and political scientist, and a Junior Fellow in the Centre of Global Studies in the Institute of Philosophy at the Czech Academy of Sciences in Prague. He also teaches in the Department of Political Science at Charles University in Prague. He analyses political and social issues in India, mainly Indian multiculturalism and the politics of identity.

Emil A. Sobottka is Professor of Sociology at the Pontifical Catholic University in Porto Alegre (PUCRS), Brazil, and researcher in the Brazilian National Council of Research and Development (CNPq). He is General Secretary of the Brazilian Sociological Association, and editor of *Civitas: Journal of Social Sciences*. His fields of study are social theory, democracy and social movements.

Richard Sťahel is a philosopher, and Head of the Department of Philosophy in the School of Philosophy at the University of Constantine the Philosopher, Nitra, Slovakia. His specialisations are the history of philosophy in the twentieth century, political philosophy, philosophy of law and the state, and environmentalism.

Oleg Suša is a sociologist and philosopher, and Senior Fellow in the Centre of Global Studies in the Institute of Philosophy at the Czech Academy of Sciences, Prague. He taught in the Department of Sociology at Charles University in Prague. He focuses on global studies, sociological theory, ecological crises and theory of modernisation.

Wei Xiaoping is Professor of Philosophy and Director of the Department of History of Marxist Philosophy in the Institute of Philosophy at the Chinese Academy of Social Sciences in Beijing. She analyses Marxist philosophy, political philosophy, and the recent economic and political transformations of China.

Index

Page numbers followed by an 'n' denote notes, and by a 't' denote tables.

Index

Index

Lucarelli, S., 83
Luhmann, Niklas, 91
Lukács, György, 135–6, 139, 140
  and culture of the masses, 140–1
  Ethical group, 127–8
  History and Class Consciousness,
    141–4
  Lenin, 141–4
  and violence, 122

Magyars, 121, 124–6
Malaysia, 67–8
Mandal affair, 171–3, 180
Mandal Commission, 171–2
Mandal-Mandir combination, 172–3
Mann, Michael, 37, 40, 46
Marx, Karl
  labour time, 61
  political and economic reform, 192
Marx-Engels Workers' University, 139
Marxism
  and Hungary, 139
  and Lukacs, 142–4
  revolutions, 34, 36
mass consumer capitalism, 81–5
mass movements, 6, 15, 69
Meiji revolution (1868), Japan, 30–1
Mexico, revolution, 51–2
Mill, John Stuart, 117n
  Principles of Political Economy, 117n
Modi, Narendra, 168, 177–9, 180
Moore, Barrington, 36
Morales, Evo, 73
multiple ownership, 187–94

Narayan, Jayaprakash, 169, 178, 179
National Civic Radical Party, Hungary, 124
National Socialism, 52
nationalisation, 136–9
Naxalite movement, 174
Neapolitan revolution (1799), 170
Nehru, Jawaharlal, 170, 179, 180
Nehruvian socialism, 168, 170, 179, 180
neoliberalisation, 20, 168
neoliberalism, 7–8
  and austerity, 56, 58–9, 73
  hyper-neoliberalism, 23
  self-destructive, 17, 89
Never-Never Girl, 63
Neves, Marcelo, 151–2
New York Times, The, 64
North Africa, 99–120

Obama, Barack, 65
O'Connor, James, 70

oil industry, 65–70, 99–100
organised capitalist social formation, 81,
  103–4
Other Backward Classes (OBCs), 171, 173,
  178

Palazzo, Albert, 109
participatory budgeting, 149, 155, 158–60
participatory experiences, Brazil,
  148–67
passive revolution, 4, 169–80, 180
People's Commissariats, Hungary, 132,
  135–41
People's Voice, The, 125, 127, 131, 140
Perrow, Charles, 91
Piketty, Thomas, *Capital in the Twenty-First
  Century*, 64
Plant, Raymond, 101, 105
Pogóny, József, 127, 131
Pogrebinschi, T., 157
Polanyi, Karl, 92
population growth, 99–100, 109, 110–15
precarisation, 83–4
primitive social formations, 102
Principles of Political Economy, 117n
Prison Notebooks, 170
privatisation, 11, 15, 106, 114
property rights, 184–5
Przeworski, A., 156
public ownership, 184–6, 189–90

Rachman, Gideon, 63
racism, 24, 93–4
Radical Democrats, Hungary, 123–6
Rashtriya Swayamsevak Sangh (RSS), 169,
  172, 173, 179
Red News, 127, 140
Research Institute of Historical Materialism,
  139
revolution
  from above, 30–4, 170
  categorising, 28–35
  definitions, 6–26
  as myth, 27–8, 32, 37, 42, 48, 52
  as progress, 8–10, 34–5
  as radical change, 6–7
Revolution of Limits, 109
Revolutionary Socialists, 131
Richta, Radovan, 76–7, 92
  Civilisation at the Crossroads, 77
risks, 76–96
Robinson, William, 82, 117n
Rousseff, Dilma (President of Brazil), 161,
  163
Rubin, Robert, 64–5

EU representative:
Easy Access System Europe
Mustamäe tee 50, 10621 Tallinn, Estonia
Gpsr.requests@easproject.com

www.ingramcontent.com/pod-product-compliance
Lightning Source LLC
Chambersburg PA
CBHW070421270326
41926CB00014B/2886